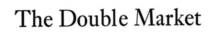

The Double Market

The Double Market

Art Theft and Art Thieves

Keith Middlemas

SAXON HOUSE

SAXON HOUSE, D. C. HEATH LIMITED
Westmead, Farnborough, Hampshire, England.

ISBN 0 347 00037 1
Library of Congress Catalog Card Number 74–24313

Printed in Great Britain by
W. & J. Mackay Limited, Chatham

Contents

Author's Note

My thanks are due to all of those who have given me the information from which this book has been written and in particular to Michael Newman, distinguished dealer in European porcelain, who first suggested the idea. Thieves, receivers, antique dealers, security agents, auction houses, private collectors, and journalists have co-operated, but it would be unfair to some if they were to be mentioned by name, and it seemed therefore better not to be specific. For the same obvious reasons, I have only rarely given sources, other than official documents and statements, for what is in the text. However, I am able fully to express my gratitude for the co-operation that was invariably and courteously given by the national police forces affiliated to Interpol, notably Scotland Yard, the Bundeskriminalamt, the F.B.I., the French Police Judiciaire, and the criminal divisions of the Italian, Austrian, Belgian, Swiss, Spanish and Portuguese police; and to M. Jean Nepote, Secretary-General of Interpol. Without this range of sources, it would not have been possible to depict the growth and operation of the double market during the last twenty years. I sincerely hope that this study may help to diminish its scope and the degree of immunity that it has possessed for so long.

Chapter 1 The Matrix

"Property is theft", the father of anarchism, Pierre-Joseph Proudhon, wrote in 1840, and it is ironical that the paintings of his friend Gustave Courbet (who agreed with him) duly became property and were stolen. One of the first signs of "developed" activity among animals is that they brutally compete for one another's goods, and the natural historian's view of theft resembles King Lear's observations on sex, without the disgust: the wren goes to it, and the small gilded fly; so does the jackal, that unfairly maligned animal, surreptitiously picking a tiger's kill; fish and birds do it, and as a rule it is only in the strict totalitarian cultures of the animal kingdom, the hive or the termitary, that a socially shared respect for "property" holds true as a social law. Otherwise, it is a matter of acquiring property and defending it.

Much of what is true of the animal world applies to human societies. Property, especially the law of property, is apt to define itself in terms of theft. Equally, property defines and articulates status: like bower-birds in New Guinea, displaying their treasures, collectors need their objects to reflect their own sense of identity and purpose. When the objects also become forms of investment and security, the conditions exist for a sophisticated market in stolen and relegitimised works of art. No book about theft, especially art theft, can profitably start with the assumption that the criminal's face is not familiar, that he is some kind of monster – or, for that matter, that he is a romantic hero. The art thief is merely a special product of modern industrial society and he will not vanish until the concept of art as investment vanishes. Since there is no immediate likelihood that it will, the Western world is stuck with the art thief as an objective fact.

There is, at the heart of all theft, a self-regenerating mechanism. No matter how hard the police work, restless, illicit enterprise will continue to satisfy an insatiable demand. Nowhere are the mechanics clearer than in the history of art theft in recent years. What has happened since 1950 is an open-ended story quite distinct from that of the plunderers of the past. In these last twenty-four years, the relationship between works of art and the market in which they are contained has altered radically. To understand the change, we need to understand factors of public demand, the mobility of works of art and, above all, the new concept of investment. The role of art as capital is a relatively new one in Western societies, and it has scarcely ever appeared in the East. Though mankind has constantly been producing works of art for more than 40,000 years, it is a curious fact that art did not come to be generally perceived as a commodity or a means of economic exchange until less than two hundred years ago. Its importance as a kind of economic fetish – for which collectors may pay £2,300,000 for a Velasquez or half a million pounds for a Monet – is the fruit of the last half-century. It is principally with *economic* art theft, with the stealing of art as capital, that we are dealing here. For it is not true that art theft has always taken place for economic reasons: the majority of the most spectacular thefts of art in history have been undertaken with other ends in view.

The nature of theft depends, to put it in somewhat abstract terms, on the thief's own experience of the object he is taking. If the thief – or the receiver – does not experience art as capital, he will seize it as something else. The most famous art thefts of antiquity were undertaken for religious, not economic, reasons. From the time that Julius Caesar conquered Greece, and brought back huge quantities of art plunder to Rome, the parade of the captured effigies of a city's gods became an integral part of the Roman triumphal procession. But this did not mean that the victorious general was exulting over the beauty of the works he had brought back to embellish the city: the captured work of art resembled the captured standard, signifying the religious castration of the vanquished state. The gods of Greece resided in their marble or bronze effigies: to tear the statue of Apollo from his Athenian temple and install it on the Capitol was to remove Apollo's benevolent attention from Athens and redirect it to Rome. In far more primitive societies than ancient Rome, it has been observed that the conquering tribe's first act after battle is to destroy or carry off the effigies and fetishes of its enemy's religion. Only the most narrow-minded aesthete will interpret this simply as an act of cultural "vandalism". (It is only when a work of art has become deritualised, stripped of its immediate religious power, that it can be assigned a new artistic value.)

The classical habit of stealing works of art as a form of religious domination underwent many changes across the centuries, and it emerged, in modern times, as an expression of political and cultural glorification – an extension of the Roman triumph in a secular direction. Tamburlane might plunder; Napoleon and Hitler "relocated". Throughout his campaigns for the conquest of Europe, Napoleon maintained a consistent artistic policy: the best statues, paintings, drawings, archaeological fragments and *objets de vertu* were to be brought back to Paris, and used to furnish his *Rome nouvelle*, the centre of the Europe he had redesigned. Naturally, the Emperor did not consider himself to be a thief. His attitude was mordantly expressed when his officers arranged for the removal of the *Codex Atlanticus*, a vast, incoherent and then virtually unstudied collection of drawings and notes by Leonardo da Vinci, from the Ambrosiana Library in Milan. Loot? Indeed, no: all men and works of genius, Napoleon decreed, were "intrinsically French", no matter what their country of origin. From this point of view, Napoleon was merely conferring on the memory of Leonardo the inestimable privilege of French citizenship, thus "completing" the naturalisation-by-residence that Leonardo acquired during the last years of his life, spent at Francois I's court at Amboise; while to France he gave the fillip of Leonardo's inheritance.

There is no doubt that through the indefatigable Lieutenant Denon – the official he placed in charge of plundering European art – Napoleon meant to transform Paris, not simply into an immense museum, but into the forcing-house of world culture. There would be no reason for the art student or connoisseur to go anywhere else, for nothing worthy of educated attention would be left elsewhere in Europe. The failure of the plan was not due to any lack of energy on the part of Denon (whose nickname, *l'emballeur*, "the packer", came to chill the minds of every collector and curator in Europe), but rather to the insurmountable administrative problems of so colossal

3

a project, coupled with the difficulties of transport and the limitations of neo-classical taste. Nevertheless, Napoleon attached so much importance to art theft as a way of enhancing national prestige that when Didot, another of his functionaries, prepared a folio presentation volume listing, on vellum, the benefits Napoleon had bestowed on France, one whole page was reserved for seven words:

L'Apollon et le Laocoon
emportés à Paris.

The "Apollo" (in terms of neo-classical taste, there was only one) was the Apollo Belvedere, which, together with the Laocoon, had stood in the Vatican collection. Because the most influential critics of the eighteenth century, such as Winckelmann, had discoursed on them as exemplary masterpieces, and because of their influence on contemporary sculpture through Canova and his school, they were key works in the canon of neo-classical taste, both for artists and collectors. The theft of these two Hellenistic marbles was thus implicitly ranked with Napoleon's battle victories and legal reforms. They were to symbolise the rebirth of ancient Rome and its heroic virtues in Napoleon's Paris. Modern Rome had to bow to the new capital as the place where future style would be generated. At this level, art theft could become an effort to change art history itself. By dint of sheer arrogance and organisation, the drift of works between one culture and another could be compressed, accelerated and directed; and another Rome *would* be built in a day. After his conquest of central Italy, Napoleon reported that

> . . . The Commission of experts has made a fine haul in Ravenna, Rimini, Pesaro, Ancona, Loreto and Perugia. The whole lot will be forwarded to Paris without delay. There is also the consignment from Rome itself. We have stripped Italy of everything of artistic worth, with the exception of a few objects in Turin and Naples!

Leur avidité, as Voltaire remarked in a different context, *était singulièrement idéaliste*. Lieutenant Barbier, who took charge of the first shipment from Holland to Paris, thus addressed the National Convention in 1794:

4

Too long have these masterpieces been sullied by the gaze of
serfs ... these immortal works are no longer in a foreign land
... they rest today in the home of the arts and of genius, in the
motherland of liberty and sacred equality, in the French
Republic.

The Dutch themselves were too stupified by his peremptory rape
of their heritage to make the obvious answer: that since Napoleon
had liberated them, they were now free men, and entitled to look
at their own art. It seems unlikely that this would have impressed
the idealists of the Louvre, who were too busy being Romans.
Hundreds of convoys were arriving in Paris from all over Europe,
laden with objects picked by Denon. From one collection in Berlin
alone he took (issuing a receipt for each object) 204 sculptures, 116
paintings, 500 gems and cameos, more than 7,000 Roman bronze
coins, 5,000 ancient and mediaeval silver coins and medals, and
1,200 "small bronze statuettes". The victims of such pillage reacted
to Napoleon as their descendants, 150 years later, did to Hitler.
Schiller expressed the German mood with contemptuous restraint,
in a poem entitled *Die Antiken bei Paris* (1800):

> What the art of Greece created
> Let the Frank by dint of battle
> Carry to his vaunted Seine.
> Let him in superb museums
> Show the trophies of his valour
> To the marvelling citizen.
> Never will they break their silence,
> Nor, their pedestals forsaking,
> Mingle with life's throng.
> He alone enjoys the Muses
> Who has ardour in his bosom –
> To the barbarian they are stone.

In 1806, a French writer stated that "within six years" the painters
of France would have exceeded the glories of Raphael, Michelangelo and Titian. This would happen through fertilisation by
plunder:

> ... we form our taste by long acquaintance with the true and

5

the beautiful. The Romans, once uneducated, began to educate themselves by transplanting the work of conquered Greece to their own country. We follow their example when we exploit our conquests and carry off from Italy whatever serves to stimulate our imagination.

The six years passed; 1812 arrived, but the promised millenium did not. Nevertheless, although one may look back with a degree of cynicism on the hopes that Napoleon's officials had of a cultural springtime induced by mass theft, it would be naïve to think that such plunder had no effect at all on France. The presence of so vast a stock of ancient and Renaissance masterpieces helped French artists to focus; it immensely enhanced their consciousness of art history; and, of course, it influenced the course of French neo-classicism, the heart of the revolutionary movement in the arts in France in the late eighteenth and early nineteenth centuries.

There is no doubt that the next great pillager of art for political glory meant to emulate Napoleon. Yet Hitler's policy was anachronistic and operatic to the point of insanity: Napoleon, at least, had a great city to build on; but Hitler hoped to make Linz, the provincial town where he had spent his boyhood, into the new cultural capital of the world – a project comparable to turning Birmingham or Boise, Idaho, into the new Jerusalem. In late eighteenth-century Paris, there had been a vigorous, inventive and complex civilisation into which the plundered works of art were absorbed. But in Linz, as Hitler knew only too well, there was absolutely nothing. Thus, if it became the "cultural capital" of Europe, its fame would be the purest testimony to the triumph of the Führer's will: like God, Hitler would have created a world out of the void. He found his Denon in Dr Hans Posse, the director of the Dresden State Gallery, and under Dr Posse's administration, the Sonderauftrag Linz (and later the Einsatzstab Rosenberg) took charge of art pillage with the same precision and minute efficiency as their fellow bureaucracies showed in the extermination of the Jews.

The story of Hitler's art thefts, culminating in the recovery of hundreds of thousands of stolen objects (ranging from the van Eyck brothers' *Adoration of the Lamb* and Michelangelo's *Bruges Madonna* to the Rothschild jewel collection) in the labyrinthine tunnels of the Alt Aussee salt mine, has been told before.[1] Superficially, it might seem that there was very little difference in motivation between Hitler and the great triumphal plunderers of the past, like Napoleon. In fact, the distinction is interesting and has a certain relevance to the theme of art as investment. Hitler's thefts signified a fetishistic, unreal belief in the power of simple *objects*. He was utterly eclectic: a jackdaw, stealing this button, this piece of blue glass, this fragment of pottery, to adorn his nest at Linz. The original context of the objects did not matter (as it had for Napoleon and his advisers). Hitler believed, or seems to have believed, that works of art were really a type of enlightenment-pill: one taken anywhere, at any time, would produce a guaranteed effect on the central nervous system. Amassing them from the conquered countries of Europe was part of the ultimate aim of changing the nature of mankind – along with the monstrous buildings in which he and his architect, Albert Speer, intended to enshrine the German soul. His works of art were freed altogether from their uncomfortable ligaments of non-German history: transformed into manipulable objects as surely and blandly as washing-machines in a vast showroom. But they were not for sale. In Linz, they were frozen for ever: an instant mosaic of art transformed, as it were, into reproductions of itself, cluttered together like the illustrations in some children's encyclopaedia.

Hitler's dream for Linz involved one important stage of what Marx had called "reification": the transformation of a work of art into a *thing*, the suppression of its actual nature and historic context. But (although fortunes were made on the side by corrupt dealers and collaborators selling works of art to the Sonderauftrag Linz and the Einsatzstab Rosenberg) the aim was not profit. The gains were intended to be "intangible", or, in the favourite Nazi cliché, "spiritual". Hitler's attitude to art thus retained a minute and distorted trace of the reverence paid to the healing powers of the imagination by German writers, such as Goethe, Schiller and Wackenroder, a century or more earlier. His occasional remarks on the subject imply that he disapproved of art dealers and wanted to extract *all* the best art from the stream of commercial transaction in order to preserve its "values". A glance at the records of Hitler's art buying would show that in his desire for a "pure" art, free from

7

the corruption of money, he was utterly hypocritical; but, to a degree, the hypocrisy was unconscious, and masked by Hitler's dim apprehension of a real problem, which he could see only through a stagnant and adolescent romanticism. He was at least fifty years too late to prevent the development he feared. In this, as he once said of Rosenberg, Hitler was "relapsing into mediaevalism".

It is unlikely that another Hitler or Napoleon will arise in the art world. The reason, which is central to any discussion of the fate of art in modern society, lies in the use of art as capital, as a means of investment. If art were not experienced as capital, it would still be plundered in some other role, either for prestige, or, as in the sack of Constantinople by the Fourth Crusade in 1204, for the intrinsic value of its materials. But it would not be stolen *as art* by the thieves whose actions are the subject of this book.

Art theft is a transaction that extends far beyond the thief. The circle is completed by the receiver, who is also the would-be vendor, and the buyer; but they operate within the *climate of opinion* about art and the relative desirability of different categories, which in turn influence the *economic climate* and determine the price. At any given time, these elements are held in a balance, but the mixture changes regularly and, of late, has hardly remained the same from one year to the next. Whether an object is "stealable" or not depends, therefore, on much more than current fashion. Let us take, as an imaginary example, a work of art that would probably always have been regarded as precious, and would have realised a high price on the open market (if it had been freely for sale) at almost any time in the last five hundred years: the *Tazza Farnese*, a large Hellenistic cameo dish which is now in the Naples Museum, and which could, with a degree of close planning, be stolen by a well-equipped gang.

The Farnese Cup was made by a Greek craftsman in the second century B.C. Nobody knows what happened to it during the next 1,600 years; but it is so large and elaborate that one may guess it was commissioned by, or entered the collection of, one of the numerous cognoscenti in ancient Rome – a type immortalised in the character of Trimalchio in Petronius' *Satyricon*, the man who knew his Greek bronzes were Corinthian because he bought them "from a dealer named Corinthus". In the fifteenth century, it was rediscovered – perhaps dug up in the excavations for a new building.

Lorenzo de' Medici bought it for 10,000 florins for his gem and cameo collection, of which he was inordinately proud. The real size of the immense sum he paid can be gauged from the fact that an ordinary painting by one of Lorenzo's contemporaries in Florence, Botticelli or Pollaiuolo, then cost between 50 and 100 florins; even Botticelli's *Primavera*, which today – according to a commission appointed in 1968 by the Uffizi, where it hangs – is worth an estimated $40,000,000, could have been commissioned twenty times over for the price of the Farnese Cup. Ghirlandaio's vast fresco cycle *Story of St John* in the church of Santa Maria Novella in Florence cost "only" 1,000 florins. Such are the vagaries of taste and patronage, and Lorenzo's ostentatious purchase of that florid, overwrought cup may serve to remind those who believe in the fictional Golden Age of Florentine patronage that Lorenzo was, in his way, as much a *parvenu* as the Texas oilmen who strive to emulate him today. But suppose that a thief had been inspired to steal the Farnese Cup from its shelf in Lorenzo's *studiolo* in the Palazzo Medici: could he have profited? Almost certainly, no. There were not enough outlets. The Farnese Cup was known to patrons throughout Italy and only a tiny number of men were systematic collectors of antique gems. Their mutual competition had inflated the price Lorenzo had to pay for the Farnese Cup, and it is unlikely that a thief could have gained direct access to such exalted figures without piquing some chamberlain's suspicions *en route*. Nor could he conveniently sell it through a network of dealers, since no such network existed in Italy at the time. Since a lower-class Italian did not travel outside his country (and only very rarely outside his home town), he could not conceivably take it to Paris or Antwerp, as a modern thief might. Hampered by lack of contacts and mobility, the best he could hope to do would be to dispose of it, for a pittance, in the market-place; Lorenzo's police were not as efficient as their modern equivalents, but then the laws of evidence and the rights of suspects were looser than they are today, and the risk would have been, if anything, worse.

Three centuries on, the thief's chances have improved. Eighteenth-century Italy is full of rich *Inglesi* on the Grand Tour, avidly buying antiquities for their collections at home. The Farnese Cup is still famous, and can be seen (if the dilettante looks for it) in numerous engravings. But – and this is the important point – the phenomenon we now know as the art market has begun to develop. Rome, Venice and Florence, the main goals of the cultural tourist, swarm with dealers, antiquarians, touts and fences. In this labyrinth of art transactions, the provenance of any object – even an object as celebrated as the Farnese Cup – can be mislaid. The fashion for collecting antique gems and cameos, which has slumped a little among the Italians, rages in London. It is not yet linked to investment, but there are no state controls on the export of works of art from Italy. Should Milord want to buy the Colosseum and shift it to his grounds in Kent, he can still do so. Thousands of paintings, sculptures, drawings, engravings and antiquities are shipped out of Italy every season. When Milord has got the Farnese Cup to England, no law on earth can drag it back to Italy; it is his. So the thief is selling it under conditions that closely approximate those in a free and legal market, and this in turn means he will get a high price for it (though the price he gets will bear little resemblance to the price Milord will pay, after the cup has gone through the back doors of a few Florentine or Roman *antiquari*).

But place the theft of the *Tazza Farnese* two centuries further on, in 1970, and the situation changes again. The desirability of the cup – as the kind of object a collector might want to possess – has dropped, for Europe's honeymoon with the Antique is over and no Hellenistic object is likely to command the kind of price, in relation to modern art, that the cup did in the fifteenth century or could in the eighteenth. It is still, of course, very valuable, and on the free market could hardly sell for less than £25,000 – most of which would come from the weight of its Medicean associations. But this is neutralised from the thief's point of view by the fact that the Farnese Cup is now even better known to art experts than it was in the eighteenth century. Its image has been duplicated in countless photographs, prints and books, and there is not a dealer or auction house whose advisers would not recognise it at a glance. Thanks to this publicity, there is no hiding place for so famous an antique; history has immobilised it, and short of a sale to the mythical millionaire in South America (of whom, more later) there is no way it can be disposed of safely. The one strategy that remains is to ransom it for insurance. But the Naples Museum is under-endowed and it is unlikely that the Farnese Cup is fully insured. Small profit there, and much risk.

Thus it can be seen from this hypothetical example that, although any work of art can in theory be stolen – unless it is on the scale of the Sistine Chapel or the Parthenon frieze – its usefulness to a thief depends on a very complex web of interbalancing factors. What is the demand on the free market? How anonymous is the work of art – or how can its identity be removed without destroying its value? Is it likely to be catalogued or recorded?

Two principles determine the balance: if it is not desirable it will not sell; if it is well known it can be traced. And in terms of these two variables, there has never been a more auspicious time for professional art theft than the period that began in 1950. The past twenty-odd years have brought an unprecedented boom in organised art robbery. It has run parallel to an equally unprecedented boom on the legitimate art market, and to a degree the thieves help the "legitimate" dealers, whether the latter know it or not, because the art market depends on a pool of homeless works of art, fed at one end by the sale of objects, drained at the other by the forming of new collections. In the last fifty years, that pool has been increasingly agitated. The turnover of works of art, through the auction-rooms and dealers, has accelerated year by year. At the same time, rather as the world's gold stock is annually reduced by friction, the quantity of available works of art by dead artists is reduced – by war, by accident, by loss, by the freezing of this or that Rembrandt in the permanent and inalienable collection of some museum. Paul de Lamerie made only a finite number of silver candlesticks, Reisener a limited quantity of signed commodes, and, as the old saw goes, Corot painted 400 pictures in his life, 850 of which are in the United States. It would sensationalise the problem to suggest that the art market, in the 1970s, is *heavily* dependent on the recirculation of stolen objects, which pass into the market by the back door and are "legitimised" by going through a sequence of increasingly respectable dealers. Nevertheless, on the basis of the evidence in this book, it is reasonable to suggest that not less than five per cent of the works of art now for sale in the world have been stolen at some point in their history. The proportion is higher in the field of simple or middling works of art – silverware, furniture, *objets de vertu*, drawings, rare prints and engravings, porcelain and antiquities – than in the area of signed paintings by acknowledged and famous artists. Not only are there more of the former around: their provenances are infinitely harder to check, and the records of their existence – if there are such records – are more confused.

Let us suppose that you, the collector, possess a valuable ancient Chinese pottery figure: a T'ang dynasty horse. It is stolen. You have no photograph of it. Of course you can *describe* it. It is a horse, sixteen inches high, made of creamy buff pottery over which a honey-brown glaze has been dripped. It is worth £3,000. Unfortunately, the collections of Europe and America abound in such horses; they are all valuable, except the fakes; most of them are about sixteen inches high and are so glazed, and there is absolutely no way in which such an object can be identified *with certainty* from the kind of verbal description that auction catalogues or inventories carry. On the other hand, if what you have lost is a painting by Gerhardt Dou (to pick a minor master) there is more chance of tracing it from a verbal description. There are more criteria: simply to recognise a painting as "a Dou" – which would be no problem for any competent specialist in seventeenth-century Dutch art – narrows the field; there are not many works by Dou extant; and when the description of subject matter ("a moneychanger counting gold with a ledger on his right and an arched window in the background", say) is added and the whole report circulated, there is a far better chance that you may get your painting back – assuming, that is, that it appears in a public sale, and further assuming that the theft report will have been widely circulated, which is not always likely.

Supply follows demand, and theft is merely another form of supply. Modern, professional art theft could not exist without the particular kind of demand for art that exists today; and this demand, quite different from that in the nineteenth century, is inescapably perverse, being wholly tied to investment. The bourgeois collector, before the 1914–18 war, was not apt to reckon his wealth in terms of the paintings, sculpture or porcelain he owned. They might serve to impress his dinner guests as an index of his spending power, or a proof of the respectability of his origins ("Amusing little Watteau, been in the family quite a while, no idea what it's worth . . ."), but, as in the case of Soames Forsyte, who knew the value very well, his wealth was not *located in* them. The pace of the market was even; a placid stream of works of art flowed through the auction rooms and was absorbed by a relaxed élite, or, in the case of most *avant-garde* painting, not absorbed. Extremely high prices were occasionally paid, though not for paintings that would command them today. Sir Edwin Landseer's *Otter Hunt*, for instance, made £10,000 (excluding copyright fees) in 1873, the year he died, and in 1887 his *Taking a Buck* was sold for more than £2,000 (in 1930, it was knocked down at Christie's for 26 guineas). In 1874 William Holman Hunt's *The Shadow of Death* went to Agnew's, with all reproduction rights thrown in, for £11,000, and in 1875 William Frith's *Supper at Boswell's Lodgings* made £4,500 at Christie's. In 1898 Burne-Jones's *Mirror of Venus* made £5,775, while in 1903 two of Sir Lawrence Alma-Tadema's narrative "machines" were sold for £5,880 and £6,000 respectively. (To convert these sums into today's sterling values, they should be multiplied by six.) When American capital entered the European art market, other prices shot up: for instance, those of eighteenth-century English portraits, French furniture, *objets de vertu* and porcelain. The prices fetched by the works of Thomas Gainsborough, for which two American investment barons, Henry Frick and Henry Huntington, competed with the obsessed tenacity of angry samurai, were especially inflated. In 1913 Frick paid Duveen £82,700 for Gainsborough's portrait of the Hon. Frances Duncombe. In 1921, Huntington surpassed him by acquiring *The Blue Boy*, that famed and meretricious portrait of the son of Gainsborough's grocer, for £148,000; it thus became the second most expensive painting in the history of the art market, after Leonardo da Vinci's *Benois Madonna*, brought by the Tsar of Russia in 1914 for £310,000. The modern equivalents of these prices would be about half a million pounds for *The Blue Boy*, and a million and a half for the Leonardo. Princes and millionaires, when seized by the urge to acquire art, were just as extravagant then as now.

But there are interesting differences. It is unlikely that any of the American barons from whom Duveen, Berenson and a host of less eminent exploiters made their money conceived of their art purchases as *investment*. They were inordinately rich and took an

13

intense and snobbish pleasure in outspending their rivals. They did not buy for resale, because they did not need to. Their untrammelled lust for acquisition clarified the fundamental law of the economics of art: that a painting is "worth" exactly what a client will pay for it, no more, no less. Works of art are not subject to the labour theory of value, since their price in no way reflects the cost of the labour and materials from which they are made. Before the development of the investment market, price was always the index of pure, irrational desire. Every time a work of art was sold, the economics of the trade (in so far as they can be said to exist) had to be invented all over again. The second-hand car dealer on the street works within far more constricted business parameters than the dealer in the gallery. He knows that if he tries to sell a Ford at £1,000, when the going rate is £750, his clients will go to other dealers, for there are lots more second-hand Fords. On the other hand, however, since there is only this particular Raphael, the dealer who advertises it knows that it is literally unique and, in theory, should name its own price. In the boom years before the Wall Street crash of 1929, it seemed that each Signorelli, Botticelli or Titian that passed from Italy to Washington through Duveen's showrooms had, like a bullet, the name of one millionaire incised upon it.

But systematic *investment* in works of art presupposes a reliable "price table" for any range of paintings by one given artist. If the system of arbitrary price through pure desire still held true, there could be no confidence in the investment trade: it would be as if share certificate 1,032 in General Motors were worth $3,000 and share 1,033 went simultaneously for fifty cents. Works of art have to be turned into classes of object, types of property. All objects in one class must correspond to one another; they must be linked, like the price of houses in the same terraced street, even if they do not exactly correspond. When Cézanne's *Boy in a Red Waistcoat* was sold for £220,000 in 1959, every Cézanne on the market, from the most finished painting to the merest water-colour sketch, responded by going up in price, although not, of course, by the same percentage. What is more, in an investor's market, the class of object to which a painting belongs can override the fate of the painting itself. This happens most of all with living painters, whose output is still incomplete. In the summer of 1970 there was a severe recession on the New York art market and the investment boom in modern American art seemed to be juddering to a halt. New York was full of painters whose works, a year earlier, were selling for between £5,000 and £15,000 – prices at which they could not now dispose of them. But since the confidence of the art-investment system, which the economics of the international art trade are now designed to support, depends on the proposition that "a Stella" or "a Warhol" *must* hold its value, dealers preferred to sell nothing rather than be seen lowering the price of a single picture. Otherwise the backlash from earlier clients would have flayed them. An exquisite irony is that this sort of crisis hurts the present and future of the live artist. For example, at the time of recession it was still relatively easy to sell a "black" Stella of 1959–60, for that series (in the telescoped history of modern art) had acquired the rank of old mastership: its historical importance was secure; it had already entered the museum of taste. It is the new works, into which the artist projects his experiences *now*, that are "insecure". To buy these is something of a gamble, an act of faith in both painting and artist. Investment can only take place when the market – the matrix of critics, dealers, auction house records – has canonised the picture, and turned it into a "work of art", a *thing*. Only its existence as an *objet d'art*, in the sinister French phrase, is left; it has become an object the consumption of which can be freely manipulated.

Now the growth of art investment (and prices) is linked to tax. As Gerald Reitlinger pointed out in *The Economics of Taste*,

> The fortunes of the mid-Victorian subject-painters . . . had been made on an expanded market for framed prints, following the repeal of the duty on glass. The English eighteenth-century school boomed in the U.S.A. after 1909, when the 20 per cent tariff on imported art was repealed. And after 1913 there was a boom in modern French paintings, following the extension of tariff repeal to living art.

However, the greatest single factor in the transformation of art into capital occurred in the U.S.A. during the 1950s. The great American collectors of the early twentieth century, such as Mellon or Frick, had already endowed their public museums. The price of major

Renaissance (and, by now, key modern) paintings was rising so fast that the inducement to give treasures away had diminished. In order to sustain the flow into the U.S.A., the Federal tax authorities introduced their system of tax deduction: a gift to a museum or public gallery could be set off against the donor's income tax, up to a maximum of thirty per cent of the donor's total liability in the year the gift was made. Even better, ingenious tax lawyers won a doubly advantageous interpretation of the law: the value of the gift was taken at the museum's assessment, not judged by what the donor had actually paid for the work; and the gift was permitted to stay in the donor's hands until his death. Only then did the gallery take possession. In practice, a collector could buy a Gorky for £1,000 in 1959, give it to some American museum in 1965, arrange with the trustees and curator that its value should be given to the tax authorities as £25,000, save thousands more in tax than he paid, keep it for the rest of his life, and win himself a name as a philanthropist. No more effective form of enlightened self-interest could have been devised. The bill, until the long-overdue reforms of 1966 and 1969, was met by other taxpayers. If the donor contrived enough manipulations of this kind he was most likely honoured by having his name engraved on a sandstone plaque in the museum foyer.

Despite the attempts to tighten up the scheme, it can still be far more profitable in the United States to give away a painting than to sell it. Equally, the tax donation system is good for dealers. When a major painting enters a museum, there it stays. It will not come on the market again. So the class of objects to which it belongs – signified as "Gorkys" – narrows. There are fewer on the market; the demand is the same; the price of Gorky's available paintings is consolidated, or grows while dealers search avidly for other classes to replace them.

Put even as baldly as this, the theory corresponds closely to what has actually happened to the art market in the last twenty years. Classes of objects in which no collector would have dreamed of *investing* have turned into desirable commodities, yielding huge capital gains. The saleroom price of certain old master prints (notably Dürers, Piranesis, Breughels and, of course, Rembrandts) has risen twentyfold or more since 1950. That of Japanese netsukes has quadrupled in ten years; the cost of inros (decoratively-worked purses, which dangled from the belt of Japanese formal dress) has multiplied eightfold. Even in Europe, where gifts to museums are not tax-deductible, there has been an enormous volume of investment in art as a hedge against inflation. Of course, it is not always the works of art that go up in value; the value of money has diminished. Ming vases pay no dividend cheques, but they provide a capital gain instead. Any object that can be designated by the magic words "work of art" has become, *ipso facto*, a repository for free capital. In the Solomon Islands, people chose cowrie shells. In certain regions of Tibet in the eighteenth century, dried cakes of yak dung were amassed as a measure of wealth. Art is our wealth; the artist, our yak.

Supply follows demand. Since the Second World War, an unprecedented number of works of art, great and small, have been released into the free market – uncatalogued and unphotographed. Because of the demand, and the proliferation of dealers, the number of times a work of art may change hands in any given year has also risen. One of the better pieces of Queen Anne walnut furniture to come on the English market in the last twenty years was bought from a council house in Clapham for thirty shillings and passed through the hands of a dozen dealers before winding up in Bond Street at 4,000 guineas. When such transactions multiply, keeping track of them becomes a labour of Sisyphus. The fabric of the art market abounds in holes through which a stolen object can be slipped on its way to legitimisation. There is plenty of evidence that a proportion of stolen works of art in the £30 to £1,000 price range are put directly into auctions, even those run by the large London houses, which, with a turnover of millions of pounds a year, cannot possibly check on all the bona-fides of their clients.

The ease and profit of art theft today are symptomatic of a dismal situation. At a time when there is probably greater and more widespread understanding of art history, individual works of art have been assigned to key positions in an artificial fabric in which the dominant factor is the awareness of commercial value.

> This knowledge is the first step in the consumption of works of painting and sculpture, which our society organises in the same way as it organises the consumption of every other object.[2]

During the nineteenth century, works of art could be invested with a kind of ethical value which the art market today still propagates. Yet the connection between the improving of museum collections at (eventual) public expense, and the cultivation of that public's "taste" is debatable. It is, at the least, curious that the dealer has become a kind of pseudo-artist, the arbiter of other people's taste. When the curator of modern art at New York's largest museum, the Metropolitan, came to sum up the last thirty years of New York art, he displayed this view with unconscious baldness. Of all the names Henry Geldzahler listed, only one was prefaced by the title "Mr". This was a dealer; but then, as Geldzahler wrote, "the dealer . . . has earned the right to be considered as a culture-hero". Nowhere is the link between capital transactions and museum policy better expressed.

Some elements of the modern art market and the policy behind certain recent acquisitions of American museums suggest that it will not be long before the audience begins to ask itself questions about the value to them of the newly-purchased group of Turkish antiquities, the Louis XV snuffboxes, the big Kenneth Noland in its chaste strip of gilt beading. To put it at its most extreme, the connection between the formation of great collections in the twentieth-century and the public benefit has yet to be proved. In the past, the individual wealth that created most museum collections was founded on the labour of the ancestors of those who now file by to enjoy them. The railways drove back the American Indian and their founders' money enhanced the National Gallery of Washington. But that is history; and it is rare to find a public authority as embarrassed by the situation as the Glasgow City Council, when bequeathed the collection of a great shipping magnate on condition that they built a suitably monumental gallery to house it in. (Twenty years later, the predominantly working-class council has only just got round to funding the enterprise.) Nowadays, with few exceptions, the public exchequer is the ultimate patron.

A sense of absurd estrangement between the declared aims of art collecting and the money that fulfils those aims endows the art thief with a certain glamour. He is not Robin Hood, but he may look like him, if suitably presented. He becomes – and in some cases is – a cousin of the Great Train Robbers, who, for several years, were popular heroes in England. The reader senses that what is stolen represents no real deprivation for *him*: it may be far more entertaining to follow the drama of the stolen Goya *Duke of Wellington* or the Vermeer from Kenwood House than to look at the painting in a museum. For the general public, art theft has entertainment value, partly because it seems to ridicule the fetish that the quality of life depends on the recovery of some stolen Meissen swans, or a vanished Soutine. The conditions that produce a barrier between art and the public – the sense that owning a work of art is a privileged activity – enhanced by the predictable bullishness of the art market and the price-tag publicity that surrounds every newsworthy painting or sculpture – give a spurious glamour to art theft. Most people can no more imagine themselves owning a valuable painting than they can see themselves possessing the millions of pounds in the Great Train Robbers' mailbags. Every art thief has, therefore, an entertainment value to the press or television as a potential Raffles despoiling the privileged élite. The truth is quite different: the thief is merely a paid agent of receivers about whom the public knows virtually nothing. So the process of theft and redistribution of works of art forms a double market in two ways: it legitimises stolen objects and it gives the public the fantasy it requires.

Notes

[1] The best-documented account of it is given by David Roxall and Ken Wanstall in *The Jackdaw of Linz*, Cassell, 1964.
[2] Jean Cassou: *Art and Confrontation*, p. 16.

Chapter 2 Making the Market

In 1961, sixteen years after the end of the war, an American columnist in the *New York Herald Tribune* could write, "Crime in the art field definitely doesn't pay – art thievery has had something of a boom in recent years, but the thieves have been generally unsuccessful in cashing in on their loot, or in fact hanging on to it." This was a curious comment on a year that had seen more robberies of works of art than any since the high days of the Einsatzstab Rosenberg, but it shows how the nature of the subject and of the double market that had grown up in this period was misunderstood. The evidence was not in doubt: "Not in memory has the world of art been hit by a series of thefts so daring, so audacious, as those of the past few months [1961] in Europe and the United States." But the question needed to be asked: were the equally newsworthy recoveries of the most notable pictures indications that crime did not pay, or that crime had not only paid but become an institution?

One fact is easy enough to establish. The pattern of theft after 1950 was quite different from that of before 1939. Robbery of major works of art was unusual in the inter-war years and even rarer in the generation before 1914. Social and economic forces controlling the art market dictated the terms. The contrast between the narrow world of buyers and sellers then and in the 1960s, when prices at last caught up with the levels obtained in the classic private sales of Joseph Duveen to a select group of American millionaires, could scarcely be more marked. In many cases, the only link between the collector and the publicity-shunning owner was the discreet, entrepreneurial figure of the dealer. Not for the paintings of the Duke of Devonshire the glare surrounding the Impressionist sales of today, with television cameras focused on the latest van Gogh to make a record. Salerooms at the turn of the century, though famous, were patronised by a small number of dealers and a select group of well-known private collectors. Works of art nearly always came to auction in collections. The typical modern sale of, say, 200 lots from almost as many anonymous clients was virtually unknown.

How this closed shop could work was shown in 1895 at the sale in London of 448 pictures from the collection of Henry Doetsch – mainly Italian primitives, then coming slowly into fashionable esteem. The audience at Christie's made a dead set against them, apparently because some had been heavily restored and others had previously been over-optimistically attributed. But Berenson had written a scholarly catalogue and it is hard to avoid the conclusion that the low prices reflected the fact that Doetsch was a foreigner and had built up the collection on what Reitlinger calls "erudite German principles". In such circumstances, when the number of paintings and works of art in circulation was small by modern standards, and when the market was a narrow preserve, theft might not be difficult but disposal was virtually impossible.

The great eighteenth-century collections in England only began to open up and disgorge a few masterpieces at the end of the nineteenth century, after the agricultural depression forced land-owners to transfer some of their remaining assets into more productive investment. The monumental sale of the Duke of Buckingham's collection, at Stowe in 1847, imposed on him by bankruptcy after a generation of conspicuous spending, was unusual. Even in the 1880s, the Marlborough and Hamilton Palace sales were characterised by sluggish bidding. In Europe the art market was still less developed: the great houses maintained and often increased their treasures. Very few, before 1914, followed the example of the Marchese Cesare Imperiale, who, in defiance of Italian law, smuggled across the frontier the superb van Dycks from the noble families of Cattaneo, Durazzo and Adorno, in a false exhaust pipe attached to his open touring car, and sold the best of them, through a French dealer, to the American P. A. B. Widener.

Thus, when the American burglar and confidence trickster, Adam Worth, stole the Gainsborough *Duchess of Devonshire* from Agnew's Gallery in Bond Street in 1876, he landed his gang with an unsaleable white elephant. The *Duchess* was on exhibition, having just realised £10,000 (at that date the second highest figure ever paid) in spite of very well-justified doubts as to her authenticity. Cut down from its original size and, in the opinion of most judges, a studio copy, quite possibly not even of the famous Georgiana, the picture nevertheless created a furore in the London art world, then witnessing the beginning of the vogue for English eighteenth-century portraits; and it became the centre of a triangular contest between Lord Dudley, Baron Ferdinand de Rothschild and Agnew's, who intended to sell it to the American financier, Junius Spencer Morgan, father of J. Pierpont Morgan.

Worth's criminal career as a successful safe-breaker, burglar and confidence trickster, though less successful gambler, set him high on the wanted list at Scotland Yard and in America, where he served one term of imprisonment. His facility for assuming the habits of whatever society he preyed on provided a succession of novelists with inspiration for their gentleman crooks – Raffles being the most direct. But Worth came into this case for reasons of loyalty, not profit. His brother John had been arrested in Paris and extradited to England for trial. When bail was offered, Adam Worth's jail sentence in America debarred him from standing surety. Lacking rich and gullible friends, he decided to steal the *Duchess* and ransom it back to Agnew's in return for his brother's bail. Working with two members of his gang, he removed it at night from the gallery without experiencing much difficulty. Agnew's offered a reward of £1,000, at that date an enormous sum. The police were set to watch the ports and railway stations and warnings were telegraphed to New York and the continent. Then a legal flaw was found in the extradition warrant for John Worth and he was freed.

There now existed no *raison d'être* for the theft. The *Duchess* was obviously unsaleable through any normal channel. Probably every likely bidder in the world had known of the legitimate sale and its result. On the other hand, there was still the £1,000 reward. Worth's principal lieutenant, Jack Philipps, tried to sell it – and his leader – to the police; and another member of the gang, arrested later in New York, tried to use his knowledge to bargain his way out. But there was no actual evidence against Worth. Under English law he could be convicted only if he were found in possession, a situation he

23

took great care to avoid. It was months before he dared ship the *Duchess* across the Atlantic, in a trunk with a false bottom, to a hiding place in Chicago, where he started his long correspondence with Agnew's.

The obstacles against ransom dealing proved to be greater than Worth had imagined. In the manner of many criminals of the 1960s, he threatened to destroy the *Duchess* if the police were told, and he sent a number of small pieces of the canvas to prove that he held it. But although there was no extradition treaty between Britain and the United States, so that Worth was not at risk, and although Agnew's were willing to deal at a starting price of £3,000 in gold, Worth had to cross the intangible barrier of confidence in Agnew's willingness to pay, and he had somehow to return the canvas, take the ransom and yet avoid the severe penalties for compounding a felony, which he would risk if he, or his agent, were caught in England. From December 1876 to August 1877 the letters from New York and advertisements in *The Times* continued, but Worth's solicitor in London proved too timid for his plans and in the end Worth had to confess to Agnew's, "I have vainly endeavoured to think of some safe way of negotiating the return of the Lady on this side of the water according to your desire (although it would be considerable expense to bring it over to England again). But I cannot see my way clear to do so without putting myself in your power and that I will not do."

Instead, he returned to his criminal career and prospered for another fourteen years, until arrested and jailed in Belgium. In prison he rejected offers for the return of the Gainsborough, but when, in 1897, he eventually emerged, ill and impoverished, he was more ready to listen. The picture was probably his chief remaining asset, and in January 1900 he contacted William A. Pinkerton, one of the directors of the detective agency. Pinkerton's played fair with him and passed on enough information to Agnew's and Scotland Yard to convince them that the deal was genuine. One of the partners from Agnew's came to Chicago, identified the *Duchess* and paid out an undisclosed amount, probably $5,000, the equivalent of the original reward. Worth died less than a year later, and J. Pierpont Morgan duly fulfilled his father's desire to buy the picture. The price of the *Duchess*, however, was now £35,000, no mean profit to Agnew's even after a quarter of a century.

In 1911, at the all-time pinnacle of competition for old-master paintings, when Duveen was busily supplying the varied tastes of Widener, Benjamin Altmann, Morgan, Mrs Gardiner and Henry Clay Frick, at prices he judged suitable to their capacity and self-esteem, the *Mona Lisa* disappeared from the Louvre in Paris. The robbery is too well-known to tell again in detail, but its sequel showed how impossible it still was either to sell so prominent a work of art or to ransom its return.

The Leonardo was stolen by an Italian, Vincenzo Perugia, who had been employed as a painter and decorator in the Louvre for six months. He was well known to the guards and had no trouble in getting in on a day in August when the museum was closed for repairs. After extracting the *Mona Lisa* from its frame, he hid it under his painter's smock and walked out. The loss was not discovered until the next day. The Paris police searched him and his house, as they did every other employee of the Louvre, but failed to find the painting, although in fact he held it there for two and a half years. Later, he returned to Italy, judging that the search had been called off, and answered an advertisement put in the press by a Florentine antique dealer, Alfredo Geri, who was mounting an exhibition of old master paintings. Perugia demanded the equivalent of £20,000 and was trapped by Geri, who recognised the *Mona Lisa* at once. The curator of the Uffizi museum was called in with his staff of experts and Perugia was arrested the next day.

At his trial, in June 1914, Perugia claimed that he had been moved by "pure patriotism". Da Vinci had been an Italian, and he had done no more than restore the Gioconda to the land of her birth – a counter-blow to Napoleon for the plunder of Italy a century before. The police seized Perugia's diary and found Geri's name in a list of dealers and private collectors, but in spite of this evidence of careful preparation for resale, his lawyer's emotional plea that the theft had been done for love of beauty and his native land – "to think differently would be to wrong the gentle, generous and chivalrous French nation" – was well received, and Perugia was sentenced to only one year in prison. Beyond the courtroom was a wider gallery: in the last months before the European war broke out, Italy, a member of the Triple Alliance with Germany and Austria-Hungary, but uneasy at the foreign policies of both, was only too happy to be on good terms with France. The less scandal the better; and after brief exhibitions in Florence, Milan and Rome, the *Mona Lisa* was restored with appropriate felicitations to the Louvre, where it remained undisturbed, the object of unreasoning homage, until its next, more spectacular journey abroad: this time to America, where it conveyed a cultural and essentially Gallic benison on the Kennedy administration.

Alfredo Geri was granted 25,000 gold francs by the Society of Friends of the Louvre; but his request for a percentage of the total value was rejected by a French court on the superb ground that, being priceless, the painting "had no value". The Louvre authorities would have agreed, for the *Mona Lisa* was not properly insured. Then, as now, museums tended to seek cover for the full value of works of art principally against loss by fire, and only to a small degree against theft. If Perugia had attempted to sell the picture back to the Louvre, he would have needed not only an organisation more competent than Adam Worth's, but also the sort of publicity and sense of national deprivation that did not become commonplace until half a century later.

The uncertain art market of the 1930s was only slightly less formal and private than it had been in 1911. "People" still sold their possessions at Christie's (Sotheby's vogue is a post-war phenomenon), and art dealing was still, in the lifetime of Duveen (by then Lord Millbank), a respectable, even exclusive profession. Prices had weakened during the world depression: in the United States neither the Stock Market nor art sales had fully revived by 1939. Europe was increasingly disturbed, and even Britain, which recovered most quickly, witnessed a reluctance to invest, an odd puritanical attitude towards ostentatious spending which reflected the presence of the hunger-marchers and awareness of the approach of war. The craving for portraits of the eighteenth-century English school had largely evaporated, although Duveen himself did what he could to sustain the market by taking care that his former clients should, when they died, pass on their collections to public bodies like the newly founded National Gallery of Washington, or the Metropolitan Museum of New York. Other fields were less protected: the works of most seventeenth-century masters declined in value, and the

26

market for French furniture, avidly collected on both sides of the Atlantic by Mrs Gardiner and Lady Cowdray, suffered a catastrophic fall. Lady Cowdray died in 1933 and the prices realised for her collection were, by more recent standards, absurd. Economic circum stances inhibited art theft.

Of course, the majority of thefts were conducted on nothing like the scale of Worth's or Perugia's operations. From country houses, châteaux, schlossen and American mansions, there had flowed a haphazard stream of more saleable objects, principally silver and jewels. A mass of middle-grade things, including porcelain, armour and weapons, unrecorded and unphotographed, must have come on the market between 1876 and 1939. But the distinction between that period and the decades since 1950 is that the double market, the *organisation* either for legitimising stolen property or for ransoming it back to its owners, did not exist. In almost every case, the balance between notoriety and marketability weighed against the criminals. Two examples will suffice.

In 1938, a country-house party were staying at Chilham Castle in Kent, as guests of the mining tycoon and collector, Sir Edmund Davis. When the servants began to clean and lay the fires on Sunday morning, they found a light still burning, a window forced open and, on the floor of the picture gallery, five frames from which had been cut pictures exactly suited to the taste of millionaire private collectors as it had been twenty years earlier – two Gainsborough portraits, a Reynolds, a van Dyck, and Rembrandt's *Saskia at her Toilet*. The job might have been done by the ghost of Adam Worth and it lacked only the shooting of the butler to set the scene for one of Agatha Christie's early detective stories; but the thieves failed to sell their loot. Ten years earlier, in Moscow, a gang had taken a Rembrandt, a Titian and a Correggio from the State Museum of Fine Arts – an expertly planned operation in which they had had to break into a room containing only the Rembrandt, through an iron grill high in the outside wall. Russian papers reported that it was the work of imperialists, who had smuggled the pictures out of the country. No sale took place in the West, however, and in 1932 four men were arrested. The paintings were found covered with a preservative wax, buried in sealed containers only a mile away, still in Moscow. It may have been true that inside the socialist state, where private property had been officially abolished, theft for resale had become an impossibility; but the contrast with Western circumstances was not marked. In the most interesting affair of the inter-war years, the thief encountered the same problems. Parts of the case, involving a painting almost as famous as the *Mona Lisa*, remain a mystery to this day.

The altar-piece of the Cathedral of St Bavo in Ghent, called the *Adoration of the Lamb*, by the brothers Hubert and Jan van Eyck, is one of the supreme works of the northern Renaissance. Painted, according to local tradition, for Jodocus Vijdts, seigneur of Pamele, in 1432, its centre panels depict Jesus flanked by Mary and Joseph, and, below them, the scene of the Resurrection. These are covered by two immense doors, each four feet by ten, with smaller scenes of Adam and Eve, choirs of angels, the Garden of Gethsemane, and, on the bottom left, two panels of horses and elaborately dressed riders, known as the Virtuous Judges. To attempt to describe the effect of the whole would be otiose; the altar-piece has justly been the glory of Flanders for five hundred years.

Its recent history has been troubled and it has some claim to be the most plundered masterpiece in Europe. What is now Belgium once belonged to the Hapsburg Empire, and in 1781 the prudish Joseph II ordered the naked Adam and Eve to be replaced by copies in which the figures were dressed ludicrously in bearskins. The centre part was hauled to Paris as part of Napoleon's cultural booty and not restored until 1815. Soon afterwards the impoverished bishopric of Ghent sanctioned the sale of six outer panels to a French art dealer, who passed them on to the King of Prussia; for nearly a century they stayed in Germany, latterly in the Berlin Museum. From there they were restored or, according to many Germans, looted as part of the Peace Settlement in 1919. In the meantime, the short-sighted clerical authorities had sold another two panels to the Brussels Museum, leaving only the centre. Not until 1921 were the twelve panels reunited.

As befits its dominant position, the altar-piece is massively constructed. The thief, who in April 1934 detached the 52 by 22-inch bottom left-hand panel (half of the Virtuous Judges), must have been something of a carpenter, because skill as well as force had been used to prise off the long iron hinges. To put off the searchers the thief had hung a placard in its place – "taken from Germany by the Versailles Treaty" – but although some Belgian newspapers raised the cry of Nazi aggression, this interpretation was short-lived. The crowd that surged into the chapel where the altar-piece stands obliterated any traces that the thief might have left, but the police suspected soon enough what would happen.

Three weeks later the Bishop of Ghent, Monseigneur Coppieters, received a typed letter signed with the initials D.U.A., demanding a ransom of one million Belgian francs and giving detailed instructions as to how this should be handed over. At the same time, to prove his credentials, D.U.A. enclosed a baggage ticket, which took the police to Brussels Nord railway station, where they found the reverse of the panel, painted with the figure of St John the Baptist. (Each of the door panels carries *trompe l'œil* representations of the saints, simulating the carved figures of early mediaeval reliquaries, and, while in Berlin, this panel had at some time been sawn in half lengthwise, to exhibit both sides.) The letter also carried the threat that, if the money were not paid, the Virtuous Judges would disappear for ever.

By 1934, admiration for the work of the van Eycks was based on a far more scholarly understanding of the later middle ages than had been current in the nineteenth century. Well aware that the chapel at St Bavo was an internationally celebrated shrine for art lovers, the Brussels police formulated their reply with caution. To trap the thief they announced through the Bishop that money would be paid and that the authorities would deal with D.U.A.'s nominee, a local priest, Father Meulapas, who had apparently been told by D.U.A. only that he was to act as an intermediary in a case involving the stolen and scandalous letters of a highly placed Belgian family. According to his instructions, Meulapas was to hand over the money to an unknown man and collect from him half of a torn sheet of newspaper. The thief would then post the rest of the sheet to the Bishop and hand over the panel to the priest. Father Meulapas would restore it to the bearer of the matching piece of paper.

The use of a priest's confessional secrecy was one of the more ingenious answers to the perennial problem of collecting ransom money without risking arrest. But in this case D.U.A. seemed unable to follow through with equivalent skill. The authorities pretended to co-operate: they duly handed over 25,000 francs as payment for St John the Baptist and offered 225,000 more for the other half. D.U.A. refused to bargain and asked for half a million at once and 400,000 later, after restitution. This rather naïve approach was taken by the police to mean that he was an amateur in financial trouble. Wary of becoming too implicated in the deal, they instructed the Bishop not to reply.

A heavily one-sided correspondence ensued until, six months after the theft, came the last letter from D.U.A. As a final threat he declared that if there were no response now "the immortal masterpiece would disappear for ever"; and he added: "nobody in the world, not even one of us, will be able to see it . . . it will remain where it now is without anyone being able to lay hands on it".

Six weeks later Arsene Goerdetier, a local baker, highly respected in the nearby town of Wetteren, suffered a heart attack. Surrounded by friends in his bedroom, he summoned his lawyer, Georges de Vos. When de Vos arrived his client was near death, and all that he heard was, "I alone know where the *Adoration of the Lamb* is. You will find the complete file in my small study, in the right-hand drawer of my desk . . .".

De Vos found carbon copies of all the D.U.A. letters there, but no other documents and no clue as to where the panel was hidden. He told the Wetteren magistrate, who passed on the news to three senior lawyers, including the Ghent public prosecutor; but for a whole month the police were not informed. During that time the lawyers conducted their own discreet investigation, taking care to safeguard the Goerdetier family name. They found the typewriter used for the letters and various oddments, including a mysterious key that did not fit any lock in any relevant building; and nothing else. The police did no better and, finally, at the outbreak of the 1939 war, the case was closed. By then a copy had been made by a distinguished restorer and hung to complete the altarpiece.

Almost at once the whole was taken apart and stored in southern France. After the setting up of the Vichy régime, it was discovered and taken, with the rest of the Nazi loot, to the Alt Aussee salt mine, and was not recovered until 1945. Meanwhile, during the occupation of Belgium, Oberleutnant Köhn of the so-called Art Protection

30

Department was assigned to track down the missing panel. Such special attention can be explained by the fact that it was still regarded as genuinely the property of the Berlin Museum; but although Köhn interrogated de Vos and others, he got nowhere. For a long time afterwards there was only silence, except that for fifteen years a Belgian policeman, Commissioner Mortier, pursued the Virtuous Judges as his personal hobby. He asked a number of questions which suggest that a scandal may lie behind the published facts.[1]

Mortier asked: why did the magistrates work on their own for a month? Why were de Vos, and the priest and friends who were with Goerdetier when he died, not questioned at all by the police? Why were some documents apparently missing from the Ghent archives, and why has the whole file of the Köhn inquiry disappeared from Koblenz? Why were the articles of a Belgian journalist working on the case in 1934 cut short after he had been summoned to the Archbishop's palace? The search for the Virtuous Judges, like the search for the remains of the Russian Royal Family, proved to be one of those stories in which every lead turned into a dead end. And what did the enigmatic sentence in D.U.A.'s undelivered last letter mean? "The Virtuous Judges is in a place where neither I nor anyone else can take it away without attracting public attention." The panel was too large and heavy for a small man like Goerdetier to move alone. Goerdetier's relations suggested that he did it to help a distinguished family out of financial difficulties – but behind this explanation lurked the subtle suggestion of ecclesiastical scandal. By the time this chapter came to be written, nearly all the participants were dead, and the only remaining hope that the Virtuous Judges would be found was that it would reappear in the manner of the Michelangelo crucifix, which an American art historian chanced to discover, coated with centuries of dirt, in the cloisters of San Annunziata in Florence, only yards from the high altar whence it had vanished in the seventeenth century. In March 1974, however, came the extraordinary discovery: as the altar-piece was being cleaned, the restorer noticed that the pigment of the "copy" of the Virtuous Judges seemed to be authentic. Further cleaning revealed the truth: the "copy" was actually the original and had hung for forty years, as Arsene Goerdetier had promised, in full view of the public, yet where no one would ever see it.

The only notable case of the 1930s to stand comparison with post-war art crime took place in 1933, when Paul Thouin, a professional burglar in Montreal, unsuccessfully attempted to ransom the Van Horne collection of old masters from the Art Association Gallery. Thouin was an expert thief, but a less able connoisseur. Having forced his way in, he slit from their frames sixteen pictures (worth at the most $30,000) belonging to a loan exhibition of living Canadian artists, and never went into the adjoining room where the bulk of the Van Hornes were. Thouin was out on bail at the time and the police suspected him, without being able to prove anything. He sent ransom letters to the Montreal papers, threatening to destroy all the canvases; and actually sliced one in half and posted it to the *Montreal Star*. At no time did Thouin ask for more than $10,000, realising from the first that he had got the wrong hostages. Some of the artists appeared keen to redeem their own work, but the case broke open when Thouin, attempting to steal from a railway truck in a goods yard, was arrested by railway policemen and shot one of them dead. He admitted to everything and agreed to lead the police to the wood near the city where he had buried the remaining canvases. Then, in jail, he slipped all justice by swallowing a strychnine pill, hidden in the heel of his shoe. In a way, Paul Thouin symbolised the end of the line that began with Adam Worth. Raffles was out; the age of the common – and professional – criminal had begun.

The war cut a great trench across the art market, disrupting all the old patterns of trade. Most of Europe was occupied by German forces; Britain was cut off, and Spain, Portugal, Sweden and Switzerland lay quietly neutral. In London prices fell fast as the bombing started in 1940. The second part of the magnificent Eumorphopoulos collection of Asiatic art was disposed of at knock-down prices at the very moment of the Dunkirk evacuation. In the United States, where the impact of war was substantially less, the art market recovered enough after the middle of the war to lead the world in the late 1940s. Even so, in quantity and real value, prices represented no advance on the 1930s. The free flow of antiques and works of art, like blood through the arteries of Western countries, had not been restored. Consequently, art theft was at a discount. Only silver held steady, a reflection of the instinct to grab portable bullion in uncertain times. During and just after the war a few far-sighted or lucky buyers picked up such bargains as a Botticelli *tondo* of the Holy Family for £6,000, or a Renoir landscape for £800.

There was, indeed, a glut on the market, induced by the war and continuously replenished by refugees, exiled from their countries by the Nazis and later the Russians, selling off their surviving possessions for what they could get. The post-war years, therefore, were excellent for art thieves in one way, but bad in another. It was easy to steal things but hard to dispose of them for adequate reward. Obviously, this was not a situation to attract the professional, who still preferred his traditional targets – silver, gold and jewels. If an astute art thief had spread a sheet on the ground and waited for fifteen years, he could have made a fortune from the detritus of works of art in Europe when the guns fell silent. But, as far as can be discovered, no such entrepreneur of the criminal world emerged, although there is evidence that many far-sighted Italians latched on to the golden caravanserai passing through Italy into Germany, or helped themselves from empty mansions and museums as the fabric of Mussolini's government collapsed.

What strikes one most about the post-1945 years is the haphazard way in which theft developed, following different patterns in different countries. The experience of Spain and Portugal contrasted sharply with that of the rest of Europe. There, a public market had scarcely existed before 1939. The great families rarely sold from their collections, and if they did, for reasons of poverty or changing taste, they took care to disguise what amounted to loss of face. Most of the few dealers in Spain had, and still have, contacts with the aristocracy, and in upstairs rooms they would show discreet customers "the property of a noble family", and offer to ship it out through the customs for a fee high enough to offset the risk of breaking the wide-ranging laws surrounding export of the nation's artistic heritage. There was little scope for a thief here, unless he ran straight for the French frontier. Given the scale of Spanish palaces, such as those of the Dukes of Lerma or the Marqués de Larios, walled mediaeval fortresses containing collections that were known only to friends and with corridors that were patrolled by retinues of servants, it is not surprising that few thefts occurred.

Instead, in equal defiance of the laws on export and the sale of church property, the despoliation of country churches and small monasteries grew. Many had been damaged in the bitter fighting and anti-clerical outrages of the Civil War and reduced to desperate poverty. In remote parishes, hill villages in the stony uplands of New Castile or Estremadura, the support formerly given by pious donations withered away. Parish priests, monks and nuns began to sell off the ornaments of their churches, the furniture or the simple and often ancient religious paintings, not so much for profit as to support themselves and their duties to the poor. Antique dealers would tour round, perhaps up the valley of the Guadalquivir to Córdoba, and return with *vargueños*, *mudéjar* furniture or paintings on copper panels, which were freely available to tourists in the early 1950s. Within half a dozen years, as the tourist industry grew in geometrical progression, demand overstepped supply, and was filled partly by fakes – crude daubs, darkened with oil and the smoke of candles – and partly by theft from the same largely unguarded churches and chapels. Since no record existed, it would have been impossible to have traced these things, even if the police or the frontier customs had been energetic in attempting to enforce the law. Sad and pitiable though this trade was, it did not represent a very large part of theft in Europe; but it did foreshadow the relationship between demand and supply from which the double market grew.

Outside the closed societies of Salazar and Franco, the dealers who had survived the war in Europe looked warily about and disliked what they saw. Germany and Italy were in ruins and under military occupation. Russian armies swamped half of Austria, Poland and Czechoslovakia. Everywhere else was austerity: on top of rationing, myriad currency restrictions had been imposed. No British dealer could take sterling to buy antiques in Europe, and French dealers could not easily buy in England even if they wished to. The war seemed to have sharpened feelings of xenophobia. Such interest as there was in the art market lay principally in collectors' own national heritage – an instinct akin perhaps to hoarding.[2] In London there was no demand for continental furniture; in Paris, none for the English style. Americans were disinclined to buy or to travel widely in Europe. American museums were still absorbing the remnants of the great collections of the pre-war millionaires. It was widely believed that art was cheap and likely to remain so – an attitude of mind confirmed by experience not only of the war, but also of the previous ten years. So, through a period of intense inflation, people sought in gold and diamonds a counter to depreciating currencies, and it is significant that the wave of jewel thefts began to preoccupy the police in the late 1940s, continuing for nearly ten years afterwards, while art theft was not perceived as a problem until the 1950s.

The formation of the Federal German Republic in 1948 and the reform of the German currency under Allied supervision greatly improved confidence in the art market. In France, and eventually in Britain, austerity receded and restrictions were cut back. The Russians moved out of Vienna in 1955; in Western Europe the Schuman Plan set the stage for the creation of the Common Market. With reviving prosperity, land values and house prices rose. Most notably in Germany and Italy, the countries hardest hit by war, but also in Belgium, Holland, Austria and to a lesser extent in France, there developed the normal concomitant of prosperity, concern with the tangible evidence of status. Just as the British *nouveaux riches* of the nineteenth century had sought out castles, real or reproduction, and stuffed their grand houses with old furniture and suits of armour, so the revived European middle class craved a link with history as a means of finding an identity. Economic position, buttressed with authentic art, would symbolise the new social order, enabling them to inherit the past without the uncomfortable memories of what the previous possessors had stood for.

Back in the 1870s, at the time of Germany's unification and industrial revolution, there had been a revival of traditional art, which can be seen as a search for Teutonic antecedents: painstaking copies of sixteenth-century drinking glasses, tall *Humpen* and green *Römer*, painted with hunting scenes and German mottoes, flooded the market. It is hardly a coincidence that the first of the post-war fashions to sweep the rich houses of industrial Germany was for pewter tankards and almost any mementos of the hunting and drinking past.

Theft of such ordinary objects caused the police little worry. Cars and jewels, far more expensive status symbols, were in illegal circulation, and a blind eye was turned towards the trade in antiques. Theft was both widespread and trivial. The markets in Frankfurt and elsewhere, run by the Allied armies since the end of the war, performed a useful service, and neither party involved in bargaining works of art and trinkets for food and cigarettes had inquired too closely into the provenance of what was sold.

Legitimate sources of genuine and reproduction articles satisfied the bulk of the demand for antiques until fashion lighted on carved wooden statues. Wood-carving is traditionally a south German art and, since the middle ages, Catholic churches and chapels had been filled with polychrome statues of the Madonna and Child and of all the saints. Few had survived from before 1500 but, covering the years down to the age of plaster copies, there was a vast range of works, from those of the master craftsmen of the Renaissance, such as Tillman Riemenschneider, down to crudely worked figures from village churches, or the little *feldkappellen* (field chapels) in Bavaria and the Austrian Tyrol. A handful of outstanding late Gothic works were recognised by scholars, but for the most part these figures were unrecorded. Depicting the patron saints of small communities, they represented in the Catholic South objects of devotion which, like the icons of Eastern Europe, acquired veneration by antiquity and folk memory, rather than by artistic merit. Yet because they fitted the same requirements as had already accommodated pewter tankards, heavily carved chests, pistols and spinning wheels, they became *objets décoratifs*, divorced absolutely from any religious connotation; they can be seen used even as menu holders in elegant restaurants.

During the centuries since the Reformers had equated Madonnas with idolatry, large numbers of these statues had passed into secular hands and many more were sold quasi-legally by Catholic churches, or looted in the chaotic period after 1945. Nevertheless, demand soon outstripped sales. Forgers working on old timbers from demolished houses built up a new cottage industry. Later, even the carvers of Oberammergau failed to keep pace. Especially in Bavaria, but also in the Tyrol, Upper Austria, parts of northern Italy, and Yugoslavia, small churches and *feldkappellen* were at risk. Most large farms in Bavaria have their tiny private shrines, and even smaller ones stand exposed in the fields or at country cross-roads. Formerly they were left unlocked and open: who would bother to enter except for private devotion? Theft was too easy and the patron saints were torn out to satisfy the cultural longings of industrialists in Düsseldorf and Essen to whom their original context meant nothing.

36

Some were not very valuable, and inexperienced thieves occasionally took plaster reproductions. But, quite apart from despoliation of the religious tradition, many of the figures taken were of great artistic value. By their own admission, the German police were slow to realise the scale of these thefts, and it was not until the Riemenschneider affair in 1962 (described in Chapter 6) that the ramifications of the trade became known. By taking a famous work of art, the most highly organised gang overreached itself. What they had done, so the police discovered, was to create a well-defined business, reaching beyond Germany, with its own forms of protection and a network of outlets through the antique trade.

Sales of antiques at auctions were not a feature of the 1950s in Germany: most of the legitimate traffic was carried on from dealers' shops or by private individuals advertising in newspapers. Unless the statues were smuggled out by the thieves through Belgium to London salerooms, or to Paris or Berne, the facilities for largely unquestioned disposal afforded by the auction-room were denied. If they were sold openly to dealers, the police would stand too great a chance of recovery, and dealers themselves would refuse to buy even authenticated objects. This gang conceived the idea of making a pool of the statues. They employed expert wood-carvers and restorers who would take, say, a seventeenth-century St Joseph, remove his head and add the head of St Matthew. A Madonna carrying the Infant Jesus would have her arms cut off and replaced by others bearing an orb and sceptre. Retouching the paint, regilding, removing or adding a halo or a crown, at once made unrecognisable statues the records of which were, in the vast majority of cases, merely written descriptions. File after file in police records in Vienna, Zürich or Wiesbaden gives simply the measurements and the date of stolen figures. Thus, in Interpol file "670/OV/453/61: Austria", we find the following entry:

> 25 March 1961, between 12.0 and 5.0 p.m. the statue of St. John the Evangelist stolen from the collegiate church of Mattsee, Salzburg. Gilt wood, holding a chalice in left hand, height twelve inches, date 1649, value about 6,000 schillings.

If this were turned into St John the Baptist or the chalice removed, of what value was the description?

The gang, with fifteen members in 1961, at the peak of its activities, was headed by a German known as "V". Part of their work was of course straightforward forgery of a higher standard than the crude productions of the south German wood-carving industry. The theft side of the business (for it *was* a business) covered virtually the whole of Catholic Central Europe. The gang's workshops were sited in Bayreuth and Nuremberg. The majority of pieces were sold to unsuspecting or unquestioning German dealers, or through newspaper advertisements direct to private clients. Only after the Riemenschneider case did the extent of these operations become clear and, following a public outcry, the Bundeskriminalamt, headquarters of the Federal German police force at Wiesbaden, set up a special regional squad (*sonderkommission*) to cover Bavaria. The greater concern shown by the Land police, and the more meticulous cataloguing and photographing of church treasures that followed, proved to be forerunners of a more general counter-attack.

V's organisation was broken up and he moved to Turkey with a false passport to escape the attention of Karl Berger, head of the Bundeskriminalamt section covering art theft. Later, Berger chased him to Istanbul, where he was caught and extradited. But V's activities represented only a small part of the pillage of church treasures in the last years before the European national authorities woke up to what was happening. The same demand for status symbols had erupted in Italy and Austria. In both cases, former wartime black-marketeers found profitable peacetime sidelines. Viennese colleagues of Harry Lime searched restlessly for new outlets after the Russian withdrawal in 1955. Austrian police records go back only to 1959, but the traffic in church thefts was by then already well established. Most statues went westwards into Switzerland or Germany, and a considerable number passed through Austria, in transit from Yugoslavia, via the small roads through the mountains of Carinthia. Inside Austria itself the records of national treasures were in such chaos that Interpol files as late as 1965 record the recovery from a river bank in Upper Austria of a haul of statues that had never even been reported stolen. In such circumstances it presented no problem to the thieves to steal in Klagenfurt or Graz and dispose of loot in Vienna itself.

The trade ramified into France and Belgium, though not into

Protestant Holland. After 1955, hardly a week went by without reports in *Figaro* or *Le Monde* of the disappearance of similar statues, crucifixes and candelabra from villages all over France. Occasionally the local curé was discovered selling church inventories to dealers, or handing over the objects and replacing them with modern copies, but most such cases passed unseen. The priests, similarly to the fathers of San Felipo Neri in a case described below, often failed to realise that, since by French law the buildings and treasures of the church are the responsibility of the state, they had no right to sell what they understood to be the property of the parish. If money were needed to retile the roof, recourse to selling statues and the like seemed easy; and many priests found modern plaster copies of the saints as good as, or better than, the worm-eaten originals. At first they also had the excuse that they knew nothing of the real value of what had gone. According to a member of France's Commission on Historic Monuments, the majority of such sales were made, in complete ignorance of market values, by priests totally exploited, like the monks of southern Spain. But the majority of crimes were probably organised from outside, and it became so serious that the French television journalist, Pierre de Lagarde, spent a year investigating the subject for the O.R.T.F. network. In 1964 he handed over to the police a comprehensive survey of the known post-war thefts, including notes on specialised gangs and many antique dealers operating as receivers.

In Italy, the receivers included a fair proportion of the dealers who had assisted Goering's pillage during the war, and also many ex-suppliers of the black market. Changing the object of their dealings from scarce consumer goods and the traffic in stolen cars to antiques and antiquities, they began to form specialised gangs, expert in separate types of merchandise. The result afflicted churches, museums and private collections to a more serious degree than in any other European country. Italian churches were in many cases more richly adorned, and with few exceptions had suffered less from bombing during the war. It seems from Interpol records that the thefts in this period in Italy were consistently of more valuable church treasures than were stolen in similar thefts north of the Alps. The case of the *Madonna* of Rieti is typical: in November 1963, an ivory statue of the Madonna dei Fiore, carved in the fourteenth century from a single elephant's tusk, disappeared. It was a particularly fine example of French Gothic style, valued – somewhat extravagantly for the period – at 200 million lire. It had stood in an alcove of the high altar, protected by an iron mesh door, held with chains and three padlocks, all of which had been forced.

The Rieti *Madonna* is only one example out of hundreds of works sucked into the vortex. For nearly a decade, however, the national pattern went either unnoticed or deliberately ignored, and no general police or government counter-measures were attempted.

For sheer size, the case of the fathers of San Felipo Neri in Naples can stand as an example of the first stage (roughly 1955–64) in the despoliation of the Italian artistic patrimony. It reveals a great deal about the ambiguous relationship between church and state, evident in Italy as much as in France. In September 1961, two priests, Fathers Guido Martinelli and Alessandro Vasco, were charged with disposing of over £500,000-worth of treasures from the patrimony of the church and its art gallery and selling them to Neapolitan antique dealers – eight of whom were arrested at the same time.

The order to which this church belongs is a religious society without vows, whose members live their communal life in greater freedom than their counterparts in monastic orders. Members of the society, founded by San Felipo in 1575, lived from their own private means, but were expected to donate all their property to the order. Since the Naples house had for four hundred years been staffed with young men of aristocratic families, it had acquired a monumental treasure of works of art, gold vessels and tapestries, and a library of over 100,000 volumes. The duties of the order, however, demanded considerable expense: they were enjoined to shelter poor students and in particular to look after and educate the myriad street urchins, the *scugnizzi* of the slums, who formed the most searing social problem of Naples.

The church had been bombed in the war, the roof burnt out, and for a while it lay open to the sky. Afterwards and during restoration, haphazard looting took place, but no great depredation had occurred before 1954, when the superiors in Rome sent the two fathers to take over from the existing prior in Naples, a cantankerous, elderly man. Martinelli became prior and Vasco steward, with responsibility for the art collection and finances. Vasco became remarkably popular with the poor in that part of Naples, but not with the former prior. Soon, anonymous letters arrived in Rome denouncing the new men for pilfering the treasure. Neither the order nor the police acted. Eventually, by his own account, Martinelli became suspicious and accused Vasco, who was deposed by his superiors in 1956 and transferred to another house of the order in Turin. Professor Molajoli, superintendent of Naples art galleries, began an investigation. During the next three years he put together a full catalogue, revealing that over 400 items, including paintings, ivory and gold crucifixes, church furniture, lamps, candlesticks, silver, many of the valuable books and even the marble walls of the chapel, were missing.

The list was difficult to compile and to begin with included the finest pictures of all – a Guido Reni, a Luca Giordano and others – but these were eventually tracked down to various state art galleries or restorers' laboratories – in itself a fair comment on the chaotic state of the records of the Ministry of Fine Arts. Some of the vanished articles were traced to Neapolitan dealers, one of whom was caught in possession of the church bells, a seventeenth-century clock and piles of illuminated manuscripts.

The despoliation was probably the most extensive since the Nazi raids and the great bulk of it was irrecoverable, having gone through the channels of the trade in the previous five years, via dealers who could claim a legitimate title. But, it was asked, was the affair in any real sense a crime? Before the nationalisation of the church's artistic property, following the prolonged nineteenth-century dispute between the Italian state and the Vatican over the temporal power of the Papacy, the fathers would have had every right to sell what was unquestionably the property of the order, to fulfil their duty in giving to the poor. Thus they justified themselves: neither had made money out of the deals and they had, through very hard times, been generous to the *scugnizzi*. The locals claimed "they were saints, not thieves". Only in terms of the nineteenth-century nationalisation of church property had they committed a criminal offence, even though they had disobeyed their superiors' instructions.

The state lost its property; so did the church; and behind them both the double market had taken shape, speeding the legitimate passage of the treasure to the villas of Milan or Ascona. The dealers had given paltry, knock-down prices. In due course the Ministry of Fine Arts was to tighten its procedures and spur on the proper recording of the Italian artistic partrimony. But depredation had gone a long way by the end of 1961 and the record was not encouraging. The demands of the Italian consumers grew with eating, like those of their German counterparts. As an indication of the scope of the traffic, in the same autumn as the arrest of the two fathers, a thirteenth-century figure of Our Lady of the Sorrows vanished from Ghent; so did a Virgin and Child from the Swiss canton of Ticino, a fourteenth-century St John the Baptist from a church near Brescia, and in Asolo Alto four carvings of angels by Brusteron, listed as Italian national monuments. By any standard these were major works of art, none of them at today's prices worth less than £5,000. Through the interaction of thief and receiver a permanent pattern of redistribution was being set up, following the channels developed by post-war racketeers but with the novel effect that at the end the object was returned, intact or transformed, but with impeccable pedigree, to the legitimate trade and a private customer. A parallel can be made with cars stolen, repainted and re-registered, and whisked across national frontiers. Thus, in Belgium in 1966, police caught two English thieves transporting statues stolen in Germany to a potential buyer in Holland. This was international business and it had run out of control long before the ecclesiastical or secular authorities responded.

But the second-hand car trade is not really a fair comparison, for it has none of the mystique of the world of antiques; nor does it offer the same opportunities for re-attribution and erroneous identification – both weapons in the receiver's armoury. G. K. Chesterton's answer to the question "where do you best hide a stolen Madonna?" still holds good: among a hundred others, of similar age, style and decrepitude. At the Sixth German Art and Antiques Fair in 1961 there were over 30,000 visitors. The succeeding year, when £1 million-worth of antiques were put on view in Munich, by over a hundred dealers, the business journal *Handelsblatt* suggested that "a new form of art dealing" was on the way. "Both sides, exhibitor and buyer, profit from this display, the one from the enormous choice, the other from the very interested, steadily growing stream of visitors." A large part of the total was made up by sacred art – in many forms, now wholly undenominational, and destined for the living-rooms of Hamburg, Rotterdam or Turin – whose provenance, to say the least, was dubious.

With ten years' perspective, the pattern is not hard to see, but at the time these thefts appeared haphazard and relatively minor instances of the crime wave. Even in the United States, owners were no more aware that they now stood in the front-line of risk. As early as 1952, a gang broke into St Joseph's Cathedral in Bardstown, Kentucky (billed by *Time* magazine as "the oldest Roman Catholic cathedral west of the Alleghenies"), and stole nine paintings including Rubens' *Flaying of St Bartholomew*, Murillo's *Crowning of the Blessed Virgin*, and the *Descent of the Holy Ghost* by one of the van Eyck brothers. According to local legend, a former bishop of Bardstown had befriended the exiled Louis Philippe, who, as King of France, had later, in the 1830s, sent him the pictures in gratitude. They had hung there for 120 years and few had been so discourteous as to query the authenticity of this magnificent gift. Inspecting the records, however, experts from the Frick Museum were dubious: the best they could do was to suggest that the "Rubens" was in fact a fine work of the Italian Baroque painter, Mattia Preti. Local worthies spurned this advice and instead went to church to pray for the pictures' recovery.

Prayer and the F.B.I. requited them. Five months after the robbery, two men were arrested in a Chicago parking lot, with four of the stolen paintings in their car. The rest were recovered from a New York dealer. In all, eleven men were held as part of the conspiracy. Led by a man described at his trial as "a former U.S. attorney", they had believed the loot worth a million dollars. An F.B.I. agent calling himself Jean-Pierre Lafitte, from the recently formed art theft bureau, trapped them by the simple expedient of posing as a ship's steward with contacts among European art dealers. To convince his "backers", he required proof that the group held the paintings – and with that evidence, made his arrests.

By the mid-1950s, American journalists were saying how incomprehensible the wave of art thefts was. Only the "gyp artists" – snatch and run operators – could get away with a small picture, they believed. Faced with the full resources of the F.B.I. if they stole objects worth over $5,000, or crossed state frontiers, to say nothing of state police, private detective agencies and insurance investigators, the thieves scarcely appeared to stand a chance. Such optimism may have been the result of shrewd F.B.I. publicity, keenly advertising the work of undercover men, but the trend was setting in a very different direction. A mass of thefts of all kinds was taking place in America: some ridiculous, like the removal of the phallus from a third-century B.C. Etruscan warrior in the Metropolitan Museum of New York, or the taking of eight small silver statues from the Brooklyn Museum, as a joke by two young boys; others amateurish – the unemployed truck driver with a small Rubens from San Francisco's de Young Museum, which he offered "for a few bucks to tide me over"; but others (the things that disappeared completely) far more serious. Nevertheless, the pundits were shaken when the Toronto Art Gallery was cleared of $1·5 million-worth of paintings in September 1959.

The gallery had been robbed two years earlier: alarm bells had brought security police running to the main exhibition room to find a massive Rubens cut from its frame. After the alert had been put out to police all over Canada and the United States, the Rubens was found on the lawn in front of the provincial parliament building. With red faces the authorities installed a new burglar-proof system – which was not proof against the professionals who cut from their frames the six best works in the whole collection, by Frans Hals, Rembrandt, Rubens and Renoir, in what *Time* magazine called "the biggest art robbery in modern times and certainly the most substantial since the *Mona Lisa* was stolen from the Louvre in 1911". Since the alarm had not been cut, it was assumed that the thieves had stayed behind at closing time, evaded the guards, worked at their leisure and escaped through an upstairs window.

A great deal of uninformed speculation broke out. The Toronto police refused to comment until, a month later, when the affair was over, the officer in charge, James MacKay, declared that he had suspected the identity of the criminals all along. Early in October he had received an anonymous telephone call tipping him off that the pictures were hidden in a private garage in the suburbs. All six were found, scratched but not irreparably damaged. When taxed about an insurance ransom deal, MacKay claimed that the police had handled the whole case and that no ransom had been paid. At the time he was believed. After twelve years it is impossible to establish whether a reward *was* paid by the insurance firms or the museum, without police knowledge. Subsequent history suggests that it was. Within months the contagion had spread all over Canada: $40,000-worth of sketches were stolen from the University of British Columbia; icons from the Vancouver Art Gallery; paintings from London (Ontario) and Toronto's Royal Ontario Museum; and the cream of the public collection at Hamilton, Nova Scotia. Some of these were found abandoned, indications that ransom attempts had failed. Others simply vanished, untraced, into the long underground passage back to the legitimate market, across the border in the United States.

Despite a number of failures, theft at this time was generally successful. For reasons described in Chapter 4, theft for ransom took its great leap forward on the French Riviera in 1961, but, from what evidence there is, it played an increasingly important, though undetected, part in the world-wide crime wave in the late 1950s. Suddenly, about 1956, the files kept by Interpol had to expand. The regular toll of statues and church candlesticks began to give way to descriptions of far more costly and memorable missing works of art. From 1956 to about 1963, when the police counter-attack began, stretched the golden years, when pillage, ransom and resale were more profitable, at less risk, than ever before or since.

1961 was, perhaps, the *annus mirabilis*: the year of the *Duke of Wellington*'s disappearance from the National Gallery in London, of the loss of a collection of Daumier drawings from the Victoria and Albert Museum, of modern Italian works from Florence, a Cranach portrait from Basle, twenty-six canvases from the Como villa of a wealthy Italian widow, and another collection from the Marquis Montedinori, to say nothing of the spectacular ransom thefts in France described in Chapter 5. In that year the Italian police, for example, made only one notable recovery.

By 1962 the fashion had spread as far as India, where a collection of bronzes of Buddha vanished from the Nalanda Archaeological Museum, and Japan, where a $30,000 Renoir was stolen from the Tokyo home of a famous publisher.

Worse still, many of the finest things lost in this period (for instance, a Rembrandt portrait from West Berlin and a Lucas

Cranach from Frankfurt, both stolen in 1959 – the former recovered from Brunswick railway station in 1961 and the latter from Munich railway station a year earlier) were found under circumstances that could only mean that they had been ransomed back – though nothing was known outside the tight world of insurance assessors about how it was done. Ransom theft was not yet singled out as a comprehensive explanation for what was happening. Instead, for fear of imitative crime, the authorities preserved a discreet silence where they could. As one official at the Metropolitan Museum put it, "The museums don't like to say things about stealing as it only aggravates the potential robberies. The Metropolitan has adequate insurance but none of the museums like to talk about that." A little more openly, a director of Pinkerton's detective agency told a reporter in 1962:

> Usually arrangements are made beforehand, before the theft occurs, to get rid of them [the paintings] through a fence in some other part of the world. A lot of this takes place under contract. A good art thief knows his property and is a connoisseur himself sometimes. Some of those who are less professional don't really know what a hard thing they have and can't dipose of it.

Only too well aware of the danger of others jumping on the bandwagon, the police said very little to anyone, anywhere. Most comment in the press was wide of the mark about the motives and means of the thieves or the direction of the market. *Time* told its readers in November 1959: "Art fences are non-existent. Art dealers, no matter how covetous they may be, cannot afford to handle such hot merchandise." According to the American journal, *Insiders Newsletter*, two years later, much of the stolen stuff was going behind the Iron Curtain to museums or to "wealthy Communist leaders who prefer art to liquid assets, since big bank accounts are regarded with official disfavour". Second in line the correspondent ranked South America, "for wealthy Latin American purchasers rarely publicise their acquisitions or send them to museums". There was very little evidence for pointing to these familiar scape-goats, and a good deal of political prejudice. Nearer home, and through unglamorous channels, scarcely different from the retail outlets of any straight merchandise, stolen works of art were being distributed through the double market, or ransomed to their owners.

Notes

1 *Europa*, November 1970. Article by Henri Schoup.

2 At a much simpler level, where the antique market merged with the market for plain furniture, carpets and bedding, turnover was lively. Faced with post-war shortages, there was for many families a clear point of balance in which old, well-made household goods came cheaper than the rationed, shoddy utilitarian stuff that was all that the manufacturers, starved of materials and designers, could produce. Some couples who married in 1946 found themselves possessors of a sound collection of antiques, simply because they set up house on what could be found in small provincial salerooms.

Chapter 3 Market Anatomy

The second decade of post-war art theft witnessed its increasing sophistication and a prolonged but rarely successful resistance on the part of the authorities in Europe and America. A columnist in the *New Statesman* wrote recently:

> Today, there is virtually a Common Market in crime. English and French thieves assist each other in Hatton Garden and the Côte d'Azur; Italian "art dealers" dispose of the proceeds of jewel, silver and art thefts, smuggling out treasures from their own country; while the lowest grade of Mafia hirelings assist between times in any skullduggery going, such as ferrying wanted men or materials along the part of the drug-routes on which they happen to operate. The Australians descend on a country like Viking raiders. Belgium and Germany are coming increasingly into the picture and enterprising thieves are taking language courses.

Art theft fits into this general scene. One not untypical month, in the spring of 1970, saw the loss of the great painting of San Isidro by Mattias Stumer, from a church near Palermo; forty of the rarest and most valuable dolls in Britain from the Warwick Doll Museum; ten paintings by modern masters from the Venice collection of Peggy Guggenheim; a group of early Japanese ivories from the house of a carpet manufacturer in Belgium; a vast number of portrait miniatures from a collector in Philadelphia – all at a time which a commentator in London later described as "a relative lull in the spate of art thefts". After the loss of three almost priceless paintings from the Palazzo Vecchio in Florence in the same month, Rodolfo Siviero, the Italian Recovery Commissioner (who had extracted one of them from a repository of Hitler's wartime loot as recently as 1963), said angrily, "After spending so much effort and the state's money to get back so many works of art that had been taken out of Italy, they can't even be put on public display without being stolen by the first thief that comes along."

The true double market now operated; in it, parallel to the normal trade in antiques and works of art, an organisation had evolved in all European countries and in America for stealing, disguising and restoring to "legitimate" sale whatever the straight market required. For many years its existence was denied, but the evidence in this and subsequent chapters is incontrovertible.

The reasons for the institutionalising of art theft are, like those for its origin, closely related to the art market. From 1960 to 1969 (when the market developed the first signs of recession) prices rose regularly and rapidly each year. Back in the 1950s the Cognacq sale in Paris had set new standards for Cézanne, and that of Brady Campbell for Modigliani, Matisse and Braque. By 1957 the boom was well under way: in that year, at the William Weinberg sale in London, Stavros Niarchos paid over £100,000 for a Gauguin. At the Goldschmidt sale in 1958, Cézanne's *Boy in a Red Waistcoat* made £220,000. Nothing would ever be the same again, said the pundits: modern art was on the way to becoming another branch of real estate.

The great increase in money values was supported by a boom in furniture, porcelain and silver. Previously depressed areas of collecting, such as majolica, revived, and Chinese blue and white porcelain began to enjoy an unprecedented vogue. Such trends were forecast by the van Doorn sale in Paris as early as 1956 and Gerald Reitlinger argues that by the early 1960s the true level of prices for exceptional *objets d'art* was, in fact, much higher than the prices realised in the salerooms suggested, because of the existence of a private market for direct transactions between individuals and museums.

Nevertheless, paintings, and particularly modern paintings, far outstripped the records of even the rarest French furniture or Chinese porcelain. On one hand, there were fewer old-master pictures than had been available earlier in the century, and, on the other, more museums, primed with more funds, strove to complete their collections before supplies dried up. The operation of the

50

tax-concession system in the United States gave a particular emphasis to modern art and an apparently permanent inflationary twist to the prices fetched by the works of living artists like Picasso and Braque. Equally, since only a handful of paintings by the greatest dead remained in private hands, spectacular and quite irrational prices were given for notable Rembrandts or Goyas. The Velasquez *Juan de Pareja*, sold in London in 1971, made £2,300,000 and Titian's *Diana and Actaeon*, from the Harewood collection, £1,630,000, prices explicable only by the fall in the value of money and the knowledge that such chances could not recur.

Restrictions (or the lack of them) imposed by governments on export affect prices just as high saleroom taxes in Europe have encouraged collectors to sell on the London market. However, the significance of these levels, when considering theft, is that they seemed to establish as immutable the investment aspect of collecting. During the 1960s advertisements for schemes to fund capital in paintings, which "guaranteed" regular dividends as high as 10 per cent, could be found even in collectors' magazines. The *Times Sotheby Index* claimed to give an accurate chart of prices showing percentage gains over the previous decade; and the margin between such statistics and the projection of future profits diminished as cupidity increased. Television programmes like "Going for a Song" attempted to stress the identification and artistic merit of the objects in front of the camera, but the competitive element, the moment of truth for the viewer, lay in the guess at its "value". A whole literature on investment has appeared in recent years, telling the amateur which objects to stockpile and on what prices he can expect to get a return for his money.

In traditional terms this phenomenon was part of the larger lunacy of the modern world, these books being of no greater value than the tips sold by touts at the local racecourse. Works of art have no value in real terms, except what collectors will pay for them. But for the knowledgeable and experienced trader, with large capital, able to survive temporary recessions, opportunities for very large and tax-free capital gains offered themselves.

Even after the war far-sighted dealers were stockpiling. Some of the main dealers in paintings in London, Rome, Paris and New York have been stockpiling ever since, off-loading stock when the market offers a truly rich return. How much is stored away in this fashion is impossible to guess. Agnew's, after all, lost the *Duchess of Devonshire* to Adam Worth for twenty-five years and made 300 per cent profit as a result. The stakes are much higher today and the firm of Agnew is now backed by the Rothschild empire. There is, of course, nothing whatever wrong with such business foresight: it is only prudent to keep a stock of fine art against a future famine. But what is practised by the great is imitated by lesser dealers. For some four or five years now, at sales of fine English porcelain, prices given by specialist dealers have risen well above the "normal" level at which they can hope to sell *at once* to their private clients. Those who live by rapid turnover and small percentage profits are hard hit, and the private collector is starved. Those who pay such prices are, in fact, stock-piling in order to off-load, preferably at auctions, as a whole collection, five or seven years hence.

In the same way as international cartels operate, and de Beers Consolidated Mines hold diamonds to stabilise world prices, stock-piling of antiques and paintings serves to iron out some of the market fluctuations and to restrict to safe dimensions the irrational demands of the collector.[1] The severest test of the stability of art as investment came at the end of the last decade. One London dealer wrote:

> In 1969 when the value of antiques stopped rising so fast, there was a sort of hiatus. By that time a lot of dealers were beginning to price their goods ahead of the market movement, so when the market slowed down everything else slowed down too. Each dealer had stock which was too expensive for other dealers to buy. For months they all sat and looked at their objects of beauty, probably wondering whether that beauty was fading. It is quite extraordinary how ugly an object of beauty can become, when it represents your working capital and no one wants to buy it.

The traditionalists who, like nineteenth-century moralists inveighing against the concept of limited liability, warned that it was impossible to *invest* in canvas and potted clay, were proved wrong in the spring and early summer of 1971 as business picked up, followed by a spiralling inflation greater than that for almost any other commodity. For those concerned with high taxation or political risks, and also for the plain collector, the question of stability seemed to have been answered: the market *could* be manipulated and the revival after the recession suggested that the *concept* of art as investment was secure.

These artificial, speculative, and highly publicised conditions were ripe for the wholly commercial practice of theft and redistribution. At the same time, increasing awareness of – or lip-service to – the social value of works of art led to an unprecedented sensitivity to blackmail on the part of the authorities whenever ransom demands (usually accompanied by threats of destruction) were made. Finally, the objects of the trade themselves became anonymous, making the task of recovery well-nigh impossible. The very finest things were drained faster and faster into new museum collections; yet at the same time the total turnover in the salerooms greatly increased. The number of professional antique dealers in English provincial towns, for example, has increased by roughly fifty per cent in the last twenty years. In France, it has reached 15,000. But standards have fallen. Many a shop which, in the decade after the war, stocked good eighteenth-century furniture, now offers with equal vigour a selection from the Regency (which may well extend to late nineteenth-century copies) and mass-produced Victoriana. At a higher price level, a whole gallery of secondary artists has been built up, including such artists as Zuccarelli, Fantin-Latour or the Koekkoek family, patient craftsmen whose merits are that they were prolific and, until warmed by the touch of modern scholarship, unfashionable. A quick comparison of the advertisements in a periodical like *The Connoisseur* for the years 1950 and 1970 will show an absolute decline in the artistic value of what dealers think worth advertising, in a period during which prices have risen 200 per cent.

The wider the field of dealing was opened to repetitive or even mechanical craftsmanship, the easier it became to hide the stolen object among other pieces the originality of which was hard to distinguish. On the wider scale, the emergence of entrepreneur-dealers, the flood of objects across Europe and the Atlantic, and the increased frequency of turnover of collections dulled the memory of experts for middle-grade works of art and made it safe for criminals to dispose of their haul, the part of their operations that had formerly put them most at risk. The enormous volume of turnover in the salerooms made it virtually impossible for staff to detect things stolen from abroad that had been entered quite bare-facedly. Occasionally, expert cataloguers would notice an identifying mark and become suspicious. Two pictures from the Queen's collection were once recovered this way at Christie's. But there is literally no way of checking the bona-fides of everyone who brings a piece in to be examined, and the presumption is that he is the owner unless proved otherwise. Occasionally, if warned, the original owner may step in: but there is no doubt at all that the vast majority of stolen things that do get catalogued are sold and become the legitimate possessions of their new buyers. In any case, in a world where many owners strongly object to publicity and where collections are increasingly held by nominee companies or banks for investment, a saleroom that enquired too closely into provenance would soon see a wave of disaffected customers depart. Auction houses anywhere rely on their clients' honesty, both in and out of the saleroom, or they could scarcely even display what is for sale.

Art theft since 1960 shows two distinct trends: first, a concentration on certain types of object (statues from churches, gold coins from museums, manuscripts from libraries) which appear to come in waves following a particular demand, as in Germany, Italy and France in the 1950s; and, secondly, a growth in patterns of theft and distribution corresponding to the legitimate trade in different countries.

The best example of the wave phenomenon is that of the onslaught on French châteaux in the 1960s. 1964 to 1967 were the best years of de Gaulle's power, and were equally prosperous for French industry and industrialists. In every market outside France, French dealers could be observed steadily pushing up the demand for and price of good eighteenth-century French furniture and *objets d'art*. It is not surprising that châteaux full of antiques were at risk. In January 1965 one of de Gaulle's cabinet ministers, Prince Jean de Breuilly, suffered the loss of all the Louis XV furniture and clocks in the principal salons of the Château de Breuilly, and nothing was recovered. In the same month, the concierge of the Marquise de Gallifret, who owns a fine renaissance château near Deauville in Normandy, was woken one night by the barking of her dog. She turned on the lights and then went back to sleep. Unperturbed, the gang, who had arrived in a lorry, found and examined an inventory of the collection and then spent most of the night loading Louis XV and XVI chests of drawers, secretaires, *fauteuils*, marble-topped tables, *bergères*, not to mention silver chandeliers and eighteenth-century barometers. In the Marquise's own bedroom they left nothing but her bed.

Only a week later, paintings worth $136,000 vanished from the château near Paris belonging to Madame Hubert Menier, a member of the chocolate-manufacturing family. Altogether over a hundred robberies took place between 1963 and 1965, mainly in châteaux in northern France belonging to wealthy Parisians, but also in the homes in central France of aristocrats such as the Duc de Luynes and the Comte de Villefranche. Then, in April 1965, the police raided the house of a country doctor, Xavier Richier, a physician at the nationalised coal mine of Lievin, and found it stacked high with the contents of a dozen looted country houses. Richier was arrested, together with his brother and a friend, both interior decorators. They admitted over eighty of the thefts (including that of a priceless Gothic tapestry from Le Mans Cathedral that had been returned anonymously by registered post), but claimed that they had committed the crimes because "the government was neglecting the masterpieces of our national heritage". The police remained sceptical. Only $1·4 out of an estimated $7 million was recovered, all of that relating to objects too well known to dispose of at once. The rest had gone to feed the French antiques market.

Writing in 1968, a dealer on the fringe of the double market described the methods of typical château thieves:

> Unlike other crimes, these thefts follow a pattern. The police know, for example, that this year the owner of Louis XV and XVI chairs will risk a visit from thieves. Last year, it was Empire stuff. They need specialists, and the Normandy gang was headed by an interior decorator, a former pupil of the Louvre school. Like the drug traffic, art theft has its rules and techniques. The actual thieves are called up by receivers acting for French or foreign clients for a particular class of antiques. Later four or five men will turn up in a lorry and attack the château – usually not a difficult job, for they are rarely guarded

by burglar alarms. Then follows what they call "make-up" – which is no more than sheer vandalism. They transform pieces of furniture; they pare off any signature, they hack up tapestries, all in quiet workshops in the provinces. Then they offer the transformed – or mutilated – things to antique dealers who exhibit them in good faith.

The breaking up of Richier's gang seems to have made only a temporary difference to the trade, just as the more intense police action has only partly checked the wave of specialist thieves working, in the early 1970s, on the armouries of castles in Austria and on the Rhine, the worst single problem of its type for both countries concerned. Unscrupulous demand for the finest weapons makes it still relatively easy to dispose of things like the Breschian horse pistol (*circa* 1620) which was taken from the Royal Armoury in Vienna in May 1970.

The traffic in and out of Britain illustrates the geographical pattern. In volume, it is still greater than the trade between any other two countries, a reflection of Britain's nineteenth-century wealth and undisputed prestige. The accumulated property, in goods as well as houses, of her affluent middle class left a residue of chattels and accoutrements far exceeding that of Biedermeier Germany or France under the Second Empire. Hence world demand has largely been met by a flood of dealers who, in the last fifteen years, have resorted to England as the great milch-cow, sucking greedily from her an inestimable quantity of Victorian china, pictures, silver and mahogany to reinforce the market for customers aching to reproduce the security and status of the Forsytes. Long-case clocks to Denmark, heavy carved oak chests to Germany, barometers and scientific instruments to Sweden, guns, ormolu and the better furniture to France, carpets and silver to the United States, marquetry to Italy, and gold – for hoarding – to the Middle East; the channels of legitimate trade fill the vacuum created by the inadequacies of each country's own nineteenth-century past, and satisfy the needs of the twentieth century.

As London became the world centre for selling works of art (mainly because of the low percentages and excellent facilities offered by the major salerooms), it also, unwittingly, sprouted the largest

56

number of receivers and became quite the biggest entrepôt for stolen works of art. British firms took over foreign salerooms or set up European offices in keen competition with the Swiss or Germans, and, unwelcome and unrelated, British criminals appeared far more frequently in the dossiers of continental police headquarters.

This trade exists for a mass market: except at the fringes, the so-called "early nineteenth century", it has little to do with the sale of fine antiques and the highly expensive old and modern masters – or indeed paintings of any great quality. Measurement is by weight rather than quality. There are dealers in London, and a few in provincial towns like Harrogate and Brighton, who export £10,000-worth or more a month – not elegant Sheraton chairs, but nineteenth-century desks, Staffordshire pottery dogs, phrenologists' skulls or whatever is required, by the gross. If the market flags, the "restorer" comes in. More "military chests" must have left England in the year 1972 than were ever made in the nineteenth century for the British Army on active service. Huge container lorries, sealed for the customs at Dover, rumble across Europe, into Belgium, Germany, and Italy. Crate upon crate of Victorian domestic *bric-à-brac* crosses the Atlantic by boat or air freight in U.S. servicemen's baggage. So long as it dates from before 1870 – give or take a few years – so long as the export manifest says so, the customs have no need to quibble.

Just how many of the works of art stolen in Britain and circulating in the world market get distributed in this way is hard to gauge. But the manner of the trade has given rise to a new sort of antique dealer, the entrepreneur with a staff of bulk buyers and a fleet of collecting vans. They advertise in local papers: "£5 to £10 paid for any bow-fronted chest of drawers; cash payment, immediate collection." These are the trend-setters, constantly pushing back the frontiers of what is acceptably "antique" into an uncharted world full of stuffed birds in cages and gilded mirrors from Victorian pubs. Some of them are unscrupulous: the temptation to make up a load with disputable pieces, bought for cash at a quarter of their market value, is always strong. Equally, the outlet is attractive to thieves with a bulky load of stolen property, for the chances of a single sale are few, and dispersal is likely to take time. By trial and error the one meets the other and the underground market is set up. There are between fifteen and twenty receivers in London who will buy up to a complete lorry-load and lay out £5,000 or £10,000 in big notes for it. They are few because big receivers tend to drive out small ones. Only a man with capital, warehousing capacity, and his own transport can undertake the business: and one or two of these graduated to antique dealing by such avenues as second-hand car dealing or the scrap metal trade. They are not often served directly by thieves, except where thefts are commissioned (see Chapter 6) but they have a clientèle of smaller traders and knockers (the term for touts who knock at likely-looking houses, offering quick cash to unsuspecting owners). The nature of their business means that they must operate from a large centre: Brighton is the second most important clearing house and roughly covers England south and west of London; Birmingham serves the Midlands, and Hull a great part of the north. (Indeed the whole legitimate Scandinavian market seems to depend on Hull: according to immigration figures, seven per cent of all people coming through the port are antique dealers.)

From the clearing house where receivers operate, there are two ways to pass stolen things back into the British trade. If the object is "hot", then it is stacked away in warehouses or, perhaps, in private garages, as far away as northern Scotland, for three or four years until the risk of recognition is past. If it is less obvious, and if no reward has been offered by the insurance companies, then it is passed from dealer to dealer until the odour of suspicion diminishes and all chance of tracing it is lost. Sometimes a receiver will "find" a piece on the police lists of stolen goods and hand it over to prove good faith.

The foreign trade takes more trouble but usually carries less risk and may well be more profitable, since it forms a direct sale to a customer who is less likely to cut the profit margin. A silver tankard may be stolen at night from a country house, reach the receiver within hours and be shipped out later the same day – probably before the loss has even been reported. Quoting "a well known London loss adjuster" in 1968, the *New York Times* wrote: "Co-operation between the British police and police overseas in cases of art theft is almost non-existent. Unless a Goya has been pinched, nobody wants to know. Interpol, to my mind, is a bad joke. Stolen treasures are safe once they have left Britain." The first part of this jaundiced estimate is no longer true, but the last sentence is irrefutable. As one American dealer with shops in London and New York, and a prison record for receiving, said in the same article: "Once the stuff is across the Atlantic no questions are asked by many dealers. They are only too happy to have the stuff to sell."

What comes into Britain is harder to document. The only obvious trends are the modern forgeries, the fake eighteenth-century paintings,[2] guns and armour from Spain, brilliantly forged rare glasses from Holland (now a common feature in smaller British salerooms) and spuriously dated paperweights from France. But the methods employed may be gauged from the erratic course of the Rubens painting stolen, in 1970, from the Singer Museum in Laren, Holland. The gang comprised two Irishmen and a Dutchman. The latter actually took the picture, having cut it from its frame and smuggled it out of the museum, wrapped round his chest under his shirt. He delivered it to his associates in a sea-front hotel in Brighton and they began to tempt the London market with an asking price of £10,000 – ten per cent of its (under-) insured value. Rumours of the sale reached Scotland Yard's Art Squad and a trap was arranged: a police agent was to view the Rubens in a private gallery and make an offer. Just when this was ready, the Dutch police arrested their thief, who squealed. One of the associates, in whose possession the picture was found, was arrested in Britain and given a stiff jail sentence at Lewes assizes; the other was caught later in France and extradited to Holland.

The channels through which the trade moves scarcely differ from those of legitimate business. Britain has no restrictions or taxes on the passage in or out of objects more than a hundred years old and worth less than £2,000. The law is at present embodied in the Export of Goods Control Order 1965; documents, manuscripts (except those of national importance), diamonds and postage stamps are excluded. Objects worth more than £2,000 need a licence from the Export Licensing Branch of the Customs and Excise, but, unless they are of sufficient importance to come under the surveillance of the Reviewing Committee on the Export of Works of Art, this is unlikely to be refused. In any case, since the overworked Customs and Excise rely largely on the honesty of declarations, the risks run by exporting the occasional dubious item through a proper shipping company are not heavy – less, in fact, than the chances of finding the proverbial needle in a haystack. A needle looks different from hay, but a single

59

shipment may contain fifty military chests, all virtually identical.

Unscrupulous dealers can only too easily slip a stolen load through customs. Even if the customs unloaded and searched one lorry in ten, the likelihood of recognition would be minute. The only stolen piece in the one unlucky lorry might have been held in hiding for months. Container traffic, first introduced by U.S. Line in 1966, poses the ultimate threat. Sealed in central London with a customs man standing by, a forty-foot metal container with 2,275 cubic feet of space for antiques can be shipped to a Chicago warehouse without being touched again. No criticism here of customs or shippers: containerisation has revolutionised the trade. In the old days a piece of furniture had to be hand-packed in its own crate, taken by lorry to the depot, unloaded, stacked, loaded into a ship hold, lifted out at the other end of the voyage, taken through customs, loaded again, and unloaded at delivery. In addition, the new service may involve multiple ownership of the contents of a single container. It poses an inordinate responsibility on the officer who may supervise the first loading; as a customs official said in November 1968, when the traffic was still restricted chiefly to the United States:

> Customs checks are very rarely made on steel containers. If the container was packed at an inland depot under customs supervision, and bears customs seals, it will not be opened. If, however, it bears only the seal of the shipping agents, it is liable to examination, although in practice it is very rarely opened. In any case, there would be very little point in this instance, since as far as I know customs are not issued with a list of stolen property. It would hardly be practical. There are some twenty ports in this country, sending out all possible forms of merchandise from coal to shoes, and shipments of works of art can be, and are, sent from many of them.

In practice, the customs do not supervise all, or indeed the majority, of containers at the time of loading, and rely largely on the export declaration, which, if the load does not contain anything worth over £2,000, does not have to be presented until six days *after* shipment. Nor do the shippers inquire: "The great majority of our customers are respected and foreign dealers that we have known for years. They have bought from equally reputable English dealers.

Naturally we have to take the invoices at their face value. Besides, there would not be time to check all the orders." But what if they are not? By the end of 1969 these fears bulked large in the minds of many upright dealers who were themselves becoming prey to art thieves.

Even harder to check is the transport of antiques and paintings in and out of a major international airport. No one knows how large a traffic goes through Heathrow airport in London. Without stopping and searching every traveller, no one *can* tell. After a major theft the ports and airports are checked by the police. But precautions do not last long, and cannot cover all the loopholes. When £20,000 worth of the finest Georgian silver was taken from Milton Park, Lord Fitzwilliam's country house, in 1968, the police tracked down two of the four thieves, who had each been paid £1,000 in cash. They established that the silver – things as fine as Queen Anne wine coolers made by David Willaume – had been handed to American servicemen at a U.S.A.F. base nearby. The thieves had been given exact instructions. (During the raid, they even dropped a paper carrying details of a similar burglary scheduled to take place at Penshurst Place in Kent. This, despite police precautions, occurred some months later.) At the time, there was a good deal of ill-feeling, but a spokesman for Major-General Clyde Box, overall commander of the U.S.A.F. in Britain, declared blandly, "We know nothing about antiques being smuggled out of the country in military aircraft. British customs have empowered us to clear military aircraft and personnel leaving our bases. Servicemen's kit and other belongings go out in closed containers and spot checks are made from time to time".

These are some of the outlets for the thousands of antiques in the bracket £50 to £5,000, probably including, for example, a Meissen tankard, painted in *Hausmaler* decoration, that was lost from Sotheby's, who had expected it to fetch £6,000. The glass display cabinets in the saleroom are open on one side only at a time, and while a London dealer was waiting to examine it, the tankard was filched from the other side by a man who disappeared at once into the crowd. By now this piece of porcelain may be anywhere in the world, although persistent rumours have located it in southern Germany.

In the same bracket come pictures worth between £500 and £10,000, except for those that are peculiarly well documented. And the quantity? I have in front of me a file half an inch thick with reports of thefts in Britain for the years 1968–70. Among them are included: "Pictures stolen from a country house" (£100,000 from the Tillotson collection, Bedford, the majority of which were later recovered); fifty-one figures from the finest collection of Derby biscuit-ware; the Dent and Sellern collections of old-master drawings; £500,000-worth of Dutch masters from Ronald Lee, a prominent London dealer; five Impressionist paintings from the Kent house of Sir Henry d'Avigdor-Goldsmid, a Conservative M.P.; collections of Georgian silver amounting to more than £500,000-worth in these two years alone; Chinese jade figures from Newton Valence House; an exceptional van Mieris portrait from a National Trust house in Buckinghamshire; a hoard of antique jewellery from Argyllshire; two cast-iron griffins, weighing over a hundredweight each; and a Murillo from an exposed country church. The column called "Too Hot to Handle" in *Art and Antiques Weekly* (which represents only a part of the total) covered a full side of print in each weekly issue. Miniatures, antiquities, first-period Worcester porcelain, Wedgwood jasper ware, flintlock pistols, lead garden ornaments, silver dishes, Italian majolica, and the takings from the Antique Porcelain Company in Bond Street, where thieves threw an iron bar through the window and the steel mesh grill, smashing beyond repair a unique Botticelli crucifix, made up in one week in January 1970 a mixed total of £165,000. The evidence of this file alone goes far to substantiate the total world turnover of £30 million a year suggested later in this book.

In Italy, more than in any other country, art theft is committed by professional thieves commissioned by receivers who almost always have a legal cover as antique dealers. The Italian police do not attempt to conceal the extent of the problem, but the concern of the state stops short of spending the large sums or engaging in the long and persistent warfare that would check it. The police are overworked and find it hard enough, at their current strength, even to investigate all the crimes being committed at present. In 1967, 1,285 separate works of art were lost and the wave was then running at over £4 million a year – *not* including the looting of archaeological sites, nor cases of illegal export, which are in practice acts of theft. Since then, the situation has worsened. According to an interview given by Rodolfo Siviero to the magazine *Epoca* in November 1970, more than a thousand robberies take place in Italy each year. This is not an official figure but an estimate based on specimen police reports for the first half of 1970. Given his twenty-five years' experience as head of the Recovery Office, this figure may be assumed to be as accurate as can be given.

Mussolini's legislation against the export of works of art has become a nuisance rather than a deterrent, and the channels through which it is evaded serve equally well the exporters of stolen property. What does not stay in Italy in the luxury villas of Emilia and Lombardy, or in the stockpiles of receivers, goes north to Switzerland. The air traffic from Rome and Milan uses Berne and Geneva as transfer points on the route to Britain and America, while objects destined for Germany tend to go via Zürich. At least as significant is the frontier route by the Italian lakes. More than a quarter of the population of Switzerland is now made up of immigrant Italian workers and, though the majority are resident, thousands cross at Como or Luino on the shores of Lake Maggiore and return in the evening. For one of these to carry a rolled-up canvas or a statue is too simple. If the risk of detection still appears excessive and no sealed container lorry is available, there is the rest of the frontier, which winds and doubles up on itself for hundreds of miles between Geneva and Bolzano in the east. Herds wander back and forth in search of pasture, and anyone with a classical education could emulate Odysseus' escape from the one-eyed giant by tying his treasures under the woolly belly of a sheep.

Getting the stuff out is therefore easy and is the province of middlemen, employed by the receivers. No Italian government could sanction the cost of sufficient frontier posts and customs officers to prevent it, any more than they could have prevented the astute gang that hired a boat to assault from the sea the castle of Pareggi, near Portofino on the Italian Riviera, and scaled the walls with grappling irons. The demand comes principally from receivers in America who have sufficient legitimate contacts to pass Italian masterpieces onto the market with a spurious provenance attached (activities that taint even the great museums), or from European dealers supplying the so-called "art investment" funds run by private banks, usually located in Switzerland, in whose collections articles are likely to remain for a generation or two until the statutes of limitations have run out. Of course the museums and banks do not *know* their treasures are stolen: they have passed through false auction sales, as did the *Madonna* of Cossito (see p. 89) or have been dressed up with respectable ancestry. Given their limited resources, the Italian police have to fall back on Interpol, unless they can intervene further down the line by attacking the receiver-dealers themselves.

It is, however, only rarely that they can bring enough international pressure to bear, for these men are too skilled at evasion and often politically too powerful. Like the hydra, they have many heads and their operations are bolstered by family or criminal connections. Rome *antiquari*, for example, deny that receiver-dealers employ thieves, and the *Gazette Antiquaria* regularly challenges accusers to name names. Yet in a speech to the Senate on 18th June 1971, Signora Carretoni cited the names of three receivers, all domiciled in Switzerland, and demanded a ban on their re-entry to Italy. All three are still free to move in and out.

Most lost collections, like the Guardis and Canalettos stolen from Signor Vincenzizzo Polli in October 1969, are given the sombre tag: "Refer to Interpol, likely destination London." And some of these have duly been recovered by Scotland Yard. Eighteen months after the robbery of ten paintings by the seventeenth-century master, Mattia Preti, from the church of St Domenico, Taverna, southern Italy, in February 1970, the Art Squad in London picked up news from the underworld which led them to Euston Station left-luggage office and four of the canvases. Later they arrested an Italian on a charge of dishonest handling, and with the help of his information the Rome police discovered the remainder. But such results are almost as unusual as the case of the thirteenth-century primitive painting of the Madonna from the Rome parish church of Santa Maria del Popolo. Once, in the year 1280, the image was believed to have stopped an outbreak of the plague and many miracles have since been laid to its credit. When it vanished in July 1970, the Rome underworld, reflecting a certain religious sympathy, co-operated. The *carabinieri*, who handled the case, heard that it had been taken to Holland on a commission basis. They succeeded in frightening the thieves so badly that they agreed to restore the picture via an intermediary; and the intermediary himself became so scared of retribution that, instead of handing over the Madonna, he abandoned it in his pension in a suburb of Rome and fled.

Fear of sacrilege is no longer a renewable restraint and despoliation is now occurring at a rate which, according to Siviero, will, within the 1970s, decimate even the incredible reserves of the Italian artistic patrimony. While the great majority of objects fall into the middle grade, in the last three years a number of truly great masterpieces have also disappeared: some, like the Titian from the parish church of Medole, later recovered (in this case by an agent disguised as a Milan businessman); others, like the gems of the Pinacoteca Civica in Pavia, or the Caravaggio from San Lorenzo di Palermo, not. Antiquities in museums seem to be particularly vulnerable. There are fewer than 2,000 custodians to patrol all Italy's museums, and there are many provincial towns whose collections are, in terms of modern criminal expertise, open targets. If the illicit operators cannot plunder an Etruscan tomb, they will plunder a museum; the San Giorgio art gallery in Rome lost 50 million lire-worth of Etruscan bronze objects in April 1967 and the small museum adjoining the Roman amphitheatre at Campania, Naples, lost the following:

> a marble head of the Emperor Commodus,
> a bust of a satyr in red marble of the second century A.D.,
> three Campanian red figure urns,
> an Attic urn with black painted figures,
> three Campanian decorated amphorae,
> two marble heads (no description).

This is a typical case, of no great value, the stolen objects now presumably forming part of a private collection; they have long ago been written off by the museum authorities. But it is more than a financial loss. The property may belong to the state; but what does Campania now have to exhibit to attract the gilt-edged tourists? To despoil Rome would take a century, but one night is sufficient to inflict a serious injury on a provincial town. Even the Ambrosian Library in Milan would have been severely impoverished if the missing folio of the *Codex Atlanticus* had not been restored. Stolen by an employee of the library who was already under suspicion of selling a picture by Jan (Velvet) Breughel, the folio contained eight scientific and technical drawings by Leonardo da Vinci. The man confessed, but the folio had reached the possession of a Florentine restaurateur. Thence it passed to a dealer, who took it to Switzerland, and, having failed to make a sale, telephoned the director of the Ambrosiana to say that he would post it from Locarno. The Italian post is not noted for the speed or accuracy of its transmissions, but in due course, and to the plaudits of a waiting crowd of journalists, the envelope was extracted from the mountain of letters at Milan central sorting office.

Certain preventive measures were announced by Signor Emilio Colombo, the Italian Premier, during the International Antiques Fair in Florence in September 1971. Local authorities were to transfer to national museums insufficiently protected works of art, and a comprehensive census of the entire artistic patrimony was to be made. This was a decade overdue, and, given the state of mutual mistrust between local and central authorities, unlikely ever to be carried out. Still, there was to be more money and more custodians; and the Premier's speech was followed by instructions to church authorities from the Vatican itself. These might have been hopeful signs if they had not been so obviously a response to political pressure.

The Premier's intervention came in a year during which theft had risen by twenty per cent on 1970 figures and centred on the Veneto region of northern Italy – the artistically rich hinterland of Venice. More precisely, it followed a week in which the patrimony sustained losses of fifty-eight paintings, including a Titian from the painter's home, Pieve di Cadore, and two Bellinis from a Venetian church, worth perhaps £2·5 million on the open market. *Il Giorno* cried, "The promises of reform, always postponed by the functionaries of the Ministry of Fine Arts, must now be implemented." On 9th September, with characteristic drama, the Ministry of Defence called up 3,000 reserve *carabinieri* to aid their recovery. With such a force abroad, thieves were caught exposed all over northern Italy, in Genoa, Bologna, and in Naples in the south – giving some indication of what stringent precautions might have achieved if only they had been put into effect previously.

66

In Germany, the fashion for church statues has been largely replaced by an interest in antique weapons and the rich armouries of Rhineland castles. Pistols, muskets, swords, pikes and armour feed a demand from within Germany and abroad, mainly from America; the bulk of the trade goes by road through Belgium or Luxembourg; Holland has a special demand for Delft pottery to replace wartime losses. According to Inspector Jahns of the Bundeskriminalamt, there is a steady export to London, where items are sold openly, but this is hard to prove and the police have not been able to identify anything from the catalogues of leading salerooms. In effect things go to where the best contacts are: in a typical case, a pair of altar candlesticks were taken through Holland to London and bought there by a Swiss dealer. He eventually sold them to the late Aga Khan, who, when they were traced, generously returned them without asking for compensation.

Some of the thieves at work are foreigners, but Germans predominate and their relationship with receivers follows the English pattern rather than the Italian. The receiver will tend to wait until a load arrives, rather than specify its contents. Consequently, the thief is usually a bigger man than his Italian counterpart. Dietz and Fuchs, who were jailed for shooting four German soldiers during an urban guerilla raid on a West German armoury in 1969, had formerly been art thieves working in Spain; and Interpol London had pursued them on the basis of information given by Sotheby's, where they had tried to sell their loot.

Germany is probably the easiest country in Europe to escape from with stolen works of art, given its long western frontier bordered by three Common Market countries, and its frontier with Switzerland and Austria in the south. It also seems to be easier there for thieves to gain respectability for stolen things, either by buying a document from a professional forger, or by sending the object to a genuine expert whose favourable verdict is then used to substantiate a claim to ownership. Only an unusually perceptive customs officer would impound a painting carrying a certificate in the (new) owner's name. Moreover the successors of V's gang have created a sub-profession of art crime: "restorers" who will alter wooden figures, paint in new details in a landscape or paint out figures, trim a canvas to a different size and generally make an object impossible even for its owner to identify. The task of the police is compounded by the manufacture of skilful forgeries, not just of mediaeval statues, but also of seventeenth- and eighteenth-century decorative pictures, not unlike the fakes from Barcelona. Jahns has arrested a man with an apparently stolen painting and traced it back to a Spanish museum, only to find that the original was hanging there unharmed.

Château thefts in France still continue, but with less intensity than in the years 1965–68. On the other hand, the drain of paintings from galleries, dealers and private collections has been a constant problem in the last ten years and no receiver of the standing of the Richiers has since been caught. Most of the identifiable things vanish over the border, since anything worth more than £10,000 is virtually unsaleable at home. Belgium and Holland are primarily used for the transit of stolen objects. In addition to the Singer Museum's Rubens, the Dutch have lost a few paintings from private collections and a number of gold coins from the Rijksmuseum. The Schott Museum in Brussels was attacked in 1965 by rather amateur criminals, who were caught later trying to sell the proceeds of other raids. The worst loss of recent years was the work of two Italians, who looted the Réné Withofs collection in Ostend, but fell into the hands of Interpol when they offered the paintings to an incorruptible Italian dealer.

Switzerland offers a contrast, having, in addition to the best entrepôt facilities, a profitable home market, exploited by a small number of receivers. Since the traffic comes in from Austria, Italy, Yugoslavia, Germany and France, there is no need for them to inquire abroad. Indeed, the demands of foreign thieves for their services have often led them to hand over criminals to the Swiss police rather than risk implication in the sort of naïvety that led two Austrians to go through the telephone directory looking for suitable outlets. The Swiss criminal network is, however, better placed to dispose of stolen jewellery, and the greater number of stolen works of art present in Switzerland at any one time are only passing through.

The private Swiss art collections are a permanent attraction to outsiders. The hoards of rich investors, tucked away in secluded villas, form the artistic equivalent of numbered bank accounts, and are as closely protected. Nevertheless the "museum" of one bank, held in a country house on the Zürichsee and containing a spectacular

68

collection of Meissen figures, was robbed in 1969 by Germans whose one mistake was to offer the pieces to the dealer in Berne who had only just finished revaluing the collection. The immensely rich Count Maurice von Bendern suffered a more painful loss. He despatched Frans Hals' *The Lute Player* from his mansion in Monte Carlo, together with other paintings from his Swiss villa, to a Geneva bank for safe-keeping. Two years later, in 1967, the Hals was taken from the vault, unwrapped and examined. Bank officials found a worthless substitute. On instructions from the police, the Count kept silent for a while. Then, increasingly angry, because he was eighty-eight and had intended to donate the Hals to the principality of Liechtenstein – of which tiny tax-free haven he had been a citizen for nearly forty years – he gave a press interview. Shortly after, the Hals was recovered in the baggage room of Geneva railway station. A thick veil of discretion covers the question of ransom.

At a different level, a gang of international criminals, Italian and Corsican, led by a Spaniard with the melodious name of La Fuente Mendoza, attacked the house of Martin Bodmer, in the fashionable Geneva suburb of Coligny, in July 1966. Bodmer, a famous collector and patron of the arts who had edited a German literary magazine and possessed a magnificent library, was vice-president of the International Red Cross. He lost ten paintings, among them a Botticelli *Venus*; and the value of £500,000 put on them seems, if genuine, to have been a gross under-estimate. Within a fortnight the thieves were caught in Marseilles, trying to sell the canvases for a laughable sum, almost on the door-step of the local C.I.D.

Spain may produce thieves, but the country witnesses few thefts. Objects occasionally vanish from the big museums: the Prado in Madrid and the Escorial suffered slight damage in the 1960s. In Portugal, theft is even rarer: the only notable loss in recent years occurred in 1967 at Vidigueira, birthplace of Vasco da Gama, where a fifteenth-century statue of San Rafael the Explorer was stolen. Thefts of manuscripts and illuminated books, however, have increased as part of a much wider, European trend; and, at the other end of Europe, a wave of curious and highly specialised thefts of antique firearms swept Sweden in 1968. Sweden's treasures had been left almost untouched, a surprising fact considering the spectacular collections of weapons on view and the trusting nature of provincial museums. When thirty-nine of the very finest pistols were stolen from seventeen different collections in July 1968, the Swedish police were taken aback – not least because all, ranging from sixteenth-century wheel-locks to nineteenth-century revolvers, were richly decorated specimens well known amongst collectors. The thieves' task was not difficult. At Göteborg, workmen cleaning part of the building housing a collection had left their scaffolding up during a public holiday and the thieves simply climbed through an upstairs window. At times they worked in daylight, and frequently ignored more valuable guns and pistols to take particular specimens to order. One was a fully inscribed presentation revolver given by President Lincoln to the King of Sweden; all were obviously selected to illustrate the development of firearms. Within Sweden they were unsaleable. Some were later recaptured by German police, but most have vanished. So specialised a pattern argues the existence of a private collector, yet no collector could be ignorant of the provenance of such weapons. Whether he, or they, employed the thieves directly can only be guessed at.

Beyond the Iron Curtain, art theft has almost ceased to exist. Persistent inquiries have failed to find any truth in the story, once propagated by journalists in America, that stolen paintings were smuggled into Russia to restore depleted Soviet collections. If anything, the traffic is the other way, as the Soviet government, to raise foreign exchange, puts on the London market such Tsarist possessions as the massive dinner service sold at Christie's in 1969. A certain number of art thefts do occur in Russia, but there are few or no outlets save in the West. The rich commissar with his secret stockpile is probably as mythical as the South American millionaire with his concrete-lined bunker full of stolen Titians. Ransom is inconceivable, because the conditions that permit it in the West do not exist in Russia.

The export of icons forms the main trade to the West, but official attitudes have changed considerably since the early post-war days when their disposal was a matter of complete indifference to the state. Then they were sold in large quantities in the "commission shops" of Moscow (where privately-owned goods could be sold at a small commission on behalf of their owners) and the government was one of the main vendors. Today, icons are sold legitimately only in the so-called "artistic salon" in Gorky Street, and any others carry 100 per cent duty at the frontier. Most of those illegally on offer in the streets are modern fakes. In 1970 the Soviet government made a formal request to Sotheby's and Christie's to avoid handling certain icons smuggled out in diplomatic bags, and one Western government has been asked to recall its ambassador in Moscow since he was caught shipping out icons by the gross.

Unless the Russian press has been forbidden to speak of those that get away, it would seem that the art thefts that take place normally fail. The students who raided Moscow's Historical Museum had to bury the Tsarist relics they took and were caught over a year later when they tried to sell them on the black market. The only serious loss in the last five years was of a Frans Hals on loan from Odessa to the Pushkin Museum in Moscow; and this was given publicity to foreign journalists precisely because the authorities feared that it would penetrate the Iron Curtain and be sold on the capitalist market. It was unfortunate that the Police Minister, V. S. Tikunov, had recently declared that "professional crime no longer exists in the Soviet Union".

A huge theft took place in 1967 of old masters of very high standing from the Brackenthorn Museum in Romania. Interpol were informed – a rarity, for Communist countries are not members – but nothing more is known. The only channel to the West is through individuals fleeing across the frontier with the most valuable portable objects they can find. Some of those who escaped from Budapest in 1956 exchanged a criminal record at home for *carte blanche* in the West, and helped themselves on the way by liberating a little of their national patrimony. Later, during the Dubček period in Czechoslovakia, refugees brought what they could and the extent of criminals shifting works of art became so disturbing that the Director General of Police in Prague asked for help from Austria in an attempt to check the flow.

The Austrians co-operated, because of their interest in maintaining good relations with neighbouring Czechoslovakia and Yugoslavia. But between West Germany and the East, before Chancellor Brandt's *Ostpolitik*, communication was minimal. When the Czech police attempted to trace a stolen mediaeval reliquary in the Federal

Republic in 1968, they had to get in touch first with their military mission in East Berlin, who passed the message via the United States Embassy to the West German Foreign Ministry before it finally reached the Bundeskriminalamt.

America has been left to the end, not because the illicit trade is small, but because in the great majority of cases the Atlantic crossing ends the line. With very few exceptions, the traffic is one way – from London, Frankfurt, Geneva, Paris and Rome; inside the United States it is a matter of redistribution, rather than re-export, and the pattern of theft is correspondingly diffuse.

The chances of recovering anything stolen in Europe decline sharply the moment the shipment or consignment has left for America. So large is the quantity of antiques entering the United States that inspection at the ports and airports is impossible. The U.S. Customs has the duty of checking only that declarations conform with the hundred-year classification of the term "antique". Except in the very highest category, circulation of Interpol and European police bulletins is a waste of time and both Scotland Yard and Interpol restrict their requests. Indeed, the warehouses in New York or at Kennedy airport are so exposed to theft that security forces are fully occupied protecting what is in transit, without inquiring into its bona-fides. One London insurer advises English dealers to crate anything going by air well enough to withstand a drop of ten feet or a night outside in the rain – both fairly frequent events. For years the world's major airlines at Kennedy airport have dithered, unable to agree on setting up a special warehouse for the antique trade, wired with an alarm and properly guarded. Meanwhile, insurance companies meet claims for damage and loss, and keep quiet in case public complaints frighten private clients into refusing to loan their possessions to exhibitions. Similar risks are run in transit within the United States: two paintings by Rubens from the Laurence Fleischman collection were stolen from a removal lorry in 1966. Much else has vanished since: in a recent case, a group of teenagers stole a lorry from its park under a warehouse in New York, their only reason for this being that they wanted a joy ride. The contents, a collection of very valuable modern paintings, might, as the police said, "have been art or pancakes". But, when they abandoned the lorry, someone else drove it off and left it minus Picasso's

The Duchess of Devonshire by Gainsborough, stolen by Adam Worth, con-man extraordinary, in 1876. Never actually caught in possession of the painting, he could not therefore be convicted. (*Mansell Collection*)

The Duke of Wellington by Goya, a sketch for the full-length portrait stolen from the National Gallery in 1961—a good year for art thieves. (*Mansell Collection*)

After 1948, German wood-carvings like this *Adoration of the Magi* by Tillman Riemenschneider suddenly came into risk of theft, and forgeries were common to keep pace with demand. (*British Museum*)

Early eighteenth-century jug, an example of German *Hausmaler* faience. Small items such as this are easily smuggled through customs, after which the authorities have little hope of tracing them. (*British Museum*)

The Lute Player by Frans Hals. Thieves stole this painting from a vault in a Geneva bank, leaving a worthless substitute in its place. The original was later recovered at the railway station. (*Mansell Collection*)

The Card Players by Cézanne, one of eight paintings stolen from the Pavillon Vendôme, Aix en Provence. A ransom of $150,000 was demanded for the safe return of the paintings. (*Litran—Paris Match*)

Detectives reconstructing the robbery at the Pavillon Vendôme (*André Sartres—Paris Match*)

An empty wall at the Dulwich College Art Gallery after paintings valued at £1,500,000 had been stolen. Elsheimer's *Susannah and the Elders* was one of the paintings lost. (*Press Association*)

The priceless *Madonna Enthroned* by Giorgione, stolen from an unguarded cathedral in Italy. The circumstances of its recovery aroused the curiosity of the Press in several countries. (*Mansell Collection*)

Three Rembrandts stolen from the Dulwich gallery: *Girl at a Window*, *Portrait of Jacob de Gheyn III*, and *The Artist's Son Titus*. (*Press Association*)

The interior of the Annonciade, a renovated sixteenth-century chapel at St Tropez, showing the door where thieves broke in to steal fifty-seven paintings, then valued at £500,000. (*Patrice Habans—Paris Match*)

famous *Children in the Luxembourg Gardens* and twelve canvases by Joan Miró and Toulouse-Lautrec. None of these have been found.

Because of publicity and the rise in prices, art thieves in America tend to concentrate on paintings. Picassos, being stereotyped as valuable, are stolen more often than works by any other artist, a reflection on how American investors have reacted to the boom as much as to the actual number of Picassos available. Since 1967 a standard pattern has developed: thieves make for a private collection, preferably one that has been illustrated or exhibited, and use the most modern technical means to eviscerate it. They then sit back, relying on the owner's cupidity or emotion to force him to accept ransom terms, regardless of police advice. Not all, however, covet modern art. More "conservative" criminals removed Monet's *Nympheas* and a dozen other admirable Impressionists from the Madison Avenue gallery of Stephen Hahn, while he was actually attending a dinner given by the Art Dealers Association of America to discuss the crime wave.

Hahn said philosophically that, since the paintings were insured for $500,000, he was expecting to receive a ransom demand. (The question of ransom is considered later, in Chapter 5.) Given the extraordinarily high crime rates of American cities and the inter-laced network of criminal organisation in the continent, there is a temptation to lay all big crimes at the door of a continent-wide conspiracy. Yet, as in Italy, the pattern seems to be that individual receivers run their own operations within certain areas; and the method of disposal is purely pragmatic.

Traces of Mafia implication are not hard to find. In February 1968 a fully authenticated Rembrandt portrait of a young man was stolen from the collection of the founder of Eastman Kodak in Rochester. Ten months later, acting on a tip-off from the Canadian police, the F.B.I. surrounded a remote airstrip in Michigan, near the Canadian border. They watched three men in a pick-up truck waiting for a light aircraft to land. One then walked over to the plane and collected a briefcase containing, as it turned out, $50,000 in cash. Classifying this as an "exchange", sufficient evidence to file a criminal charge, the police moved in and in the back of the truck found the Rembrandt, assigned to a collector in Montreal who had sent his emissary with the money. Together with the leader, a

Chicago import–export broker, two Mafia members were arrested, both members of the Bonanno "family". Another Bonanno figured prominently in October 1969 when seven men were arrested, together with their receiver, allegedly the "biggest fence on the East coast". More than a million dollars' worth of miscellaneous antiques were found on the premises of their warehouse – a front for the distributive machinery for stolen art.

The most interesting major theft in the United States – and an exception to the rule that redistribution is confined to North America – has been the ransacking of the Tillman collection, a story that is by no means clear, even five years after the event. Georg Tillman, one of the great *cognoscenti* of the twentieth century, built up in the 1920s a superb collection of German porcelain: figures of the Böttger period, 250 superb examples of du Pacquier porcelain from Vienna, and decorated faience from other rare eighteenth-century German factories such as Frankfurt and Bayreuth. He bought only the finest things, from all over Germany, Poland, Austria and Czechoslovakia, and his section devoted to *Hausmaler* faience (pieces bought from or smuggled out of the factory and decorated by gifted artists in their own freelance styles) was unrivalled in any public collection in the world. Wisely, he shipped it out of Germany in the late 1930s and retired to Holland. Having built up another collection of ethnographica which he left in Amsterdam, he fled to Britain in 1940. The porcelain collection went to New York, where it was stored in a warehouse belonging to the Lincoln Company.

In the succeeding twenty-five years, the Tillman family had the packing cases inspected once, in 1958. Despite occasional rumours in the mid-1960s, it was not until two or three identifiable pieces appeared on the market that they became alarmed. Finally, in June 1969, the cases were opened and found to contain rubbish, covered at the top with a few pieces to disguise the loss.

About 1960, apparently, the warehouse had been taken over by the Mafia and the whole collection dispersed slowly and discreetly during the next five years, through the agency of one or more New York dealers, to private collectors in Germany, Switzerland and Brazil. The F.B.I. have so far failed to track down any of the thieves and the dealer principally concerned has died in curious circumstances. The case is, in fact, dead and, for reasons connected presumably with

Mafia corruption, likely to remain so. A few pieces of porcelain have been traced in private collections, but not a single item of the *Hausmaler* faience has been seen since, a fact that may indicate either a single very wealthy entrepreneur who will sit on it for twenty years, or one of the great losses of art of all time.

The collectors may have bought in good faith, but they have every right to be disturbed at the situation. Although the Tillman pieces had never been exhibited, their superb standards were known, and there is evidence that some of the new owners were anxious enough about the effect on their standing socially and among other collectors to have met recently in London to discuss what to do. No one would willingly court the obloquy that would follow if he were known to have participated, however unwittingly, in such a carve-up. The investments of such collectors will be hard to put on the market for a generation or more: museums would scarcely buy, even if the Tillman family had by then lost their legal right to recovery.

In the United States and Canada, art theft is still a by-product of criminal organisation. The big receivers are importers of what is stolen elsewhere rather than managers in robbery itself. Almost impregnably secure, they can afford to be lax. One American importer who visits England each year is known to boast quite openly that a high proportion of what he sells in the States is "bent gear". In Latin America and in Mexico, art theft is oriented towards North American demand. The seventy pre-Columbian gold figures of animals and birds, dating from the Coclé culture, that were taken from the National Museum in Panama in 1966 have either gone to collectors in the United States or been melted down for their scrap value. Looking farther east, the contagion has spread: Australia and Japan, being modern capitalist states, reflect the trends of Western Europe. Picasso's well known nude called *La Belle Hollandaise*, dating from the end of his Rose period, was stolen from the Queensland Art Gallery in Brisbane in 1967. Art theft is well known in Sydney and Melbourne; while in Tokyo the Mitsubishi Bank distributed calendars for Christmas 1969 with a reproduction of a missing Toulouse-Lautrec from the Kyoto National Art Museum, and recovered it – at a price – within a month.

Such is the appearance of robbery during the last ten years. Before turning to the criminals who make up the double market, and the exclusive, highly profitable area of ransom, it is worth making some tentative calculations. The thefts mentioned so far comprise less than a quarter of the cases important enough to rate a column in the main European and American newspapers, and perhaps less than a twentieth of those given a separate card index in the Interpol principal file. According to most police art squads, recorded thefts represent only half to two-thirds of the actual total, and, of those recorded in each country, Interpol is notified of less than ten per cent.

The proportion of the total number of stolen works ever to be recovered remains very low. If the highly valuable paintings that form the basis of ransom demands are excluded – since the thieves' intention is usually to return them – the true dimensions of the failure become clear. As a general rule the figure of recovery may be taken as less than ten per cent – rather higher in the case of things fine enough to reach the Interpol clearing-house; substantially lower for more ordinary ones. Over ninety per cent disappear into the vast dim river of the double market and emerge having lost what is most precious to their former owners, the attribute of individuality.

When it comes to assessing the volume and value of stolen objects in circulation, it is impossible to do more than make a guess. At the time of the major thefts of the early 1960s, one American journal estimated the value of what had been stolen in the world in 1960–63 at $12 million. That total included only cases serious enough to be reported in the press.

The files of unsolved cases in the Interpol library give a more informed but equally selective analysis. To take the case of sculptures: in the years 1956–69, a total of 1,267 objects were reported stolen, including 517 from Italy, 129 from Austria, 33 from Germany, 47 from Belgium, 43 from the Netherlands, 21 from France, 16 from Switzerland, nine from the U.K., one from Greece and 38 from the rest of the world. But the inadequacy of these statistics is shown at once because many German and most Greek thefts were not reported to Interpol in those years. For sheer numbers, Canada came second with 413 – all of which were taken in a single robbery. The figures for pictures, engravings, furniture, tapestries and *objets de vertu* are equally unhelpful. Nor can one place much credit on press reports such as this, dating from April 1968:

76

Police evidence is mounting that a high proportion of the $60 million worth of antiques stolen in Britain has been smuggled into South America, Europe and the United States. Loss adjusters estimate that in the last year art and antique robberies have risen by more than thirty per cent in Britain, which has the biggest reservoir of fine art in the world.

Is this $60 million based on the actual price paid by the former owners, or the price charged by the new? Does it include, for example, the bronze figures of British monarchs from the Buxton fountain in Parliament Square, four of which were stolen in 1960 and four after its removal to Victoria Tower gardens some years later? Art theft takes place on such a wide scale and covers such a varied range of objects that a "value", even in round figures, is not to be found.

A better indication comes from the Association of Art Dealers of America, who estimated their New York members' losses, in the first six months of 1965 alone, as $100,000. What one can say, tentatively, but on a basis of evidence, is that roughly five per cent of all antiques, paintings and *objets d'art* on sale anywhere in the world have a dubious provenance; that is, they have been parted illegally from their original owners, and passed, perhaps through half a dozen separate hands, to a point at which they can be offered for legitimate sale. In nine cases out of ten, even if such an item were recognised, it would be legally and practically impossible to restore it. We are talking of a not inconsiderable part of the total trade; of an illegal market worth (on pre-theft value) as much as £30 million annually (£5 million each in Britain, Italy and the United States); in terms of actual *profit* to criminals, £10 million. The greater part of this goes to receivers. To put it another way, there are possibly thirty receivers in Britain, 100 in the United States, and 200 in Europe engaged wholly or partly in the double market and making on average £30,000 a year each, tax free.

Notes

1 The same is broadly true of the art investment funds that grew up in the boom years of the 1960s. These include Artemis, headed

by the Banque Lambert in Brussels, and Modarco, virtually an investment fund, based in Panama, whose shares are handled by the Banque de Paris et des Pays-Bas in Geneva.

[2] The methods of these manufacturers are not without interest. *Art and Antiques Weekly* reported in September 1968 that London dealers had been receiving letters from the offices of Petit Artisanat, Avenida del Generalísimo Franco in Barcelona, offering "antiquary type" paintings.

"We have pleasure to send you herewith a couple of photographs of oil paintings. We are looking around Spain and buy this category of painting. We are not in a position to guarantee the authenticity and even we assume that they are not real antiques, but of course there is no doubt of their artistic quality. We export these paintings to the United States of America and we know that they are sold as antiques.

"We would like to have some connection in your market. Please be so kind and inform us in respect of your possible interest towards what we are offering. If you are in a principle susceptible to be interested please let us know and we shall arrange a visit to London, the idea being that we may discuss in detail on this particular. The prices range between $75 and $250 per painting, the frame included."

Further inquiries produced an assurance of high quality, but a polite refusal to give certificates; the pictures "were being bought from collectors throughout Spain" and the prices were all right – weren't they? One wonders whether any reputable firm accepted the offer to enter into fraud. I have seen a set of these pictures sold at auction as genuine, in a Sussex saleroom, for prices mercifully not more than 50 per cent above those quoted in the letter.

Chapter 4 Thieves and Receivers

The workings of the double market can be understood only by examining those who operate it, for the relationship between thief, receiver and eventual client is just as important a consideration as the rise in demand and prices, the anonymity of salerooms, the investment boom and the pattern of crime. By a quirk of fashion, the thief has always attracted the public interest. Raffles is an archetypal hero whose remoter heirs can still be found stereotyped in television serials. Whenever art thefts occur, the newspapers repeat the classic story of the *Mona Lisa*. The receiver has, since the days of Fagin, had a harder press, and, as the double market has become a business organisation, he is not likely to be reinstated in the future unless he perfects his technique so finely that he acquires commercial glory as an entrepreneur – illegal but essential to the continued existence of private art collecting.

Yet the professional art thief has no distinguishing marks, no special mentality, no gift of connoisseurship. He is simply a thief, a mechanical manifestation of the demand of a certain type of society for symbols of status, wealth and culture. He has no glamour, except what the public invests him with, or the narcissism of the underworld reflects. Whether he ransacks a house as a hired hand to bring his receiver antiques, or whether he employs his own men and does his own research in the illustrated articles of *Country Life* and *The Connoisseur*, is irrelevant as a means of analysing art theft. The man might as well be repainting stolen motor cars, or stripping stolen gems from their settings.

The reasons for the public distinction between thief and receiver are very simple: thieves are frequently caught, receivers rarely, so little is known of their methods; and the need to dramatise the subject can be sustained in depicting a robbery, but not so easily in considering the dangers and tensions confronting the skilled distributor of stolen property. Not even a convicted receiver would consent to be interviewed for this book. Of those who are caught, few get sentenced to the full measure of their crime; and they retain, in any case, a vested interest for the future in protesting their innocence. According to the evidence of every police headquarters in Europe, the receiver will resume his trade when he comes out of prison: it is too profitable a métier to relinquish. For the same reasons, the thieves who work closely with receivers have an equal interest in silence. Only the vain weathercocks of the underworld and those on the fringe expound their techniques in public.

Two further difficulties face the analyst. The law of libel is far more useful a defence to a receiver whose public face as an antique dealer is assured, and whose resources enable him to brief good counsel in the courts, than it is to a convicted thief; and the complexity of protective relationships makes it hard to do more than guess at the extent of actual business organisation behind the receivers themselves.

At the outset, the common attribution of art thefts to the Mafia or the Union Corse should be challenged. Both organisations have, at times, taken a share in the art market: the former disposed of the Tillman collection, the latter engaged in ransom thefts in the south of France in the early 1960s (see Chapter 5). Two young Italians, caught by the Art Squad and charged in London in 1972 with importing stolen religious treasures, claimed to have been tortured with cigarette burns by a Mafia receiver, and *mafiosi* appear regularly in Interpol notices of Italian thefts. But these are special cases, where unusually high returns offered themselves to a "family" already habituated to dealing with stolen property or highly valuable illegal traffic such as that in heroin. Sections of the Union Corse became involved during a period of transition, after the great jewel thefts of the 1950s on the Riviera, and before perfecting the heroin traffic in and out of Marseilles, the basis of the "French connection". Yet art theft was never so profitable as jewels and drugs and was dropped as soon as more profitable alternatives appeared.

The organisations that support the double market did sometimes share a common origin with *mafiosi* and Corsican criminals in war-time black-marketing and collaboration with the Gestapo. For example, Italian *antiquari*, who had helped fill trunks for the Einsatzstab Rosenberg, continued the illegal side of antique dealing long afterwards. But the characteristic art-theft group today depends not so much on a "family" as on a single man, whose personal protection is governed by financial considerations, not by loyalty. Such a man will possess connections in the underworld, access to thieves, and a discreetly public esteem as a good buyer, established over many years; in addition, he will maintain an equally important series of relationships in the legitimate antique and fine-art trade, with dealers and salerooms, and, above all, with a personal register of private clients and collectors, sharply divided between those who never suspect the vendor and those who will buy at bargain prices without asking unnecessary questions. In addition, he will have the tools of his trade: expertise in porcelain or paintings, large reserves of cash, transport, and unlimited and carefully located storage facilities. Finally, he will be protected by an impenetrable façade as a straight businessman, by knowledge of all the intricacies of the law of receiving and possession, by access to the best legal advisers in time of trouble, and not infrequently by direct corruption of the police or government authorities.

Thus the trade is centred on the receiver, whose own methods have come very close to the confederated or "white-collar" criminal techniques evolved since the war in the United States. Directed by experts of this calibre, with substantial funds, the actual robbery has been reduced to a skilled occupation. Specialisation and division of labour help to ensure secrecy. Modern technology is available: thermic lances to attack safes, the science of restoration to obliterate identification. Since the profit is far greater for the receiver than the thief, the former can stand the loss even of hundreds of pounds by scratching, restoring or slightly altering a painting, rolling off engraving on silver, bleaching or even stripping furniture, so that it becomes unrecognisable. It might be worth his while, for example, to replace the piece of wood carrying the *maindron* or stamp of a French cabinet maker, even if this reduced the value of a piece of furniture from £10,000 to £5,000. Very high fees are paid for this skilful work to corrupt restorers, who may also be active members of a gang. It has also been known – in Italy and Germany especially – for a restorer to be a front for criminals, so that when a particularly fine but dirty painting comes in for cleaning from owners who appear ignorant of its true value, a copy is substituted. (A seascape that had always hung on the stairs in semi-darkness, covered with a heavy varnish, turned deep chocolate, the details of the ships hard to distinguish and the general appearance dingy and Victorian, is not likely to be recognised after restoration and cleaning, and the risk involved in substitution is correspondingly low.)

Professor Donald Cressey suggested five years ago that the export to Europe of the sort of crime threatening to undermine the American political and economic system could be only a matter of time.[1] In the art-theft world in the last decade, increased mobility, technical skills, the "task force" concept, and a high degree of specialisation have led to a situation in which confederated crime presents an elaborate structure, with the profits of crime used to buy immunity from arrest and prosecution. This point was reached in Italy about 1969. France, Britain and Germany have apparently not yet succumbed, but one recent study has predicted that corruption of police and political authorities is the most likely growth area for British crime.[2] In such an organisation, the old relationships of gang leader and thief have been subsumed into a worker–management pattern, behind which lie respectable backers whose direct involvement is virtually undetectable, and who resemble the shareholders of a limited liability company. It is therefore quite inappropriate to portray the art thief or the receiver as a romantic hero or a monster. They are both squalid manifestations of a special case of modern economics.

But who are these entrepreneurs? Like the bosses of the international narcotics trade, their names appear only on the rare occasions when they are arrested. Even then, they set themselves apart from ordinary criminals. In the assize court of Aix en Provence in April 1970 one appeared: seventy-nine year old M. André David, art collector, respected antique dealer, holder of the Légion d'Honneur, the Croix de Guerre, and the Médaille Militaire. "His love of works of art", a psychiatrist declared, in evidence for the defence, "is bound up with a deep contempt for some owners of these works, those who do not understand their language. For David believes that fine pieces of furniture and pictures speak." Almost, it appeared, a crime of passion. David had collected an Algerian *broquanteur*, or junk dealer, Toto, his half-brother, and Busiqua, a Corsican restaurant owner, from the flea market in Aix and instructed them, "When you have something bring it to me." He told the court, "I thought the three went to the front doors of houses when they were in fact going through the windows. Sometime later, when I heard that a gang specialising in clearing out châteaux had been arrested, I asked Toto to stop supplying me – but the thieves were arrested and I concluded my suspicions were unfounded."

Nevertheless, when the police arrested the three, they were in David's van, carrying a load of stolen antiques from the Château d'Espanon, home of the Marquis de Castellane. Where were they going? "To M. David." But David denied all knowledge: he had lent them his car, true, "but I have nothing with which to reproach myself, not even book-keeping errors". Was he imprudent, or, as the public prosecutor maintained, a big receiver who kept a record of all the principal collections in the area? Bewildered by expert testimony, the court felt unable to decide, and handed down a sentence of ten years to Toto, but only a suspended sentence and a £7,000 fine to M. David.

Greater success attended the prosecution in the case against the gang of château thieves led by Doctor Gustave Richier, but only because they were caught in possession of so much, and because the other members, Marcel Binh, son of a private dealer, Claude Mabillotte, unemployed lorry-driver, and the doctor's brother, an interior decorator, broke down and accused each other from the dock. Richier, epitome of the small-town, middle-class practitioner, precise and conventionally dressed, had been the brain of the gang, but its protective cover, as opposed to its methods, remained amateurish.

In Britain, respected and apparently respectable dealers have been exposed in various malpractices over the years, chiefly for combining in the "ring" to rig prices in the salerooms. Until the furore occasioned by a series of particularly outrageous ring operations in 1970–71, the existence of the British Antique Dealers Association was no certain guarantee of professional standards of conduct. But the principal receivers lie mainly on the fringe of the trade, battening on a whole series of small traders without shops who work as knockers and middlemen, like small fleas on the backs of bigger ones. Almost without exception, import–export of antiques forms a major side of their business. A necessarily disguised portrait of one of the principal London receivers is given in Chapter 7. The only one successfully prosecuted in recent years maintained an antique shop at Amersham, the disposal centre for the proceeds from a series of thefts from country houses all over England – Caesar's Castle in Westmorland and Montacute House in Somerset among them.

In Italy, the *carabinieri* recovered an enormous haul of church treasures, stolen in the north between 1957 and 1962, when an art expert from Padua was arrested with a gang numbering eleven thieves and a dozen antique dealers. In that instance the expert, who had acted as intermediary receiver between the thieves and the dealers, brought down the whole network after his arrest for the theft of a crucifix from the cathedral in Pisa. As the police picked up the dealers one by one, each squealed sufficiently loudly to give other leads and swell the total. Over three years of investigation, more than £500,000-worth of identifiable objects was returned, together with some others that had been mutilated for easier resale. Nearly all were on the Ministry's list of *Oggetti d'Arte Trafugata*.

But, as with criminals of any category, the small men are the ones who normally get picked off. One example is the former employee of a New York gallery who set himself up in business as a dealer with a stock of over 250 paintings stolen from Herbert Arnot Inc., largest commercial importers of works of art from Europe. He lasted only a few months. The receivers who bought a Picasso water-colour, a study for *Les Demoiselles d'Avignon*, in Philadelphia, returned it and confessed when one of the gang was shot dead by police during a motel hold-up. The only major receiver to be imprisoned in the United States since 1965 is the California businessman (see p. 74) who ran his warehouses like a chain store for stolen paintings.

The gradations between thief and receiver are as many as individual criminals. There is, for instance, the con man "so distinguished looking, we were almost ashamed to arrest him", as the New York police said of one who shopped extensively at Macy's and Lord and Taylor, and shop-lifted $30,000-worth of works of art which he then sold to antique dealers on the pretence that he represented a broadcasting network and was authorised to dispose of the props that had been used in various television shows. There is the bogus priest, well known in every country: "Father Cantry" who, in clerical disguise, charted out the Jesuit college at Grantham and returned at night to take a Renaissance painting of St Jerome. Such figures belong to any age, but some come very close to being entrepreneur-receivers. Six Yorkshiremen set out to become dollar earners with a product that, the prosecuting counsel said at their trial in 1969, "was intended for the export market in a manner of which the government would scarcely approve". All over the West Riding they had looted garden statuary and antiques, the bulk of which were recovered just before they were due to be shipped to a buyer in America. A year later, at London airport, after weeks of planning through Interpol, C.I.D. men raided the luggage of three Lebanese and found £50,000-worth of stolen treasures, including jewel-studded icons from a chapel in Syria. A further £100,000-worth was sequestered in their offices in Beirut, and a number of mothers superior and priests had to fly to London in order to reclaim the possessions of their churches.

The top flight of thieves are hard, permanent criminals, highly trained in robbery and intelligent and disciplined enough to organise an efficient task force. Their one – and very common – weakness, is an addiction to gambling on a grand scale, a trait that prevents them from turning profits into the trading surplus of the true receiver. Few are strangers to prison: "Z", the principal thief of a gang described in Chapter 7, has since been arrested on a straightforward charge of burglary and will probably serve four years in jail, by no means his first nor his last term. He may graduate to being a receiver and lift himself out of the danger of having to do the actual theft, or he may degenerate with successive sentences into an old lag. He is essentially the same type as V, head of the church thieves in Germany; Karlheinz Berg, also a German, arrested in Vienna by the Austrian Interpol Bureau on a charge of stealing a Rubens, and finally extradited and imprisoned in Holland; or Sacheverell Stanley Houghton, who pleaded guilty in 1969 to being valuer and assessor for a gang working on English country houses and was sentenced to three years in Albany prison. According to the prosecution, his job was to point out the objects worth stealing and he was paid on a

commission basis by the gang. He might have been a good valuer
– the loot from Tew Park was worth £20,000 – but what he actually
sold brought poor returns: a mere £1,700 for three-quarters of it.

This point differentiates quite clearly between thieves who belong
to a syndicate, and take a proportionate share in the rewards, and
the hired hands – the common thieves, such as the five Italians from
Ferrara who cut down the Titian *Christ Appearing to his Mother
after the Resurrection* from the parish church of Medole, and were
caught by a straightforward police strategem. There is a huge
gallery of thieves of this type: Anthony Waldron, unemployed
croupier, and Dudley Kemp, unemployed farm worker, serving
five years each for their part in the robbery of the Tillotson collection;
Jan Koch, doing five years in Marberg jail for icon thefts from
Yugoslavia; and the five men from Port Richmond, New York, who
were seized while haggling over a stolen Goya.

The price mechanism operating in this section of the double
market bears harshly on the men who take the greatest risks. Some
idea of the fall in theoretical value of a work of art in its journey
through the double market can be gained from the confession of a
man arrested in Rome in 1970, who admitted to stealing a painting
valued at 18 million lire, which had been resold by his receiver to a
client for 5 million lire. The client must have been strikingly incurious
if he imagined such a sale price to have been honest. It is also significant that in this case the thief's commission was a mere 280,000
lire (£190).

On the other hand, thieves in Italy are more often directly hired
by receiver–dealers than is the case in the rest of Europe. Dr
Gandolfo, head of Milan C.I.D., said recently, "Crimes are committed
by well organised groups with plenty of funds, working on behalf
of collectors, Italian, German, Swiss and American. The thieves
work to the order of these groups." His judgement is confirmed by
Dr Luglie, head of the police school in Rome. It is correspondingly
difficult for thieves to strike out on their own, in the face of the
criminal establishment. They may dislike working for low rewards,
but they lack the contacts. Those who approached G. B. Meneghini,
the wealthy estranged husband of Maria Callas, with an outstanding
fourteenth-century altar-piece found themselves arrested at once;
and another group, unable to find an outlet, simply abandoned in a

lonely farmhouse in the Campagna a full length portrait by Hans Holbein the younger.

If the double market is wholly successful, then any given work of art will have been fitted with a spurious pedigree before it ever reaches the private client: either he will buy from a perfectly honest dealer, perhaps fourth in line from the receiver, or he will be offered something from which individuality has largely been removed. But higher in the price range, and especially with paintings, the transition from vendor to collector is less easily managed.

The existence of the oil sheik, gazing on walls covered with stolen tapestries, or of the mad millionaire with a bomb-proof concrete-lined cellar in Brazil, cannot be proved or disproved. Judging from what was said at the Eichmann trial, and from persistent rumours of wealthy refugees hiding under the Stroessner dictatorship in Paraguay, leading Nazis in the Third Reich did secrete substantial funds in Latin America before 1945, a few of them living to claim them. Possibly works of art formed part of the dispositions made in the event of German defeat. The Nazis' attitude towards paintings was, albeit hypocritically, "pure", and they may have sought to safeguard the German heritage in this way. Of the hundreds of works missing from European countries, many may still be in the possession of ex-Nazis; yet none have apparently returned from such sources except the two Pollaiuolos mentioned in Chapter 8 – and these were German soldiers' loot from a Nazi collection. It seems strange that there should be no substantiated record of the transport of stolen art to South America, especially as the routes of the Nazi pillage inside Europe are well documented. While it was not impossible to transfer funds through complaisant banks in Switzerland and Portugal, the transport of large crates across the Atlantic in 1945 would have been a very different matter.

According to Esterow in *The Art Stealers*,[3] one of the finest detectives in the Sûreté, Charles Lapron, tracked down such a secret collection in the late 1920s, and arrested the "owner", Pierre Duval, with his mistress, in a villa on the Italian Riviera, munificently furnished with the proceeds of a dozen robberies from the rich collectors of Paris. The story is a good one, but much embellished over the years, and the original records have long been destroyed. The cold fact is, Duval appears to have been a thief with at least two previous convictions, rather than a buyer from other thieves.

But do certain private collectors now buy knowingly on the illegal market, as newspaper reports assert? Does the stereotype of the crooked millionaire represent a form of wishful thinking, disguising the real efficiency of the means that transmute theft into legitimate resale? Facts are hard to come by. One rich Italian, trapped by Rodolfo Siviero into handing over the *Madonna* of Cossito, seems to fit (see p. 89). But the jet-set trappings, the houses in Switzerland and Uruguay, disguise the fact that he was actually a receiver, seeking to sell the triptych through a New York dealer. There is a theory that the Caravaggio *Nativity* from San Lorenzo in Palermo (see p. 121) was taken as part of a campaign to supply the demands of galleries and museums in Latin America that in the last few years have been improving their stock. While this is an interesting variant on the individual collector explanation, it lacks credibility where a work of such importance is concerned.

What of the several buyers of the Tillman porcelain? They acquired the figures with some semblance of good faith. They may have been suspicious, but the pieces emanated from an apparently reputable New York dealer, and the contents of the collection, which had never been exhibited and not seen for nearly thirty years, were not precisely identifiable. The best source of information available in Britain, a person who has worked both for gangs of art thieves and for the police, claims that the crooked millionaire exists, but can point to the existence of only one, who, knowing that things are stolen, buys at his own price from dealers who do a certain amount of receiving and may indeed supply him with what he wants. There may be others: the great strength of the double market is that it is almost impossible to prove that a collector bought in *bad* faith. In America, the Rembrandt from the Eastman Kodak collection was on its way to a Canadian private buyer when the emissary, carrying $50,000 in cash, was arrested during the handover. Such cases become known only by chance. If pictures of this quality are bought, at bargain prices, to be held secret for a generation or more until the statute of limitations in the country of origin has run out, then they are not likely to emerge until the 1980s or 1990s.

And what part does commissioned theft (including possibly the

Madonna of Santa Maria del Popolo, recovered on its journey to an unnamed collector in Holland, or the *Ephebus* of Selinute) play? Most police officers concerned with the market believe that commissioned theft does take place. Yet again, there is no specific evidence, only hints about who "may" buy;[4] nothing has been pin-pointed in recent years in a private collection, if one excepts the two pictures claimed back by the Italian government from the Thyssen-Bornemist collection in Switzerland because their export had contravened Italian legislation – a form of theft perhaps, but not one detrimental to Thyssen himself. However curious the circumstances of acquisition, no one would suggest that the Boston Museum *procured* the theft of the ancient Turkish gold treasure they first displayed in 1970, nor the contentious Raphael portrait of Signorina Maria della Rovere. The normal method of disposal – if anything on this scale can be described as "normal" – is that followed in the case of the thirteenth-century altar-piece stolen from Cossito in Northern Italy in 1964. The *Madonna* was first altered and retouched in a Milan workshop, then smuggled into Switzerland by the receiver, who was also a director of an auction house, registered in Liechtenstein. A catalogue was printed for a sale in which the *Madonna* figured prominently. Copies were circulated, but only to members of the syndicate, and no actual sale took place. Nevertheless the supposed auction, and the catalogue entry, gave the *Madonna* a sort of provenance, enough for a second partner to launch it on the American market at a price of £135,000.

Beyond the ring of the professionals lies the open field of the private thief, the amateur, the magpie and the psychopath. Just as most museums in the world have suffered disasters from people with a mad destructive impulse, so, occasionally, pictures vanish for no reason apparent to the sane. The *Black Boy*, Gainsborough's portrait of the fourth Duke of Rutland, belonging to the Sickles family of New York, was burnt seventy years ago in an outdoor oven by an Austrian maid in revenge for a fancied insult. In 1964 a Boston court had to decide whether Thomas Gezork, a Polish-born art student, was fit to stand trial for the theft from the Boston Museum of a unique piece of Greek jewellery, a third-century B.C. gold filigree earring in the shape of Nike, the goddess of Victory, riding in her chariot. Two psychiatrists testified to his schizophrenic personality, but were unable to judge whether he had been sane at the time of the theft. Fortunately the earring was recovered months later, after a hard winter, buried in damp earth and hidden in, of all things, a Campbell's soup tin.

Earlier studies of art theft have concentrated largely on the excesses of the irrational. Not that Vincenzo Perugia or Arsene Goerdetier were certifiably insane: their exploits simply made better stories than the routine crimes of a large number of professionals. For all the space taken up in headlines by the trial, in 1962, of Gerald Greene, a University of California student who stole Paul Klee's *Jung Waldteufel* from the Maitland collection in Los Angeles, the affair was trivial. The Klee was recovered by efficient co-operation in the art world and an advertisement in the *Burlington Magazine*, for Greene had been foolish enough to give his real name when he sold the painting to a highly respectable German dealer. But during the trial the state attempted to prove that the Klee was worth more than $5,000 and that it had been transported through the southern district of New York – that is, that Greene had committed two Federal offences. The clash of rival experts over the definition of whether the Klee was an oil, a water-colour or a print, and whether it was worth $1,000 or $25,000, taught the public a cynical lesson about the modern art market. Eminent lawyers wrangled over the precise specification of a work of art composed of oil, gesso and water-soluble paints on a square of linoleum; and the prosecutor's attempt to define a work of art foundered in a torrent of ambiguities:

> A painting is not a loaf of bread or a can of beans or a Cadillac convertible or a share of General Motors stock. These other things are things that are widespread. Everybody has at least some of them and they are traded every day, everywhere, and their value is readily ascertainable because there is a market on every street corner for cans of beans and loaves of bread and in every town there is a place to buy cars. But paintings are different because they are unique. There is nothing else like them. A single painter in his lifetime can turn out only so many of them and, once these are done, there can never be anything quite like it. But something more comes into the value of a

painting because a painting is a work of art and the painting is worth something because it evokes something in us, in the viewer. What may leave one viewer cold, may to another viewer be the most significant sort of statement about our lives and our existence; so a painting meaning much to one person may not be worth very much to another person.

But that does not mean that paintings have no value and a painting's value is not ascertainable, for paintings too are sold. They are sold at auctions. They are sold by professional dealers to each other. There is trade among museums. There is trade among connoisseurs and paintings have a good market rate just like other forms of property.

Works of art are peculiarly vulnerable to the thief intent on only a single crime, particularly if he does not intend to sell; and while the proportion of such losses is small compared to the quantity processed by the double market, it is not insignificant. A man who steals for sheer lust of possession is virtually undetectable. The "impecunious art student" who took Rodin's *Psyche* from a London gallery and returned the statue four months later with a few lines quoted from Yeats and a ten-shilling note towards the Tate Gallery's subscription for Rodin's masterpiece, *Le Baiser*, was never caught – nor did the police expect it. Two missing portraits by van Dyck were found outside the Musée des Beaux Arts in Aix en Provence in April 1958, with a note to say that they had been taken to win a bet; and an outrageous thief who stole a painting by the modern Italian artist Giorgio Morandi, from the Pitti Palace in Florence, left a copy of the original stuck to the frame with sellotape, a note on the back: "Thank you very much. I love Morandi. 18.3.64." Museum officials spent their time angrily denying that a copy could hang in public view for six weeks without being noticed. Sergei Claude Bogousslavsky sneaked Watteau's *L'Indifférent*, a tiny painting of a carefree youth in a rose-coloured cape and blue doublet, out of the Louvre in 1939 and kept it for a time before handing it back to the Paris police, explaining that he had just wanted to remove the ill effects of hideous museum restoration.

Apart from the eccentrics, there is a flourishing group of amateur criminals who, according to the professionals, risk their livelihood by creating the publicity the double market strives to avoid. Thus, a man calling himself Dr Otto Petter drew attention to himself in October 1965 by posing as an art dealer and carrying in his car statues of saints which he had tried to sell to other dealers; he was duly arrested by German police. Major David Baxter, stationed with the Royal Army Ordnance Corps in Oxfordshire, pleaded guilty at Oxford Quarter Sessions in 1969 to stealing an antique revolver worth £4,500 from the Pitt-Rivers Museum in Oxford and another worth £6,000 from the Castle Museum in York. Rumours that these two were for sale had reached Scotland Yard Art Squad earlier in the year. Only when they visited the Pitt-Rivers Museum did they realise that the revolver, a muzzle-loading English flintlock, *circa* 1640, with an almost unique mechanism, had been replaced by a forgery, made to order by a Chinese workman in Hong Kong during Baxter's service overseas. The forgery was so good that only the lack of patina on the metal pointed to the substitution. Baxter had written a book on firearms and had ready access to museums. While in York he found that security was lax; other weapons followed, from provincial museums. Under questioning he handed them in, and confessed at his trial, "My intellect told me that sooner or later I would be found out. I showed all the weapons openly to friends, relations and dealers. Now that the chain is broken I feel a sense of relief."

Protestations of high-mindedness or innocuous love of art have, of course, formed part of the criminal's defence ever since Perugia stole the *Mona Lisa* and pleaded a political motive. Juries have tended to be sympathetic, feeling perhaps a certain sense of identity with men who wanted no more than to possess a masterpiece for a few hours before handing it back. Nothing is more likely to prejudice the survival of the masterpiece, but the attitude has been much encouraged by the legal necessity to prove intent actually to steal. If Charles Garrett, a chauffeur and butler, whose house was found to contain £50,000-worth of assorted paintings and *objets d'art*, had not pleaded guilty to charges of theft and asked for forty-five similar offences to be taken into consideration, he might have been hard to convict, for in the two years of his collecting mania he had made no attempt to dispose of the articles.

The magpie thief is an agreeable rarity. One young Frenchman used to drive off in his large convertible at weekends, cross the Spanish border, and come back with chandeliers, church furniture and tapestries to decorate his modest flat in Toulouse. But the majority of amateurs are confidence men, like Franco Bertucci, a salesman and former detective from the Roman police force, who acquired a Raphael miniature, painted in 1501 when the artist was only eighteen. Its owner, Professor Tullio Gramantieri, had refused offers as high as $75,000. In two and a half years the police found no trace, but in September 1950 a dealer in Rome was visited by an unknown customer, who offered him the miniature for a mere 2 million lire ($3,000). Suspicious of the low price, the dealer stalled, arranged a future meeting and called the police. When Bertucci was caught, his *modus operandi* was revealed. He had consulted the professor about another miniature, which turned out to be a forgery. During the interview, Gramantieri had courteously produced the Raphael to emphasise an argument – and, on his return visit at night, Bertucci had known exactly where to look.

At the end, there are no heroes, only villains. Adam Worth's ghost is recalled only by the sentimental. Yet it is hard not to admire the logic of the Australians who, "like raiding Vikings", pulled a single confidence trick on a major London saleroom. At prices totalling nearly £9,000, they bought four paintings. After the sale they went to pay and asked the clerk at the desk if they could take them at once. Could their bank vouch for the cheque? But of course. A telephone inquiry to a provincial branch produced the answer that more than £9,000 was available in the account. The pictures were handed over. In the afternoon, before the bank closed and when a new cashier had come on duty, another Australian went in and cashed a cheque for the total; and the whole gang left by air that night, after blandly showing their saleroom receipts to the customs. The saleroom can sue through the civil courts, but for such a sum the pursuit to Australia is hardly worth it.

Cases concerning the sad, often frightened men tempted by little-known valuables in their care make pathetic reading. One such case concerns a former vicar of Upwood in Huntingdonshire, who left a trail of depredation behind him during his tenure. First, he sent the Portuguese silver-gilt plate belonging to the church to Sotheby's, claiming his archdeacon's approval and giving instructions not to

93

put its provenance in the catalogue. Later he reported the theft of a communion service, and showed the police a similar set of chalice and patten to help their search; this was, in fact, the lost service, sold afterwards to a firm of church furnishers. Finally, he exchanged the chalice from another parish church in an antique shop in Cambridge. Inadequate stipend and family disasters led him to prison; the judge at his trial declared, "If you examine your conscience and ask yourself what is the most despicable sin a clergyman can commit, surely the answer would be to steal the holy vessels of which you were put in charge."

Theft of church plate was once a matter for excommunication and vestigial reverence may explain the survival in Britain of so many sixteenth- and seventeenth-century chalices. But no supernatural sanctions restrain the custodians of public collections, the experts who, if they chose, could strip many a provincial museum with poor records and inadequate display. Most museums in the world show only a fraction of their collections, while the rest lies in the vaults below. It is very rare for lapses to occur among the staff of Western collections (but see p. 66) or national museums,[5] but the illicit sale of antiquities has been a profitable pastime in the museums of Beirut and Cairo since at least the end of the nineteenth century. Small duplicated objects could be bought ten years ago in either capital almost at the back door, and the trade has not been checked by the perfectly legitimate sales that sometimes take place in order to relieve storage problems.

In the Middle East such breaches of security rank lower than in the West; hence the affair of the holy books of the Armenian Patriarchate in Jerusalem, which were catalogued at length and with considerable scholarship by Sotheby's in 1967. These manuscripts, the best of which had been illuminated by the monk Thoros Roslin between 1262 and 1269 A.D., had been secreted in a safe to which only the most senior members of the Armenian hierarchy had access. Keys for the separate locks were all held by different officials. Very few scholars outside the Church had ever seen the manuscripts and Sotheby's failed to realise what their sale implied – until an English bibliophile queried it with the Armenian authorities in London. At once a protest was made. The Most Reverend Bassak Touman threatened legal action. The manuscripts were withdrawn and returned to Jerusalem. Three years later they were at last put on view to the public, together with other items from the treasury – jewel-encrusted books, gold and silver work and reliquaries. But what inquest went on within the hierarchy is not known.

In the same way, the Norwegian authorities have had to handle with the greatest discretion the unseemly story of a robbery at the Munch Museum in Oslo. The paintings of Edvard Munch, Norway's only great artist, have spiralled upwards in value in recent years and now rarely make less than £20,000 each on the few occasions when they come onto the market. By far the greatest collection of his work is in the Oslo Museum, and its curator was regarded as the greatest authority. No *catalogue raisonné* of Munch's work existed, and collectors seeking authentication usually sent their pictures to an official. Sometime early in the 1960s, a trickle of paintings began to come onto the English market and, in many cases, certificates were later issued from Oslo. Scotland Yard traced thirty, sold above-board at high prices in London between 1961 and 1968. But for a single slip, the official might have escaped, but his illegal dispersion became known when he went on holiday. One painting came back for verification. The deputy director recognised it as from the museum collection, and went at once to the police.

The official was given a jail sentence of five years, but the embarrassment of the Norwegian government had only begun. In the face of popular outrage that the most famous national collection could be so easily ransacked, questions were asked about security and the absence of a proper inventory. Scotland Yard could do no more than give the addresses of those buyers who had bought in good faith, and leave the Norwegian government to sort out the mess by buying back what they could.

Notes

[1] Donald Cressey, *Theft of a Nation*, New York 1969.
[2] Peta Fordham, *Inside the Underworld*, London 1971.
For a discussion of art theft and corruption, see Chapter 9, p. 175.
[3] Milton Esterow, *The Art Stealers*, New York 1966, pp. 229–32.
[4] The only commissioned theft that the author has come across,

occurred for different reasons. The owner of a fine collection of Japanese art, being short of money, arranged with the underworld to have it stolen. He duly received his cheque from the insurance company. Ironically, a few of the pieces were later recovered, and he had to repay their value.

[5] A long-serving employee of the Victoria and Albert Museum in London was arrested in 1961 for piecemeal thefts stretching back over many years; and in 1963 John Rewald of New York's Museum of Modern Art recovered, from the museum in Cézanne's old studio in Aix en Provence, a portfolio of his early sketches, sold ten years before for $80.

Chapter 5 Ransom on the Riviera

As Adam Worth and Arsene Goerdetier found in the past, ransoming a notable painting to its owners is far harder than stealing it. A more modern exponent, a nineteen-year-old Belgian student inspired by the exploits of Max le Jaguar, hero thief of a Radio Luxembourg programme, encountered the same problem after lifting the famous Rubens, *Studies of a Negro Head*, from the Royal Museum in Brussels in 1964. Probably the best-known stolen object since the *Mona Lisa*, the painting appears on every 500-franc Belgian bank-note, but André Benguies' real folly was to telephone the museum director with his demands from the main post office in Brussels, leaving time for the call to be traced.

Nevertheless, to a well-knit conspiracy, with ample funds, ransom offers unusually high rewards, attracting over-bold receivers and big criminal organisations in a lean year. The object is to steal something of outstanding value – something that is unsaleable through ordinary channels, that most private collectors would not dare to touch, and that any competent dealer or saleroom would identify at once – then return it, for the reward, to the owner or the insurance company. The standard fee of ten per cent for recovery, say, of a Cézanne might now be as much as £20,000, a sum paid quite legally, and legally retained by the informant – unless he could be proved a contact of the thieves. All the cases described here would have presented little difficulty to any competent burglar: nothing like the elaborate methodology of *Rififi* or *Topkapi* was required. Indeed it is essential that the stealing be easy: those looking for ransom either employ minor criminals and pay them off quickly, or put in their own men who, for the security of all, must not be caught. Once the loot is hidden, the risks are even less. Nearly all the deals with insurance companies in the early 1960s included a form of immunity, whether or not this contravened the spirit of the law.

Ransom has three substantial advantages over ordinary theft. First there is a willing buyer, because most insurance companies prefer paying ten per cent of a recovered picture's value to the full amount for total loss. Secondly, publication of the price of similar objects – usually pictures – at auctions gives the thieves a fair idea of what to expect; and this tends to be confirmed when the reward figure is advertised. Thirdly, the thieves have a ready form of blackmail at their disposal: pressure on the insurance companies or the owner by suggesting that the canvases themselves will be destroyed, and pressure on governments to recover works of national importance and prestige. The emphasis deliberately placed by the legitimate market and the critic on the significance to art history of certain paintings thus makes them vulnerable in an entirely novel way.

On the other hand, it does not take long for insurance companies to wake up to the danger of cumulative blackmail. In any case, some notable collections are under-insured or not insured at all, except against fire. Even the most sophisticated thieves have to bell the cat – to find someone who will run the risk of negotiating and claiming the reward. Finally, the gang may have to hold on to the loot for months, or buy the best legal advice they can. All these handicaps were present when the ransom racket broke out in the already highly developed underworld of the French Riviera in the early 1960s.

After the war, jewel thefts and smuggling emerged as the staples of organised crime in the string of rich resorts from Monte Carlo to Le Lavandou. The gross proceeds have since been surpassed by those from the processing of opium into heroin for the American market at secret laboratories in and around Marseilles, but in the 1950s all the headlines were taken up by the regular raids on the rich who came to gamble at the casinos or lie on the discreet private beaches of Cap Ferrat or Juan-les-Pins. Marseilles is the administrative headquarters of police for the whole region, and its chief, Commissaire la Vallette, grew used to hearing the misfortunes of

98

losers who had salted away wealth in diamonds while they still ruled states that have now disappeared from the map.

The Riviera underworld is dominated by Corsicans. Napoleon's birthplace may be one of the most beautiful islands in the world, but its people have traditionally been driven by poverty to leave the soil and go to France, where, also by tradition, they have shown peculiar aptitude for two vocations – crime and police work. Family connections and the survival of vendettas from Corsica itself help to explain the intimate knowledge each side has of the other. Whether the Union Corse is the counterpart of the Mafia is not easy to assess. Officials of the Marseilles C.I.D. are in the habit of claiming that they have never heard of any "Corsican Union", other than the perfectly legitimate political associations of Corsicans living in France. Yet recently M. Michel Poniatowski, who has since become Minister of the Interior, accused the "Corsican Mafia" – a worldwide organisation of fifteen "families" on the *cosa nostra* pattern – of controlling the greater part of the drug traffic in France today.

The Corsican lobby in the National Assembly, the deputies Peretti, Sanguinetti and Giacomi, protested vigorously; but the recent disclosures of Corsican involvement in the Latin-American drug connection, the shooting of Lucien Sarti in Mexico, and especially the arrest in 1971 of August-Joseph Ricord, allegedly head of the heroin traffickers in Paraguay, support Poniatowski's allegations. Ricord's history included a flirtation with art theft in the last years of the war, as the Vichy régime collapsed. It is not coincidence that the majority of thieves actually arrested for the Riviera robberies were of Corsican origin, nor (according to French police) that the gang that achieved the ransoms was led by a member of the pre-war Spirito–Carbone–Sabiani Paris crime syndicate. The same sources are now prepared to admit that widespread infiltration of the police and customs service had occurred in the late 1950s, particularly in Marseilles.

By then, the great milch-cow of cosmopolitan jewellery was running dry. Hauls like the $800,000-worth stolen from the Begum Aga Khan in August 1949 had receded into the province of myth. Insurance companies tended to insist on stricter security and owners were likely to find themselves restricted to wearing their more splendid pieces only four or five times a year. The rest was paste;

and the Marseilles police recovered from their embarrassment at finding the Begum's jewels on the steps of police headquarters, after a telephone call in January 1950. By way of silver and *bric à brac*, the Corsican families graduated to stealing pictures. The first major loser was Armand Drouant, art dealer, painter, and collector, whose villa at Villefranche was looted of thirty paintings, worth $130,000, in January 1960. Two months later, seven paintings, including a Modigliani and a Utrillo, valued all together at $60,000, disappeared from the Municipal Museum at Menton. On 23rd March, canvases worth more than $600,000 were snatched from the "Colombe d'Or", a famous restaurant at St Paul de Vence, a village in the hills behind Cannes.

In the 1920s, the "Colombe d'Or", originally a sixteenth-century inn, was re-opened by Paul Roux as a restaurant, and, besides the tourists who drove up from the fashionable resorts on the coast, a cosmopolitan clientèle of artists and writers came to stay there and eat on the terrace overlooking steeply terraced hills. Roux was a friend of many of the best *avant-garde* painters of his day. Some of the lesser-known and poorer artists left him pictures instead of paying, but the heart of the collection, the twenty superb examples that hung in the dining room, were bought, cheaply enough, from Braque, Soutine, Utrillo, Leger, Picasso and Modigliani.

Roux died in 1955 and left the collection to his son, François, who still owns the restaurant. The pictures were never insured: the premium would have been enormous and the family regarded them, like the inn itself, as a feature of their lives rather than as an investment to be safeguarded with burglar alarms. Ironically, after the Menton theft, Roux thought about carrying the dining-room pictures upstairs each night, but they were too bulky. Instead the heavy chestnut-wood shutters were barred and the doors securely locked. The thieves came twice to spy round. Roux actually took a rather indistinct photograph of two scruffy characters walking away from the private terrace. Another member of the gang stayed the night, and sat in the dining-room, incongruous among the smarter guests, until the shutters had been closed. He signed the register with a false name, but gave his real profession, that of stonemason.

Perhaps it was he who patiently sawed through the half-inch thick shutter, opened the catch and let the others in. They came in a small lorry, parked outside the main door, and took all twenty pictures from the one room – three Braques, three Legers, a Picasso, Modigliani, two Buffets, a Miró, Dufy, Matisse, Bonnard, Utrillo, Valadon, Laurencin, Rouault, Derain and Bezanne. One might have said they had good taste, but they left equally splendid paintings in the passage outside. As one said at his trial, "What do I know about paintings? I am a barman. We nearly left the Picasso on the doorstep, because it was hard to get into the van." All five were arrested in a matter of days, after boasting of the job while drunk in a Nice bar. Roux managed to identify three: petty thieves from the coast. The pictures had vanished and for nearly two years the police waited, pressing very serious charges, but offering to mitigate them if the paintings were found.

The inquiries of Inspector Antoine Sarrochi, who took charge of the case, led deviously to the Corsican background, and to a bizarre case of vendetta execution. The police were questioning a retired gang leader, Jean-Thomas Guidicelli, sometimes known as "Grosse-Tête", at his villa "La Dunette", at Cap d'Antibes. Guidicelli had become a local philanthropist since his retirement, and mayor of his home town, Pietralba in Corsica. He had nothing to do with the theft, but the black police Citroën parked outside was seen, and when he next walked out into his garden he was shot dead. Even murder led the police nowhere, although the discovery of a private harbour under Guidicelli's house, from where he used to run a launch loaded with smuggled cigarettes, created a local sensation.

Meanwhile, as soon as it became clear that the collection was uninsured, the principals behind the gang sent ransom notes direct to Roux, asking for $30,000. Then, and later, the Roux family kept their silence, but there are well-authenticated reports that a ransom of in the region of $10,000 was paid. In any case, on 14th February 1961 an anonymous caller, dressed as a priest, told Marseilles police to expect a letter containing a baggage ticket. This duly arrived with a note: "use this and you will get a surprise". At the main railway station in Marseilles, police found all but one of the pictures – that one being by a minor artist, Bezanne.

By the time that the trial was held, in December 1961, the great robberies at St Tropez and Aix en Provence had taken place; and the prosecution demanded maximum sentences as a deterrent: eight years' solitary confinement for Louis de Coene, alleged to be the leader, and for a Corsican, Michel Paoli; and five years for the others, including the supposed receiver, Roger Cardinale. In the Alpes Maritimes Court at Nice, the three men identified by Roux pleaded guilty. Coene, a wealthy resident of Nice, was defended by an outstanding Paris advocate, Maître René Floriot. The Italian lawyer who defended the others cited the case of the thief who had stolen the *Mona Lisa* in 1911 and been sentenced only to eighteen months, the inference being that a man who could get away with despoiling the rich was no more than a misguided folk hero. In the end, de Coene and Paoli were acquitted and the rest given short sentences of up to three years. The public in the courtroom applauded the lenient verdict.

Neither side mentioned the question of ransom. The police spoke vaguely of "an international gang of art thieves". The reason for keeping quiet was easy enough to find: more than a million pounds' worth of the finest French modern paintings was at that moment in limbo, hidden quite possibly by the same people as had organised the "Colombe d'Or" crime and thus in imminent danger of destruction.

In the summer of 1960, after a series of underworld tip-offs, Interpol had warned police all over Europe that the number of art thefts was likely to increase. "We took great care to see that art galleries were aware of the danger," the Paris police affirmed afterwards. "The people responsible did not take our warnings seriously."

Museums and police might well have been alerted by practical experience: shortly before the Nice trial, $20,000-worth of paintings had disappeared from the private Art de France gallery in Cannes, and a major robbery, very similar to the "Colombe d'Or" one, and also taking place in St Paul de Vence (at the home of Aimé Maeght, a Paris art dealer), had been prevented only because local police, on the tracks of chicken thieves, happened to disturb the thieves as they loaded pictures into a car. Minor criminals, these were arrested in a barber's shop the next day, but they refused to talk or to incriminate the men behind them. Yet no protective measures were taken.

The small town of St Tropez, then hardly touched by the suffocating hand of fame, was still recognisably the fishing port discovered by the painter Paul Signac, whose boat was driven into the harbour during a storm in 1892. In the next thirty years, the artists had St

Tropez and its special quality of light and colour to themselves. Fashionable Parisians would say to Matisse, Bonnard, Marcquet and others of the "Mediterranean school", "Are you going to spend the summer in the Sahara?" The last of them, Dunoyer de Segonzac, now in his eighties, lives in close seclusion outside the town yet still paints every day. In 1955, Georges Grammont, a millionaire industrialist and an inspired collector of the Mediterranean school, left his collection of a hundred paintings and sculptures to St Tropez. The municipal authorities scarcely knew what to do and had little money to spend, but under the direction of a sympathetic architect, Louis Sue, they renovated the Annonciade, an exquisite sixteenth-century chapel on the waterfront, and made it one of the most perfect small galleries in Europe; it contains, by any standard, the most notable collection of modern art in France, outside the collections of the great museums of Paris and Grenoble. Apart from Sue, however, enthusiasm was lacking. Few people attended the opening, when Segonzac was appointed curator, and the municipality was surprised when the Annonciade became their principal tourist attraction. They debated whether to provide a guard and a burglar alarm and failed to find the funds. Instead, seven keys to the main lock – an attractive piece of eighteenth-century ironwork – were distributed.

During the night of 15th July 1961, thieves broke in and loaded into a 2CV Citroën fifty-seven of the finest paintings, worth not less than £500,000 at 1961 prices – at that time by far the largest theft to have taken place in Europe. The burglary was easy; the lorry was stolen and later jettisoned; and no investigation took place until the next morning, when the cleaner saw bare patches on the walls. A ransom demand for 50 million old francs (£40,000) was made at once, in a handwritten note addressed to Segonzac at the Hôtel de Ville.

The gang was believed at the time to have tried to sell the collection privately and to have attempted to interest East European governments. In Western Europe, publicity made it impossible to dispose of it. But their immediate demand for ransom makes the idea of a resale operation inherently unlikely. The pictures, however, were insured only against fire, not theft; and, although the Annonciade itself was owned by the state, the contents belonged to the municipality, which had no hope – or intention – of paying. Instead, Segonzac announced that he would open a public subscription aimed at a total of 10 million old francs.

Destruction was threatened. The thieves took one painting and cut it to pieces, returning the sections to Segonzac, bit by bit. When a third of the painting had been reconstructed, he recognised it as one of his own early water-colours. The public lacked interest; the subscription list flagged when it had barely reached half of Segonzac's figure – let alone 50 million francs. Stalemate followed. The police were not unduly hurried. It was not, they admitted, an affair of murder or even of the Algerian O.A.S. While the gang also procrastinated, Inspector Sarrochi set himself firmly against loose talk of paying a ransom, and most of the press comments at the time ranged speculatively over mythical private collectors who would enjoy their loot in secret. The police knew, with fair certainty, who the members of the gang were, and waited; the gang themselves, dismayed at holding a white elephant, began to look out for something that *was* insured.

Meanwhile, with what seems in retrospect a touching faith in the security of public exhibitions, the town of Aix en Provence prepared to put on view an international collection of Cézannes – twenty-two oils, twenty water-colours and nineteen drawings. Questioned about precautions on a local radio programme, soon after the St Tropez robbery, the deputy mayor of Aix replied – "we have armed guards".

Cézanne's birthplace had not been kind to him in his lifetime and its local museum refused to hang any of his canvases until after his death in 1906. Since then, Aix has done something to restore the balance, and Cézanne's old studio outside the town, looking across at the stark triangle of the Mont Ste Victoire, *Leitmotiv* of many of his landscapes, has been restored with great sensitivity – so that it still seems as though the old man with his floppy hat and baggy trousers might come in at the door and take up where he left off at the easel. The 1961 exhibition, an outstanding celebration of Cézanne's œuvre, originally organised by Professor Novotny, author of a scholarly biography of Cézanne and director of an art gallery in Vienna, was brought to Aix at the instigation of M. Leo Marchets, artistic adviser to the city.

The exhibition filled the top two floors of the Pavillon Vendôme, a seventeenth-century villa standing in a large garden, surrounded by trees. Many of the paintings had come from private collections in America, as well as galleries and museums on both sides of the Atlantic. The "armed guards" did exist and were made available by the local police. But one was on leave on the night of Sunday 13th August and the other sat downstairs near a telephone. He did not patrol the top floor because he did not wish to disturb the only other occupant, the woman curator. Outside, the gardens were brightly lit and four floodlights illuminated the façade. The thieves climbed easily into the garden, found a window open, and, by the light from outside, took six paintings from the second floor and two smaller ones from the third – one of these being the famous *Card Players* from the Louvre.

Nothing was discovered until daylight. Aix was then in the middle of the long summer weekend, coinciding with the festival of the Assumption. In spite of this, the owners and the insurance company, the Union Stadt Versicherung A.G. of Vienna, were told at once and police headquarters in Marseilles put Inspector Sarrochi on to the case. Just about the same time as the press arrived, two owners, a Dutch woman and an American couple, drove in to Aix to lament their losses, and another, more interested in his investment, telegraphed demanding immediate payment of the insurance.

The thieves could hardly have involved a more cosmopolitan series of interests. The Louvre *Card Players* was fully insured by the French government. Nearly all the others were under-insured by their owners – the art galleries of St Louis (*Portrait of Marie Cézanne*), New York (*A Peasant Seated*), Cardiff, and Zürich (still-lifes), and the three from private hands. The burden, estimated at £700,000, thus fell on the insurance company, which had taken the overall risk of the exhibition on a "nail to nail" basis – covering transit as well as the time the pictures spent in the Pavillon Vendôme. Looking back, with the benefit of later evidence, it is clear that the thieves knew that the exhibition was insured, and that their primary aim was to negotiate a ransom. They were not disappointed. In spite of a reconstruction of the crime, staged in the Pavillon on the day after the robbery, the police found out very little except that the thieves had had a remarkably easy passage. Analysis of the methods of scaling the building may have helped Sarrochi identify the gang

105

as Corsicans from Marseilles – but subsequent developments in any case connected the Aix theft with that at St Tropez. After a week of false trails and the usual crop of eccentrics ringing with news that the haul had been passed to a millionaire's safe deposit in a Zürich bank, Marseilles police prepared to arrest the gang on suspicion, hoping that the threat of trial on a swingeing indictment might persuade them to restore the pictures.

At this moment, the French government intervened. Total destruction of works of art had always been the reserve card in the thieves' hands. Remembering the carved-up Segonzac from St Tropez, and fearful both for the national heritage represented by the Louvre Cézanne and the reputation of France in the international art world, André Malraux, Minister of Cultural Affairs under de Gaulle, instructed the police to put first priority on the safe recovery of the pictures. An official from the Ministry and representatives from the Louvre went to Aix, closely followed by Henri Seyrigh, Director-General of the Department of Museums.

Meanwhile, the gang presented a ransom demand for $150,000, which the Viennese insurance company at once turned down. A complicated exercise in bargaining began, in which a Paris attorney represented the Union Stadt Versicherung, and an unnamed accomplice the gang. From Paris, the Sûreté asked the company not to pay anything and tried to put an embargo on the negotiations. A stiff fight took place between the Ministry and the Sûreté. During that time the ransom demand was dropped to $100,000, and the police successfully blocked an attempt to sell some of the pictures individually to receivers in Marseilles and Paris.

The thieves were caught in a difficult position, from which they were shortly freed by the offer of a ten per cent reward, made, despite police protests, by an insurance agency in Marseilles. The Viennese company had already paid out $1,300,000 to the owners. In April 1962, eight months after the Aix robbery, an anonymous caller left a message at Marseilles police headquarters, telling the police to watch a blue-green Peugeot 404 parked in a street in the city. For twenty-four hours detectives hid nearby, but no one appeared. When they searched the car they found all eight Cézannes wrapped in newspaper on the back seat.

Irritated beyond measure at the restrictions imposed from Paris, the Marseilles force was still unable to make an arrest, because the fifty-seven St Tropez paintings were still at risk. On the other hand, the gang refused to lie low. In the months of waiting they had made an attempt to rob the Narbonne Museum, where they failed to seize a distinguished collection, including works by Pieter Breughel, Boucher and David, only because they could not pick an elaborate eighteenth-century lock on the main door of what had formerly been the archbishop's palace.

Fresh negotiations began for the return of the remaining St Tropez pictures, while the police again stood by, watching the Ministry give its blessing to what was happening. In this case, however, the reward was small – Segonzac had managed to raise only $10,000 – and the thieves' morale was high after their earlier success. Segonzac himself almost gave up hope, and in the Annonciade small plaques were fitted to the blank spaces on the wall, giving the title and artist once represented. The authorities, however, still had one card in their hand: they could promise immunity from prosecution if the pictures were restored. Whether this actually happened is not susceptible of proof. In November 1962, Malraux's private office was sent a message to inspect a derelict barn at Villiers-Saint-George, a village in the country outside Paris. The letter read: "We ask forgiveness for having taken these works. By returning them now we hope that our cases will be dismissed."

All the pictures except the mutilated Segonzac were discovered, cut from their frames and rolled up under the hay. The Louvre restored them for the Annonciade free of charge. Some had been damaged by having been rolled with the painting inside instead of outside, and all needed to be relined and framed. Segonzac had the great pleasure of seeing them rehung in the Annonciade, now equipped with a modern alarm system, before he retired from his post as curator. Indeed, almost everyone except the insurance company gained from the transaction: the St Louis restorer found a second Cézanne painted on the reverse of the canvas bearing the *Portrait of Marie Cézanne*, and his museum neatly doubled its original investment. Even ministerial intervention seemed for a while to have paid off.

The Riviera art thefts of 1961 passed rapidly into criminal mythology. Cases of ransom, though not uncommon in France, have not recaptured the initial bravado, or success. But the failures – for example, that of a retired army officer who removed a collection of drawings by Fragonard, Boucher and Tiepolo from the Besançon Museum in 1966 – suggest that only second-rate criminals have tried.

Greater doubt hangs over the robbery of eighteen Impressionist pictures from the Chardean collection in November 1970. Monets, Manets and Renoirs contributed to a valuation figure of 10 million new francs (£760,000), but they were not insured. Unlike the St Tropez affair, all were recovered quickly from a disused Métro station in Paris. Whether the thieves found it worthless to hold them, or whether a reward was paid, is not certain. Apart from this one crime, the tacit compact made thirteen years ago is still effective. Ransomers in France steal children in preference to works of art.

Chapter 6 Contagious Theft

The long-term effects of the bargains struck by the French Ministry of Cultural Affairs bedevilled the tranquillity of the art market for years. Until then, private collectors as well as museums, though perhaps reluctant to part with their paintings for a loan exhibition, had tended to regard the display of their property as something of a social duty, even as a service to culture. The risks opened up by ransom demands, above all the threat of total destruction, alienated them, and they became mistrustful of requests for loans and increasingly preoccupied with concealing the very fact of ownership. Fewer and fewer collectors have been willing to let their possessions be photographed or exhibited: too often, those stolen have been precisely those better known to the public. Equally, insurance companies became wary of covering exhibitions, particularly in provincial towns with a low security rating. Premium rates were stepped up all round. Since only national collections can afford the most sophisticated burglar alarms, the provinces suffered both in terms of display and costs.

The most devastating result, however, was that these cases showed publicly the undoubted willingness of some insurance companies or governments to submit to blackmail. A figure of 65 million old francs can now be put on the ransom paid out for the Aix Cézannes. The Riviera thefts were headline news, while uninhibited speculation about ransoms developed in Britain and America. Knowing the Corsican underworld, the French police were able to stop up the loophole privately, but elsewhere the authorities were not prepared. Seven major cases of theft for ransom took place in 1961–62, in Sicily, England, Germany and the United States. None were connected directly with the Riviera criminals, although the Corsican element should not be ignored. But the speed of infection is a measure of modern communications, not of a continent-wide conspiracy. Like prospectors flocking to the Klondike, a series of inventive criminals seized on a single theme as if they had been waiting for the chance.

Pittsburgh, capital of the American steel industry, has an unfortunate record as regards patronage of the arts. The parsimony of the city authorities lost them the Mellon collection, later offered to Washington D.C., and the Frick collection, which now belongs to New York. After the last war, David G. Thomson, a vastly wealthy retired steel baron, offered the city 330 paintings from his collection of modern art, if they would build a suitable gallery to house it in. They refused, and he sold the lot to a Basle dealer. Thomson was not only one of the most noted collectors in America, but a man with a highly developed judgement. In the 1920s, he had built up a fine collection of works by Paul Klee, which he sold in 1961 to the West German state of North Rhine–Westphalia, rather than to his native city. A benefactor of the New York Museum of Modern Art and the Carnegie Institute, he was probably better known in Europe than his own country.

His house in the South Hills residential suburb was fitted with a supposedly fool-proof burglar-alarm system, but on the night of the robbery, in July 1961, the Thomsons were out at dinner, and had forgotten to switch it on. Ten paintings – including six Picassos – vanished. One, *The Bathers*, measured five feet by four. All were cut crudely out of the frames and badly damaged; a Matisse had a hole punched in it, a Picasso oil was ripped nearly in half, and a Picasso collage was completely ruined. Thomson immediately offered, directly to the burglars, a reward of $100,000 for the paintings' safe return, excluding at this stage recovery by the police or a casual find. The reasons for the offer were understandable: Thomson was not the only one to fear that petty thieves with no idea of the value of what they had taken might simply burn them if they failed to get a few dollars from a junk dealer. His action won support from, amongst others, Gordon Washburn, director of the fine arts division of the Carnegie Institute, who scouted the idea of such an unskilled job being done for ransom.

Other authorities in the art world saw the danger of a high reward offered in such a way for pictures that were far too well known ever to reach the legitimate market. Their forebodings were justified six days after the robbery, when a letter came from a man calling himself "Sally", claiming to represent the thieves; after Judge Henry X. O'Brien, of Alleghenny County, had offered to act on behalf of the owners, Thomson made a public statement to the press, leaving no doubt that he would fulfil his bargain and ask no questions.

The Federal Bureau of Investigation regarded these proceedings with intense hostility. From the beginning they had suspected professionals ignorant only of how to treat pictures. At first, however, they could find no reason to intervene and the case was investigated by Alleghenny County detectives. But the implications were so serious that the F.B.I. assumed control on the pretext that, by crossing the state line in order to commit the crime, the thieves had committed a Federal offence. Joseph M. Chapman, director of the recently formed bureau investigating art theft and forgery, took charge.

The F.B.I. gradually put together a picture of a highly professional gang working mainly on private houses in suburbs in the Pennsylvania–Ohio area. The man "Sally" – later identified as Ralph Charlton Hobbs, a forty-five year old unemployed salesman – followed up his letter with a telephone call on 1st August. A complicated series of negotiations, counter-moves and sub-plots followed, conducted by telephone, and newspaper advertisements signed "Sally". Hobbs instructed Thomson to come to New York and book into the Manhattan Hotel. Thomson was told that he would receive the pictures and should be ready to hand over the $100,000 in small notes. "I'll call you at the hotel," Hobbs said. "I'll want to make sure I'm talking to Thomson, so we'll use this code. I'll ask you 'Is Ben Bolt there?' and you say 'Ben Bolt's not here. This is his manager, Spider.'" (Ben Bolt was a boxer in a well-known comic strip at the time.) Instead, Chapman was disguised with grey hair and a false moustache to look like Thomson, and he and another F.B.I. agent waited in the hotel room, keeping in radio contact with twenty-five more policemen dotted around the city. Hobbs duly called, went through the patter agreed, but then plied Chapman with questions about the inside of the Thomson house. Still not satisfied, Hobbs told him to go to the second floor of the New York public library on Fifth Avenue. "There's a Los Angeles telephone book – you'll find instructions there."

At the library, Chapman found nothing, but a note that he left was taken by Hobbs shortly after. Now under the surveillance of at least four policemen, passing as porters or librarians, Hobbs took his car and drove south on the New Jersey turnpike. A convoy of police cars surrounded him, two in front heading for Pittsburgh on the assumption that that was where he was bound, and two behind. The standard of tracking must have been high: Hobbs did not know he was being followed, either then or during the next month while he lived quietly in Pittsburgh, placing the "Sally" advertisements in a local newspaper.

Thomson refused to pay any money before he was certain that the pictures would be returned. On 7th September, Hobbs rang again and asked him to pick up a parcel in the Greyhound bus terminal, "to prove that you're doing business with the man who can return them". The key was in a telephone booth in downtown Pittsburgh. F.B.I. agents duly collected Picasso's *The Bathers*. Weeks went by, and North American Insurance paid out £189,000 on the entire claim. The pictures had been grossly under-insured, but by agreement with Thomson they would, if found, be redeemed for that amount. The company agreed to pay for restoration – a clause that gave rise to great recriminations later.

The gang then began to put pressure on Hobbs. In November, when they had been sitting tight and unrewarded for nearly four months, he went openly to the Thomson house and demanded to be paid for the restored Picasso. Thomson refused. Two days later, Hobbs responded: there would be a further delay. Meanwhile, the F.B.I.'s inquiries came to a head and, on 13th December, fearing that a stalemate might induce the gang to destroy the pictures, they arrested Hobbs in Bridgewater, Pennsylvania. His story was that he was only asking on behalf of two men who had stolen the pictures and had since died.

Hobbs was charged with transporting *The Bathers* across the state line into Ohio and back. The next day, police swooped on a motel outside Pittsburgh, too late to arrest the thieves, who had left some hours earlier, but in time to find all the paintings rolled up in a mattress cover under the bed.

No money had actually been paid to the thieves and the insurance company took possession and stored the pictures in the vaults of the Mellon National Bank. Thomson, however, claimed not only for the cost of restoration, but a hefty sum in depreciation, on the grounds that a picture, once seriously damaged, could never recover its true value. In refusing, North American contended that, even when restored, the pictures would be worth much more than the insured value of $189,000. A committee of art experts gave its judgement in favour of the owner, but litigation dragged on for two years before the Thomson collection was again complete.

The F.B.I.'s concern about the payment of a reward on a "no questions asked" basis had been justified even before Hobbs was arrested. On 10th September 1961, a man carrying a pistol hidden inside a bunch of gladioli pushed past the maid who opened the door of the Bel-Air mansion of building millionaire David E. Bright in Beverly Hills, Los Angeles. He tied up the girl, locked her in a lavatory and expertly cut out from their frames five of the pictures hanging downstairs – two Picassos, a Modigliani, an abstract, and a pastel on board by Degas, which he left behind in the kitchen since it could not be rolled up. All five had been exhibited locally; the remainder, though impressive and valuable, were not touched. Not surprisingly, when the Bright family returned, they refused access to reporters and photographers. Bright did concede, however, that the collection had been valued at over $2 million.

An unsigned ransom note arrived shortly afterwards, bearing a threat of destruction. Within a week, Los Angeles police tracked down a Palm Springs estate agent, Edward Henry Ashdown, aged thirty-nine, whose finger prints matched those found in the hall of the Bright house. At first he claimed to have been a guest of the family, but later broke down and admitted both the theft and writing the ransom note. In mitigation, he explained that he had done it to draw attention to himself, and he showed the police a nearby garage where he had hidden the stolen property. He was charged with robbery and grand larceny and released on $5,250 bail.

What happened then can be explained only on the presumption that Ashdown was working with Mafia connections, if not actually to their orders. According to the Los Angeles police, he broke bail and flew to Sicily, arriving there on 23rd September. Three days later, the country mansion of Baron Gabrielli Ortolandi di Bordonaro, a wealthy Sicilian bachelor and art collector, was ransacked. The Baron was away, shooting on another estate, and the only person living in the house was a deaf elderly concierge, living in the court-yard. An unknown number of thieves scaled the outer wall, forced a side door with a crowbar and made their way accurately through the house to the principal salon, where they picked twenty-three paintings and carefully cut them from their frames. They left no finger prints and took only the best: among them *The Sacred Family* by Mabuse, a Titian, a van Dyck and a Rembrandt, as well as some silver and a few especially fine pieces of Capo di Monte and Chinese porcelain. "Whoever they were," Ortolandi told the press, "they were led by art experts." Not even the Mabuse had been insured; the value of what was lost was estimated at $320,000.

No art theft on this scale had occurred in Italy since 1944. The Italian police threw a net over all the exits, ports and air terminals and the Alpine frontier, then contacted Interpol, the French Sûreté, Scotland Yard and the F.B.I. The F.B.I. checked with Los Angeles and Ashdown was found to be missing. Armed with a photograph, the Sicilian police arrested him in Palermo. Once more, he admitted the theft, gave the same excuse as before and enough information for most of the loot to be recovered. The Californian legal authorities pressed for his extradition, on the ground that the Bright case had been committed first, and in due course Ashdown stood trial at Santa Monica, where he was given a sentence of from two to ten years' imprisonment.

The Sicilian robbery had been planned well in advance, but Ashdown's principal backers never even came under suspicion, so unused were the authorities in Italy and the U.S.A. to the intrusion of syndicated crime into the field of fine arts. In Germany, they proved equally shortsighted. The well-established trade in looted religious carvings from southern Germany reached a peak in the early 1960s. Then, in August 1962, V's team exceeded their normal brief and dismantled a nine-foot sculpture by the famous sixteenth-century artist Tillman Riemenschneider; it had been hanging in a chapel in Lower Franconia since 1524. One of the most celebrated early Renaissance sculptures in Germany, the Riemenschneider *Virgin and Child* signified a great deal more to the Catholic South

114

than the little carvings from the *feldkapellen*. (Indeed it was only after the masterpiece had vanished that the extent of the earlier depredation was realised.) The Bavarian state police sounded an international alarm, but failed to find anything except some fragments of the stone floral wreath that had surrounded the statue. Weeks passed, and eventually Henri Nannen, editor of the magazine *Stern*, took matters into his own hands and announced that *Stern* would ransom the Riemenschneider, no questions asked, for 100,000 marks ($25,000).

Two months after the theft, Nannen had a midnight telephone call from a man calling himself "Leininger". If half the ransom were placed under the wheel of a steam roller in a Hamburg street, the thieves would leave half the sculpture in a parked removal van nearby. Strict instructions were given not to inform the police. Nannen's deputy editor, Reinhardt Holl, went alone to the rendezvous, left the money, walked over to the van, and found the pieces and a smaller sculpture by a pupil of Riemenschneider neatly laid out in the back. A few days later, a second call indicated that Nannen should leave the rest of the ransom in an open field near Nuremberg. He complied, and recovered the remaining bits. When the news was published – by the thieves' instructions, a fortnight later (and *Stern* made the most of its public service) – church bells all over southern Germany pealed out in celebration.

Within a year of the first experience, in France, ransom thefts in a dozen disguises had appeared all over Europe and America. In 1962, the Lefevre gallery in London was robbed of a magnificent exhibition of Impressionist paintings which, with one exception, were found intact in a luggage locker in Leicester Square Underground Station. Imitation is contagious: one need look no further than the press and radio publicity given to the Riviera thefts. Rumours of reward and ransom were bandied about, in spite of the efforts of the national police forces, who, both then and later, showed themselves a good deal more far-sighted than either insurance companies or government departments.

In Britain that year, the most spectacular instance of theft for ransom occurred on 10th July. The O'Hana Gallery in Carlos Place, Mayfair, was holding a summer exhibition of nineteenth- and early twentieth-century paintings. Jacques O'Hana had put together a striking loan collection particularly well representative of Renoir, and added a number of pictures that he had bought himself at the sales of the Somerset Maugham and Alexander Korda collections at Sotheby's. The exhibition was highly praised by the critics for its discerning selection, and in the first six weeks more than 250 people a day bought the illustrated catalogue. Someone amongst them mapped out the surroundings with the utmost care.

Between 1 and 4 a.m., thieves drove a van down the narrow side-alley that runs off Carlos Place between the Westminster Bank and the Connaught Hotel. The driver stayed inside, blocking the alley, while the others used a jemmy to break open a door leading into a back yard. Here, on the side of the building, was a fire escape, which led also to the first floor of the bank, and the gang were able to lower themselves down into the enclosed yard at the back of the O'Hana Gallery. They forced the back door, which had no burglar alarm, and went quietly to work, cutting twenty-three of the chosen pictures out of the frames and taking a dozen smaller ones with the frames still in place.

The theft was not discovered until daylight. While detectives searched the exhibition rooms for finger prints, O'Hana discounted rumours that the pictures were on their way to a millionaire eccentric and, quite correctly, explained that it had been a highly professional job, done by men who were as selective as he had been himself in arranging the exhibition. Twelve Renoirs had gone, including the portrait of the model, *Andrée assise*, one of his most famous nudes, painted in 1904. With them, others by Braque, Picasso, Cézanne, Monet, Utrillo, Bonnard, and Kandinsky; and O'Hana's own Vuillard, from the Korda sale. The gallery was covered for £250,000 insurance at Lloyds, but the market value of the missing works was later given as £350,000. At once the assessors, Grayston Kelly & Co., offered a reward of £20,000 for information leading to recovery.

Nothing more happened for two weeks. In public, the police expressed surprise that such obviously unsaleable pictures should be stolen. Off the record, they agreed with journalists that the thieves might try to collect the reward. At midnight on 26th July, an informer telephoned Scotland Yard to say that he "had heard" that the loot was to be moved that night; the police were told to raid the loft above a wholesale warehouse, once a Salvation Army hostel for dockers, down by the Thames. Three hours later a flying squad burst in to find two men apparently guarding the room. On a bed, wrapped up in three bundles and covered with a cheap blanket, was the whole collection.

The two men refused to talk and proved scarcely more voluble at their trial. The police gave evidence that they were only middle-men. At the time one had said, "I'm obviously in trouble. Do you think I've got the money to buy this stuff?" Meanwhile, the original informant claimed the reward. No one else was caught, no names were brought out into the open. The pictures went back on exhibition, with a radar security system; and perhaps someone, somewhere, felt a chill as he read the report of the trial at Marlborough Street magistrates' court, where one of the accused said, "Look, it's my responsibility. Someone told you they were there and I had them. I've got an idea who it was, so leave me to fix it in my own way."

The O'Hana theft was simple, perfect and in its own right a criminal masterpiece. Ten years afterwards, it is still impossible to find out who organised it, or who eventually collected the £20,000 reward. The technique was simple and fool-proof, but hard to repeat; even the dimmest old lag might become suspicious if offered a few fivers to mind a bulky package, or drive it from one place to another. Future bargains might take an unconscionable share of the reward. The operation also contained a high element of chance, for the police might have missed the rendezvous, or the small men might simply have run off. There have been few such cases since, although the thief on probation who stole a Frans Hals from Longford Castle in 1969 seems to have been betrayed in a similar fashion.

For four years after the O'Hana robbery, there was a lull. The mid-1960s saw the illicit market choked with stolen property and a widespread police counter-attack. Except for the most well-organised gangs, with their own regular receiver and a disposal network, the going was tougher than it had been before. Publicity, experience and rising insurance premiums put private collectors on the defensive. Public galleries and museums whose security arrangements had scarcely altered since the nineteenth century rapidly brought themselves up to date; and those who next tried the insurance racket – at Dulwich in December 1966 – came grievously unstuck.

The picture gallery at Dulwich College in south-east London possesses a collection that is unique of its kind. Containing some 600 pictures, it ranks almost with the National Gallery in splendour and richness. In seventeenth- and eighteenth-century art, its coverage is scarcely surpassed by the great European museums. Yet few people know even of its existence. For the thousands who file up the steps of the Tate or the National Gallery, only dozens make the five-mile journey out of central London to the single-storey, grey-brick Italianate building next to Dulwich College. The collection was begun by the founder, Edward Alleyn, in 1626. 150 years later, Stanislas II of Poland gave a London art dealer, Nicolas Desenfans, *carte blanche* to buy enough paintings to found a Polish national gallery. In 1795 the king abdicated, leaving Desenfans with a vast but not indiscriminate pile of canvases for which he had not been paid. He tried to sell, but the Revolution and the Napoleonic war cut off France, his own birthplace and the most promising market, and on his death he gave them to a friend, Sir Francis Bourgeois. When Bourgeois died in 1811, he bequeathed the majority to the College, with a fund to provide for their maintenance in perpetuity. Impressed by such pious munificence, the College employed Sir John Soane to build a joint gallery and mausoleum, to hold both the pictures and Sir Francis himself.

At the time of the 1966 theft, the gallery had already been robbed once, and the governors, headed by Sir Gerald Kelly, a former President of the Royal Academy, had had installed a new burglar-alarm system, covering all the windows and doors – though not the pictures themselves. However, on New Year's Eve 1966, thieves parked a stolen car on some waste ground at the back of the gallery, climbed a high wall, drilled a neat hole of eleven by twenty inches in a panel of the main door, and squeezed through, avoiding the burglar wire on the lock and an electronic eye, set at waist height. Once again, the *modus operandi* was entirely professional. Within a few minutes they had removed three Rembrandts, three Rubens, and two works by Gerhardt Dou and Elsheimer. The bigger canvases were taken out of the frames on the stretchers, not cut; and for perhaps another hour, the thieves meticulously unpinned them from the wood. So much care was unusual; leading the police to think that a true lover of art was involved. Nothing but the best had been touched: the Rembrandts were perfect and entirely authenticated: the *Girl at a Window*; one of the several portraits of Titus, Rembrandt's son; and a portrait of Jacob de Gheyn. Likewise, the Rubens were small, easily hidden, and more desirable than his vast fleshy apotheoses of the gods.

In terms of crude cash value, the Dulwich theft outshone that of Aix en Provence. Obviously it was done for ransom: so, at least, reporters were told by Sir Charles Wheeler, President of the Royal Academy, and other distinguished figures, including Sir Kenneth Clark and Sir John Rothenstein. The police were more reticent, confining themselves to the statement that the burglar-alarm system was wired direct to local police headquarters. What was not said publicly became embarrassingly clear later: the collection was not insured and there could be no assessor to offer a reward. According to the Chairman, Lord Shawcross, the College had been unable to afford the premium: as an educational foundation, it was already making a loss, and was about to make a public appeal for modernisation. There could therefore be no question of a reward from the Trustees, although Lord Shawcross offered a token £1,000.

Realising their invidious position, the thieves adopted the same technique as at St Tropez. Instead of blackmailing Dulwich, they brought pressure on the artistic establishment, and telephoned the Secretary of the Royal Academy at his private house with a demand for £100,000, failing which the eight paintings would be destroyed.

Whether high-level negotiations might have followed the French model and involved the government is speculation. Soon after the theft, Scotland Yard received an underworld tip-off and on 3rd January raided a flat in Southwark, south of the Thames, where they found the two larger Rembrandts and a Rubens stacked under a bed. The rest, being smaller, had been put in a suitcase and taken elsewhere. Several men were held for questioning. The next day, another tip-off led a squad car to Streatham Common, where the remaining five pictures were found, almost unharmed, under a holly bush.

Only one man was arrested and it must be presumed that the rest of the gang turned in the pictures because the storm was fiercer than they had expected. Well aware of the possible political repercussions, Scotland Yard had worked with the utmost urgency.

Fortunately for Dulwich College they were up against a weaker team than the specialists operating in 1969–70, whose career is described in the next chapter. These would not have scrupled to destroy a Rembrandt if their ransom had failed.

The ransom epidemic did not end, even in France, with the original surfeit of criminal success. In Britain, the Dulwich story, highly publicised, proved that ransom was futile when applied to a public collection, insured only against fire and accident. The underworld could assume that the same risks applied to smaller, provincial museums (especially since the one man arrested after Dulwich received a swingeing eight-year sentence) and, after Lefevre and O'Hana, to loan exhibitions. But private collectors, adequately insured, enamoured of their possessions, moved into the front-line of risk.

Elsewhere, given the steadily rising prices of modern paintings (it was no accident that everything stolen, from the Picassos to the Titian in Sicily, had either a high and indisputable price tag or a strong local sentimental value), receivers had an inducement to plan ransom operations. Art theft had always been a relatively secure form of crime, because the law in most countries demands proof of possession and, unlike stolen cars, pictures are easy enough to hide. Under Italian, English, French and most American state law, it was then possible to pay, if not actually to advertise, rewards on a "no questions asked" basis which positively invited thieves to cash in.

From analysis of recent cases where ransom was asked, it seems that the Thomson case had become a precedent in the United States. When T. Edward Hanley, the elderly and ailing owner of one of the more diverse and original modern collections in America, was robbed in August 1968 of well over a million dollars' worth of paintings, his wife at once offered to pay "a reasonable sum of money with no questions asked". Her husband was not to be told, she insisted: the shock might kill him. A week later all were recovered hidden in the country outside Bradford, Pennsylvania. No arrests were made and, not surprisingly, detectives refused to discuss any aspect of the case. Other rewards have proved equally effective. $10,000 brought back a number of Chinese jade carvings to the Norton Art Gallery in Palm Beach, and $5,000 part of the Thomas Fenwick collection to Cleveland, Ohio. The most recent ransom occurred in December 1972. A dozen fine modern paintings vanished from a collection in New York State. The F.B.I. suspected who the thieves were but could not find the pictures and had no other evidence. In due course, local police were approached by an intermediary, who claimed that the theft had originally been done for a private client who had since died. The gang then offered to return the pictures, but asked the police to guarantee them freedom from arrest. The District Attorney of New York State, Carl Ruggieri, consulted the F.B.I. and decided to use his powers to waive prosecution "in the public interest".

Fundamentally wrong though these concessions are, they are probably inevitable in a legal system that sets so high a value on the rights of property ownership. The American authorities have not succumbed often enough to create a problem of the magnitude of ransom theft in Italy during the last four years. One of the most celebrated paintings by Caravaggio, which disappeared from a church in Palermo in 1971, is only the latest in a series of more than thirty works of art in the "unsaleable" category to have completely disappeared. Nevertheless, in the avalanche of thefts in Italy, failed ransoms form a minority. The Bellinis stolen from Venice in 1971 were recovered in the ruined annexe of a disused hospice on an island in the Venetian lagoon, after a midnight boat journey by the *carabinieri*, whose information arrived almost immediately after the Italian Committee for the Preservation of Venice had offered a £3,000 (8 million lire) reward. So it was with the Titian from Medole, after a transparently unnecessary car chase. Always the authorities assert that only local criminals are involved. But what else can they say?

Scepticism is reinforced by the more recent loss of the Giorgione *Madonna Enthroned*, the most valuable and, to the history of art, probably the most outstanding painting stolen since the *Mona Lisa*. It had hung until December 1972 in the wholly unguarded cathedral of Castelfranco Veneto, despite earlier attempts to break in, and despite three warnings from Francisco Valcanover, the regional superintendent of the Ministry of Fine Arts (a fair comment on the state of co-operation between Italian civil service departments). Totally priceless, it was also totally unsaleable. The experts disagreed about the motive; Siviero set in motion his recovery network, believing the Giorgione bound for a crank collector or an international receiver. Colonel Felice Mambor, of the *carabinieri*, suspected that the same gang, with the same motive, was involved as in the thefts a year before. The municipal authorities offered £5,000 reward, and information duly reached Colonel Mambor's squad that the Giorgione was about to be smuggled into Switzerland. There followed another splendid car chase, shots, and the escape of the driver leaving an empty car. A mile away, the *carabinieri* found the painting, securely packed, in a house, and arrested, as the driver of the stolen car, an unemployed youth who was standing nearby. The Italian press were not the only ones to ask questions about such a curious trail of evidence, and to suggest that Mambor's squad (which, it turned out, had also recovered the Titian and the Bellinis) had come too close by half to the informers, if not the thieves themselves.

Chapter 7 No Questions Asked

In the past, ransom has provided an all-too-convenient explanation for a number of unsolved art thefts. Proof has not been offered; hence an account of the career of a particularly well organised team of English criminals may be of value.

Success at ransom in any country requires a congenial state of law and a conducive system of paying rewards for the return of stolen property. In the period after 1968, Britain offered facilities on both counts. While the law relating to theft was tightened by Section 23 of the Criminal Justice Act 1967, in order to prohibit rewards offered on a "no questions asked" basis, the "usual conditions" (standard form in reward advertisements)[1] still did not include provisions to make payment by insurance assessors contingent on the arrest and/or conviction of the thieves. At the same time, the old common-law offence of compounding a felony was abolished. An accomplice in crime could no longer be charged with a serious offence if he gave information that led to the recovery of the stolen property and subsequently claimed the reward himself. It was thus made easier for insurance companies and loss adjusters to pay rewards without probing too closely into the bona-fides of the informant. This fortuitous relaxation of the law was exploited to the full by criminals whose knowledge (or legal advice) was as sound as, and prescience greater than, that of some of the loss adjusters with whom they began to deal.

Insurance companies do not talk about their clients or their practice. Only occasionally the defence is dropped, as in London in January 1971 when the senior partner of one of the main firms of assessors (or loss adjusters) took the stand as a witness for the prosecution in the trial of a man charged with dishonestly handling pictures stolen in five raids during the previous two years. From what he said then, and from other sources, the practice of paying rewards "for information received" appears to be an exercise in fine judgement where professional ethics, duty to the client, and the spirit and practice of the criminal law merge. Nothing is certain; there are no rules; judgement for or against the practice depends on a series of arbitrary assumptions about the rights of individual property in relation to the rights of society as a whole, and about the unique value or status of the stolen works of art. Jewel theft is, in contrast, a simpler matter to deal with, since anything but the Kohinoor can be replaced. It was precisely the element of moral blackmail involved in negotiations over stolen works of art that helped to blur the edge of ethical conduct and elevate the job of informer into a public service.

The principal function of a loss adjuster is to act for the insurance company that has covered the loss. If possible, he will try to recover the stolen property, and it is common practice to offer a reward, in the region of ten per cent, for information leading to recovery. Since all information, apart from that resulting from pure chance – such as an honest man's stumbling on a hidden cache – comes from the underworld, it is inherently tainted. Yet there is no alternative. So long as the adjuster is satisfied that it does not emanate from the thieves themselves, he is entitled to pay part or all of the reward. Hot information is never sold cheaply: insurance rewards are vastly higher than the sums – in Britain rarely, if ever, topping three figures – paid to informers out of police funds. The total paid out in the five cases in 1969–70 was £16,500, and the accuracy of the informant was correspondingly high.

In theory, such information comes from sources close to, but not actually from, the criminals. Such sources include: a conversation overheard in a pub; a betrayal by a woman revenging herself after a quarrel; or information offered by one of those informers who work half in, half out of the underworld, and who, as like as not, end up floating face downwards in the polluted reaches of the Thames, the Seine, or the Hudson River. Loss adjusters have a network of contacts, tenuous and involuted as a spy network. What loss adjusters do *not* know are the bona-fides of the men who offer information. False names, addresses and number-plates, conversations by telephone with X or Y, rendezvous at night and messages left for collection in empty cars are the stock-in-trade and signify no proof, either way. Squalid as the circumstances are, the practice is useful, and without it both insurance and police work would be tied hand and foot. According to the evidence of Cecil Hart, senior partner in Hart and Company, during his inquiries after the Great Train Robbery in 1963, he had dealings with more than a thousand informants. Seventy-five per cent of informants are those also used by the police, and for obvious reasons they prefer to remain anonymous. Sometimes they meet the insurance company with a policeman, who may vouch for them, and in this case there is a form of authentication. But if not, or if they make contact for the first time, there is nothing, beyond the instinct of an assessor with years of experience, to prove that the information does not come from the thieves themselves. What more can he do than trust his informant's word or signature?

Loss adjusters form a small, discreet, responsible profession, with their own code and qualifying examinations, and the business of saving other people's money and, in a nebulous way, furthering the public good. They faced a criminal mentality, able and perceptive enough to take advantage of legal loopholes and swift to learn by example, and had to deal with thefts of works of art the value of which totted up to that of a small oil tanker, all in a matter of fifteen months.

The organisation that took advantage of them is still in existence, although it is unlikely that its operations will start again. In so far as it had a distinct form, the team consisted of a receiver and a number of housebreakers, and it had some similarities (and a very vague connection) with the Great Train Robbers of 1963: in each case a coterie of criminals came together for no particular reason except that they had first met in prison, and stuck together like an extended family because they trusted the rest of the underworld even less than they did each other. The receiver, an antique dealer of nearly twenty years' experience, built up his fortune as one of the entrepreneurs exporting antiques from London. His criminal record goes back almost as far and includes a five-year jail sentence for fraud. Horse and dog doping have been attributed to him, as well as receiving on a wider scale than concerns works of art. Someone who knew a little of the team, described him thus:

X's organisation was all over this country. From the Midlands down to the West Country. He organised the disposal; I think, to begin with, he probably financed a hell of a lot, but of course it got beyond even his pocket in the end. He wasn't only taking goods from these people (his own thieves); in the end it got so well known, people were coming up from the West, Brighton and God knows where, all over the place. They'd say "Got a load for you". . . . He needs a lot of cash. At the same time, he has got to get rid of it. I know for a fact that he's got God knows how much stuff stashed away. There's no one else on that scale. It's either in a garage that he rents elsewhere, or a friend of his owns a garage somewhere. He's got the key to it, he just dumps it there and forgets all about it until someone comes up. And, you know, he sometimes doesn't even look to see what he has got when he buys a load – it's incredible.

As for the others:

You see them all going around in their flash cars. These little middle dealers and thieves, they can't run these cars and go on at the rate they are. Y gambles like a maniac. They all do, all these people gamble like absolute crazy. Now, you talk to a thief, he has either got to gamble, or he has got to go and burgle. Gets a kick out of this, you see. Now X gets his excitement in dealing in stolen goods. Same as he gets his excitement by putting money on a horse. He wants to make money, but he has expensive women and so on. . . .

Y gets perhaps £1,000, £2,000 [from a burglary]. He spends it within a week and then goes and does another job and that sort of thing. Whereas Z – a tall man, well-dressed, great womaniser, goes to all the smart hotels, mixes with the well-to-do. Possibly picks up little lots of information where to do his next job. I think he is a person that keeps a percentage back, but again is a terrific gambler and has to carry on doing it. Partly for the thrill. . . . They take their holidays on the Riviera: one has a flat there in his girl-friend's name.

Seen from the police angle, the picture is slightly different: the receiver more of a frightened pawn in the hands of the principal thief, Z, a dominant bully, powerfully built, undeniably impressive, with an excellent organising mind, perhaps the most skilled housebreaker operating in London. By comparison, the others are small men, carrying a style of life too large to sustain. The Corsican is supposed to run a chain of hotels and to carry a gun; another lives off a high-class call-girl; a third boasts a past as a professional bullion thief. But their reputations feed on collective triumphs; each member is built up by association with the team. Awe grows in the underworld in direct proportion to the value of what they steal, and other criminals enhance their own importance just by knowing such men. The myth requires them to be dangerous – "You know, if the insurance money hadn't been paid, these boys really would have burned the stuff." Perhaps that was true: they understood very well how vulnerable to blackmail private collectors were; how they could extort from them perhaps as much as, or more than, the insurance company would pay, to save a lifetime's obsession from the flames.

> Most of the dealings were done at [a well-known gambling club]. That's where you see all the big fences and crooks and so on. They went too far when they got into this insurance thing. It was O.K. They would have pulled it off once but you can't go pulling it off two, three, four, five times, just like that. You know, they *would* have gone on and on. . . .
>
> X will never stop being a receiver. And if he is not taken now, and though the whole office gets smashed all around him, I would say in three years' time, he will build an even bigger empire. He will have learned something because he has a mind. There is no doubt about that. A very good mind. And if he is not caught this time, I'd say the next time you try and catch him it's going to be very difficult. In fact virtually impossible. . . . You have got to catch him with the stuff.

In such cases, the police are hampered by the plain fact that they can prove theft only if they catch a gang in possession of stolen property. From the moment of getaway, the thieves have every advantage; but as picture and reward begin to approach each other, like tunnellers through the base of a mountain, the risk increases. The services of an intermediary are vital. Information is given; the fish bites; one picture is surrendered as proof; the assessors agree to pay the whole reward; the rest are found, usually in the left-luggage

127

office, or a baggage deposit, in a railway station; and in due course the whole ten per cent is handed over. In theory it sounds simple. In practice, as our informant said, once is easy, twice, less so. The police suspect and shadow. The highly efficient Criminal Intelligence section of Scotland Yard (who never give evidence in court for fear of becoming known to their quarry) watch every journey of the gang. A bulky roll taken to the boot of a car invites a police swoop. Suspicion divides the gang: will the insurance pay?; can the go-between be trusted not to betray them, collect the reward and disappear?; are the police themselves infiltrating, using informers or, worse, putting up as a potential "buyer", a double-agent who will demand to see the whole loot before making his offer, and, when he is shown it, give the signal to spring a trap? Torn between mistrust and greed, thieves go through an elaborate pantomime to ensure secrecy. A simple promise that the police will not be told is scarcely enough. The go-between becomes the most suspect of all; and a secondary stage may evolve where he employs yet another informant to collect the reward, in order to safeguard both the gang and the faith of the insurance assessor. Nothing, after all, could be more impressive than a truthful endorsement of the words, "In signing this receipt, I categorically assert that I had no hand in the stealing of this property or the purchase of it from the thieves".

Not all the art thefts that astounded London commuters reading their evening papers between January and September 1969 were connected; but when the police first began to suspect a link, they concluded that a single gang had master-minded them all. A crime wave all of its own, attracting harsh publicity, threatened to get wholly out of hand. The sequence began with a relatively minor theft of two paintings by the eighteenth-century French artist François Boucher from a house in Chester Square. At £20,000, their value did not rank in the top flight, like the Rubens from the Singer Museum in Laaren which was occupying Scotland Yard's small Art Squad at the time. The case was dealt with by Chelsea police; and in due course "after information received", the pictures were found in a locker at Victoria Station. The next, six months later, aroused no more attention. Mr Vasco Lazzolo, the artist, was robbed: three paintings, worth £6,500, were taken, and later recovered in the same way.

After that, complacency disappeared. On 23rd January 1969, Mr Lionel Jaffe, an American film producer, returned from a visit to the cinema with his wife, to find his house in Eaton Square ransacked. From his collection of modern artists, seven pictures – by Picasso, Rouault, Dufy, Leger and Chagall – were missing, together with a Henry Moore sculpture and some jewellery. At £110,000, the estimated value confounded journalists sceptical about a criminal network. Detective Sergeant Len Silk, of the Art Squad, eventually pieced together the thieves' complicated and meticulous escape route, which involved at least two stolen cars and the storing of the loot in a number of different houses west of Earl's Court Road. From the picking of the front-door locks to arrival at the temporary resting-place in Ealing probably took less than an hour. Once again, there were no leads. Silk had suspicions but no proof. Mr Jaffe was angry and upset; insurance assessors offered a high reward; and within a short time all the works of art were recovered, under a gas stove in a deserted house in Hackney.

These three thefts were all done by the same thieves. The police had no idea who was giving the information and they had as yet no informers who knew how the gang operated. But the smoothness and ease with which pictures were being restored undamaged, and rewards paid, disturbed them.

The case that showed what could be done to bring ransom theft to an end originated in quite different circumstances. When Lord Rockley's flat in Connaught Square was looted of a £135,000 collection of seventeenth-century Dutch masters by a gang posing as removal men, such evidence as there was suggested the same blend of calculated skill and risk. A ten per cent ransom was demanded, half from Lord Rockley, half from the assessors, accompanied by the usual threats of mutilation or destruction. The Art Squad, however, after a year specialising in picture thefts, was developing fresh sources of information, and in this case they discovered that the demands came from a gang of lorry thieves, imitating the work of the specialists. This gang soon ran out of ideas when both the owner and the assessors proved unresponsive, and, lacking the experience to do anything else, they began to look around for a receiver or a private buyer.

Police funds can be applied to a wide variety of uses and, in the twilit area of recovery of something as fragile and vulnerable as a work of art, the money can be used as bait. An intermediary, P, became the "private buyer". From considerable experience of the underworld, he spoke the jargon of thieves, yet carried the authority of a man accustomed to spending thousands for what he called "bent gear". He was shown a single picture. Later, arrangements were made for him to view the whole Rockley collection. Three cars were to meet him at a secret rendezvous, carrying the paintings.

The police had to plan their operation with immense care. If they arrived too soon they might fail to catch the gang in possession. If too late, they would have to arrest the go-between, or risk revealing his identity. Early in the morning, a dozen plain clothes men in civilian cars waited unobtrusively outside a house in North London, knowing that one of the gang was to drive off and bring the pictures back, and that the others would then follow to the rendezvous. They watched the first car drive off. When it came back, several men began to talk outside the house. The police swooped, searched and retired in considerable embarrassment, having found nothing. The operation disintegrated, for no better reason, so it was discovered, than that the guard in the house where the pictures were stored had overslept.

The "private buyer" was now suspect, and useless for the future. On the other hand, the lorry thieves were out of their depth, marked men holding a now undated and uncashable security. For a week they stuck out against a series of indirect but sinister police warnings, and then gave way. Another telephone call, another remarkable recovery: in Norwood Crematorium.

It is still not certain whether the Longford Castle robbery in May 1969 fits into the sequence, or whether it was simply a traditional country-house job, where the thief grabbed the smaller objects and ran, too frightened even to try another room. Longford Castle, home of the Earl of Radnor and one of the finest Tudor houses in the south of England, contains a collection matched by very few of the notable families of England. Two of the grandest examples were sold at the turn of the century and both, Holbein's *Henry the Eighth* and a van Eyck, now adorn the National Gallery. The Velasquez portrait of *Juan de Pareja*, sold at auction for £2,300,000 to meet death duties, was the talk of the London art world in 1972. It seems possible that the thief was paid to steal a pair of Holbein miniatures that were actually on loan to the Victoria and Albert Museum. Instead he broke into a downstairs room, snatched a number of small objects and pictures, none of great value, and the Frans Hals *Portrait of an Old Woman*, which hung on one side of the fireplace. The pair to it, *An Old Man*, was left untouched. Lord Radnor had only recently inherited the estate, on his father's death, and a modern burglar-alarm system had not then been installed.

The Hals was little known outside the *cognoscenti* of museums, and it is conceivable that it could have been sold, after a year or two, to an over-eager American collector anxious to improve his tax rating by generosity to his home town's museum. In spite of a security check at the customs and an intensive search by Wiltshire police, not a single trace was found. Then a ransom approach was made, and whether it came from the real organiser of the burglary or an enterprising outsider who had nothing to do with the theft is not known. Lord Radnor was told that if the insurance company would not pay ten per cent of the £75,000, he must do so or say goodbye to the Hals. Angry and deeply shocked, he refused and passed all the information to the Art Squad.

In spite of hints that a gang was involved, there were puzzling angles to the inquiry. Usually there is some "buzz" among informers after a big robbery – most of it vague and fanciful. Here there was nothing except a remark made by a man already on trial for another robbery that he had heard someone in a pub in London discussing the set-up at Longford Castle. Silk remained convinced that the picture would slip onto the illicit market. Five months passed; and the Wiltshire police heard the curious rumour that an old lag, recently out of prison, had a prize piece for sale.

The thief, a man of sixty-five who had spent a large part of his life in prison, had been out on probation for a short while in May 1969. He stole the Hals, hid it, and went back to finish his sentence. Hence the silence. In March, he came out, blinked at the light, and looked round for a private buyer. Again, whether he was acting on his own or giving his backers the slip is not certain. If the latter, he may simply have been exposed to the police by his assistants.

The problem of nailing him without losing the picture gave Wiltshire police the chance to play an entertaining and subtle game of counter-bluff. A young, attractive policewoman was given an alias as "Dot Watson" (reminiscent of Sherlock Holmes?) and put in as an agent for a private collector to gain the thief's confidence. Thinking she was an underworld art expert, he confided in her, tried to find out the value of the Hals, and eventually took her to where it was hidden. In April 1970 he was arrested and duly sent back to prison for another five years. The Hals was restored, the Radnors gratefully entertained the South-West Regional Crime Squad to lunch, and Longford Castle was wired with the most modern radar alarm system.

Two important developments grew out of this robbery. Lord Radnor became an admirable example to other losers: he had shown the utmost probity and public spirit in refusing to do a deal for ransom and in passing all his information to the Art Squad as well as the local force. And in London, the resources of the Central Department of Scotland Yard, that section that deals only with very serious crime, from armed robbery to murder, were put behind the three-man Art Squad. Very soon after the theft at Longford, Wiltshire police and Scotland Yard held a joint conference. As the pieces were put together, the line was seen to go back at least eighteen months and perhaps as far as the Dulwich and O'Hana cases.

The whole question of rewards and the law was discussed and the police decided that it was essential to smash the racket at once. They had no power to forbid the payment of rewards on a selective basis: to do so would have struck at the foundations of their own network of eyes and ears. They had to wait for the next job; and Detective Chief Inspectors Peeling, of the Central Department, and Lambert, of the Art Squad, and Sergeant Silk began to play a cool, level-headed game to trap the thieves and smash their contacts with the insurance assessors. In this sense, as the gang reached the high point of its career, the police, for the first time, held an advantage.

Losers may be classified quite simply into those who co-operate and those who exercise their legal right to rescue their own property, in ways that enhance the risk for others. Sir Roland Penrose stands very high in the first category. A poet and a well known painter, as well as a great collector, he helped to found the Institute of Contemporary Art and has been its chairman for more than twenty years. He was a great patron of modern art in the 1930s, encouraged the Surrealists in England and organised the International Surrealist Exhibition in 1936. A friend of Picasso, as well as the author of a standard biography of him, he helped the Tate Gallery buy the magnificent *Three Dancers* from Picasso's own collection; and he organised the memorable Picasso Exhibition there in 1960. When the thieves broke through the front door of his house in London in April 1969 and stole twenty-five pictures, he refused to have anything to do with rewards unless the information led to the recovery *and arrest* of the gang. This, in spite of the fact that the collection was greatly under-insured, and in spite of the sentimental value of works like Picasso's *Weeping Woman*, 1937, and those by Braque, Chirico, Chagall and Miró, some of which he had bought from the artists themselves.

"By making a deal you are just encouraging other kidnappers," Penrose told the press; and Tyler and Co., City loss adjusters, made it perfectly clear, when the reward of £7,500 was advertised, that arrests were essential. No doubt the thieves were surprised when they realised that the total insurance on the £300,000 haul was only £75,000, but they had no intention of submitting tamely, as the Rockley lorry thieves had done. Penrose was tested to the utmost – at one stage the gang chipped from one of the lost pictures a fragment of canvas, bearing the signature "Picasso".[2] The parallel with St Tropez and the mutilated Segonzac was loathsome, yet the risk was run.

Since the assessors refused to pay out except after an arrest, most of the approaches came direct to Penrose, who passed the information straight to the Art Squad. It thus became possible to feed a bait to the thieves. Each time the receiver, X, rang up, Penrose was asked to say, "You must deal with my agent." Let us call this man "Q". He had never met Penrose but he knew enough about him to carry off the deception. Why he should court danger is a difficult question. The risk appealed to him just as fear mingled with excitement touches even the most hardened thief; also, he needed immunity himself.

Until a few weeks after the Penrose theft there were no indications as to who was responsible. Q was then approached by the receiver, and asked to contact Penrose directly – to say that he knew something and to sound out the likelihood of a deal. Obviously, the gang could make nothing from the assessors. Q pretended that he knew Penrose personally, and that he could dress up the ransom as a friendly offer; but, without actually contacting him, returned to X to explain that the assessors knew all about the previous ransoms, disguised as insurance claims, and had no intention of paying out. Q insinuated that he would be able to extract money from Penrose instead. Until then, he had imagined that X held the pictures, but it now became clear that Z, the principal thief, was hanging on to them, and that he no longer trusted his own receiver. Q had therefore to convince, separately, each member of the gang.

For this, the Art Squad had been waiting for months. Patiently, they played the fish and did not forget to watch their own informant as well. The gang clearly distrusted each other; and they asked Q to find out Penrose's conditions. He returned with a long list – that he was to see the pictures, make notes of each individual one, and take the sizes. None of these emanated from the owner; they were meant to ensure that Q was taken to where the pictures were – at which point the police would swoop and arrest the gang for possession.

The gang were suspicious from the beginning, but the lead was the only one they had. X took the list of "conditions" and showed it to the others, then burnt the note and offered Q a single painting to take back, as identification. Q refused, swearing that Penrose would never pay out without assurance that the whole collection was safe. He was told to wait two days. Finally the condition was rejected. Bluffing hard, Q threatened to go back to Penrose. When that bluff was called, he had no choice but to drive to the block of flats, go into the hall and pretend to have seen the man he had never actually met. All the time, he was being watched, until the gang were satisfied enough to do what in thieves' jargon is called a "dummy run".

Q met the receiver in his antique shop one evening, three weeks after the theft. Outside, as discreet as the thieves themselves, a police squad car was parked. Motor cyclists and more cars waited in reserve for Q to give them a signal if the dummy run were real. Inside, the men chatted uneasily, probing each other's guard. The first time, confidence was low on both sides. After a while the receiver drove Q off to a restaurant, where the thieves were sitting, introduced him and ordered a meal. For three hours, during a long

134

dinner, the talk ran on, the gang testing the informant and his background, and the links with the owner. Underneath the screen, they were waiting for the police to raid.

The police expected nothing else. In this sort of cat-and-mouse game the longest patience wins. They sat outside the club and, when the party broke up, made no move to follow. Instead, they met the informant afterwards, encouraged him and assured him that the operation was going well. From their own experience, and from their other check sources about the gang, they were certain there would be another test, another dummy run.

Perhaps they had underestimated the credibility of the informant's acting, or the gang's need for urgent cash. Q was told to expect nothing for a few days and went off for the weekend. On Saturday morning, X telephoned; this time the journey was real; the pictures had been moved to an abandoned house, waiting for inspection. When the message finally got through, the rendezvous was postponed till the Monday.

Very little was left to chance. The police build-up was completed in the morning, without using wireless in case the gang were listening in on the police frequency. Q was to meet the gang in the afternoon and they were to drive him off. Once he had satisfied himself of the pictures' authenticity, the "deal" with Penrose would go through.

Just as Q was about to walk into the antique shop, a plain-clothes policeman stopped him. The pictures had been found – the news was already in the early edition of the evening papers. Q was on his own, to bluff in earnest. He stalked in, angrily accused the gang of leading him up the garden path. They swore he was wrong and promised they were ready to set off. He told them to go and buy a paper. After a heated argument, Z did. His fury at the news seemed genuine. Perhaps he did see £10,000 falling through the floor. On the other hand, was the whole thing a little too pat? This did not occur at the time to the informant, acting his way out of an extremely nasty situation. In the end, they split up, he pretending to believe that it was bad luck and aggrieved at his lost reward. What the gang thought, no one knows; but until Q rang them the police were afraid for his life.

The irony of the thing is painful. Neither the thieves nor the police knew that the derelict house in Ealing, where the paintings had been roughly hidden, had been scheduled three months earlier for demolition, starting that very day, 1st July. Just as Silk was briefing two squads of police for the run-in, the telephone rang. Builder's labourers had begun work, clearing the cellar, and turned over the twenty-five canvases hidden in a heap of rubbish. Thinking they were merely junk, they nearly threw them on the bonfire outside, but eventually decided to show them to a nearby antique dealer. He recognised them at once and the word got through just in time to stop the operation and save the informant's cover.

It says a great deal for the patience of detectives that this story could be told without regret. The coup would have been spectacular. Instead, a reward was paid to the finders by Sir Roland himself, and the police sat down to wait. Something had been gained, in spite of failure. Each member of the gang was a marked man, but did not know it; and, most important, the police had a line on the link-man between them and the assessors. The counter-offensive was under way.

The gang kept quiet for three months, and then struck up on a more modest scale. On 3rd August 1969, £12,000-worth of pictures disappeared from Lord Sainsbury's house in Bryanston Square, and, in September, £35,000 of paintings, drawings and lithographs, belonging to Sir James Colyer-Fergusson, from Onslow Square. In both cases the missing collections held great personal value. Lord Sainsbury was insured. Sir James was not; but he offered a reward through his solicitors. In due course the Sainsbury pictures were found in the left-luggage office at Gerrards Cross station, and the Colyer-Fergusson ones in an empty flat in Sloane Square.

The police search had narrowed down to a single man. On the night of 11th December, just after he had been handed £2,500 in £10 notes by Cecil Hart, Peeling and Silk took Bernard Oxley, a thirty-seven year old garden-ornament manufacturer from Folkestone, for questioning.

Oxley was tried in January 1971 at the Old Bailey and acquitted on five charges of dishonestly handling stolen works of art valued at more than £500,000 during 1969. He said in evidence that he had not acted dishonestly in receiving reward money totalling £16,500. What emerged was this: Hart had handed over the rewards in cash, usually meeting Oxley at night. The first contact had been made by Oxley, after the 1968 robbery. Hart had not known who he was or where he lived, and had made it clear that he could not deal without knowing if Oxley were in touch with the criminals. Hart also took the precaution of telling Chelsea police, who were seeking the lost Bouchers, and after they were recovered he paid out £500. Later, he gave Oxley – each time under a different name – £12,000 for the Jaffe pictures and £400 for those of Vasco Lazzolo (although Hart's were not then the assessors).

By the time of the Sainsbury robbery in August 1969, the heat was on. The loss adjusters advertised a reward of £1,600, but when Oxley approached him, Hart warned that he would again refer to the police. Oxley promised that there would be arrests. Finally, acting for Sir James Colyer-Fergusson's solicitors, Hart advertised a reward of £4,500 (this was in September); and it was after he had handed over the bulk that Oxley was first questioned by the police. According to Hart, Oxley tried to enlist his help to get the police off his back. He also gave him a list, which Hart passed on to Scotland Yard, naming three thieves supposed to have been connected with these thefts. Oxley's defence was that his information came at second hand. He was not implicated with the gang; and he had always been told by the loss adjusters that his activities were legitimate under the law. "I wasn't doing anything wrong, so why the aggro?"

Hart was not, of course, in any sense on trial, but the curious coincidence that the same informant had been right five times out of five needed a little explanation. In both the Sainsbury and Colyer-Fergusson cases, Hart had seen, spoken with, or written to the Commissioner of Police, Sir John Waldron, and other senior officers, including Deputy Assistant Commissioner du Rose, to confirm that he was about to pay the reward. Knowledge, however, did not imply approval by Scotland Yard. The assessors were within their rights, and Section 23 of the 1967 Act, and the police could do nothing to stop them. Whether they were within the spirit of the law is another question and one pertinently raised by the judge. Hart thought so. Traditional insurance practice bears him out. These cases, on the other hand, were unique.

Although there was only one arrest and no conviction, the Art Squad may yet have won their fight. At the material level, as Q said, "It has not been as great a success as either of us would like. At least we have got back between us probably greater value in stolen gear than anyone else; I should think half to three-quarters of a million pounds worth. Just out of this little team. But we have only scratched the surface." The paintings were all restored, safe from the threat of destruction and all the public outcry that would have burst out if "irreplaceable masterpieces" had been put in the front-line of law and order. Much more important, though thieves went loose, is the possibility that the loopholes in the law may have been narrowed. The police intended to expose insurance practice to public inquiry rather than attempt to charge thieves – whose identity they knew perfectly well – with merely trivial offences. There will always be thieves, because ordinary theft is a part of life. Theft for ransom is not. So great a temptation, in some ways so easy to respond to, merits exceptional counter-measures. The trial revealed that, although insurance assessors pass a variety of examinations, negotiations with informers are not among the subjects covered, nor do they form part of the formal code of the Institute. From subsequent history, it seems that the professional code has been tightened up.

While making allowance, in this sequence of thefts, for the fact that one firm was caught off balance and exploited by exceedingly skilful criminals, there are still questions to be asked. Even if, as Hart said, there is no other way of dealing with informers, should the interests of private property override the public interest? What is said of paintings could hardly be said of stolen cars, but is there really something so life-giving and unique about a painting? However hedged about with restrictions and safeguards, the system of rewards for information contains a basic moral and social conflict: put a condition of *arrest and conviction* on a case and the amount of information drops to near zero. Pay up without it and the masterpiece returns. Somewhere between, there may be a marginal zone, neither outside the public interest nor endangering what the world values as art; but to play on that field requires exemplary losers, quite unusually skilful police and an informant prepared to risk his neck. Failing these, most of the advantage is held by the villains.

Notes

1 A typical example is the following:

£800 Reward

Stolen 19th/20th January from Forty Hall, Forty Hill, Enfield. 2 paintings in oils, 'Venice' and 'The Upper Reaches of Grand Canal', by the School of Canaletto, measuring 15in × 18in, framed, glazed and backed. The above reward will be paid by

Hart & Co.,

23 Lawrence Lane, London, E.C.2.
(606 3266)

subject to the usual conditions.

[2] The picture was restored and eventually signed again by the artist.

Chapter 8 Recovery

So far, criminals and the illegal traffic have dominated this account of art theft. What of the movement back, from thieves to losers? The proportion of recovery is low; and tracing a stolen work of art does not always lead to its restitution, because of the conflict of differing legal systems and the lapse of time. In recent years, recovery has become the province almost exclusively of national police forces, save in rare cases such as the French Ministry of Cultural Affairs' intervention to preserve the Aix Cézannes. But, at the end of the Second World War, other institutions and agencies worked to recover at least 80,000 works of art from the Nazi rape of European treasures. The aftermath highlights many of the difficulties hindering restitution: identification, official inertia, and the complexities of international law.

The great bulk of what had been stolen under the auspices of the Nazis turned up, mainly as a result of the patient work of the Allied Military Fine Arts and Monuments Commission's recovery centres. Later, the Americans, notably General Lucius D. Clay and Robert D. Murphy, Ambassador in Rome, distinguished themselves by applying political pressure where the wheels of bureaucracy refused to move. Most of the stolen works went back to Italy and France, but a large number were recovered by Holland, Belgium, Denmark, Norway, Czechoslovakia, Poland and Austria, as well as by émigrés and refugees scattered over the Western world. Often the circumstances were bizarre. Such was the case of a cartoon by Lorenzo di Credi, which, along with others of the Uffizi Gallery's irreplaceable drawings by artists of the Italian *quattrocento*, was hidden in a Tuscan villa to escape the German advance on Florence. The villa was occupied and a private in the Wehrmacht stole the cartoon. He was still carrying it when, in 1944, he was captured by the British. An English soldier bought it from him for a can of fish and the Credi went with the Eighth Army all the way to Germany, where the soldier acquired a German girlfriend, and gave her the cartoon as a parting present. She hung it in her kitchen and later sold it to a local shopkeeper, who sold it to a German art dealer, who sold it to a wealthy collector in Tangier. The collector, wanting to make sure that his *trouvaille* was real, photographed the cartoon and submitted a print to the National Gallery in London for authentication. The National Gallery notified the Italian Recovery Office (it was a well known drawing, fully catalogued) and the collector generously circumvented what might have become a tedious legal imbroglio by returning the Credi to the Uffizi.

It is not possible to calculate how many drawings, water-colours and "minor" works of art underwent the same dispersal, without being returned. In 1966, the Italian Office for the Recovery of Works of Art (set up by the Allied governments in 1945) published an illustrated catalogue of 700 items that were still missing from Italian collections after a quarter of a century. Most of these had vanished with the transport trucks of the Wehrmacht's 35th Infantry Division, which retreated from Poppi in Tuscany on the night of 22nd August 1944, and got clear through the Brenner Pass into Germany. A small portion of the load was abandoned at the village of Campo Tures in the Dolomites; the rest has never been seen again. It includes several important Hellenistic sculptures from Roman collections, such as the *Niobe* of Palestrina and the *Venus* of Leptis Magna, but the majority of missing objects are paintings by, among others, Raphael, Memling, Titian, Perugino, Bronzino and Tintoretto; there are numerous fifteenth-century tapestries, and a collection of important Italian renaissance furniture, majolica and metalwork. Perhaps the most valuable piece of *orfèvrerie* in the list is a silver-gilt platter, bearing "The Triumph of Amphitryon", attributed to Benvenuto Cellini; this was part of the vast spoil removed from the Abbey of Monte Cassino by the Hermann Goering Division in October 1943.

The Recovery Office's 1966 catalogue contains details of the residue of 3,600 works of art listed as missing in the catalogue compiled after the war. The Germans returned a bulk shipment of

1,941 pieces to museums in Naples, Rome and Florence in 1949; others have drifted back, turned up, or been unearthed by the unflaggingly persistent Dr Rodolfo Siviero, head of the Recovery Office.

In his efforts to get back the Italian treasures, Dr Siviero (who works under the title of Minister Plenipotentiary, Chief of the Foreign Ministry's Delegation for the Retrieval of Works of Art – a name more impressive than his actual powers) encountered endless difficulties, not only from the Germans, but from the Italians themselves. The tangles of Roman bureaucracy are well-nigh impossible to unravel: the simplest action must frequently be cleared through several government departments, and the ones responsible for the care of Italy's artistic patrimony – the Ministry of Education and the Ministry of Fine Arts – are understaffed, dull and apathetic. Moreover, Italian bureaucracy still contained a number of former Fascists, as Bonn's did former Nazis; many of them resented Dr Siviero's fishing in troubled waters. (At least two of the Fascist officials who had co-operated with the Germans in organising the looting of Italian museums were still in office in the 1960s). Siviero, a well known art critic and author as well as a skilful detective, had helped to set up a partisan resistance organisation in the war and narrowly missed execution by a German firing squad. He began tracking down the stolen art treasures in 1943, with Allied help, and the fact that he was so patently on the "right" side may explain some of his later difficulties.

The problem of government indifference is worse than clandestine interference. When Dr Siviero's office published its catalogue in 1966 – financed privately, in default of government money, by a Florentine bank – a senior official of the Ministry of Fine Arts went on television to "refute" it; only eighteen paintings, he claimed, were missing, together with two sculptures and one drawing. This, the official went on, was why the government had cut the annual budget of the Recovery Office from £17,000 to £6,000. The record of governmental stinginess to the Recovery Office is impressive. After Siviero set it on an official footing in 1946, he organised a mission to Germany, for preliminary investigation of the problems of recovery. The Italian government did not, on that occasion, give him the money for transport, nor did it pay for his journey to America in 1962 to recover pictures stolen from the Uffizi.

In 1953, an agreement was reached between Italy and West Germany on the return of stolen works of art. Konrad Adenauer and the then Italian Premier, Alcide de Gasperi, signed it; West Germany undertook to search out and return all works of art that had been either looted from Italy, or sold to Germany illegally (that is, in contravention of Mussolini's previous legislation) before the occupation. At first, the Bonn government showed goodwill and enthusiasm. Italian officials did not. The Recovery Office's budget was not only cut down: in 1966 its establishment was reduced to one of eight, assisted by the unpaid services of some of Italy's leading art experts. Rome even refused to appoint expert representatives to a joint searching commission that the Germans intended to set up. At this point, according to Siviero, "the Germans began to understand that the Italians did not care about the problem, and turned stubborn themselves". The last important negotiations between Bonn and the Recovery Office took place in 1959, when Siviero had the humiliating task of "bargaining off" fourteen Italian pictures in German collections, including two Raphaels that had been illegally sold, in exchange for the return of a hundred other paintings which the insatiable Goering had appropriated for his private collection. Finally, the West German government – which had never allowed Siviero's team to inspect the storerooms of German museums, the obvious hiding places for unidentified loot – proposed that the whole operation be wound up as from June 1970. It is a measure of Italian official irresponsibility that this was agreed to at once; and it is fair to recall similar official reactions to the floods in Florence in 1966 and the prolonged dilapidation of Venice.

The sequel is even more disheartening. When the Recovery Office identified and traced ten more sculptures and paintings to private collections in Germany and Switzerland, the Italian Ministry of Fine Arts refused point-blank to authorise their recovery or pay the travel and shipping expenses. Friction between Siviero and certain Italian dealers became acute. Many *antiquari* had collaborated with the Fascists; at least one of them, the late Alessandro Contini-Bonacossi, had been made a count by Mussolini in return for his "services to culture" – which comprised an immense bequest of furniture, paintings and tapestries to the Castello Sant' Angelo in Rome. One Florentine gallery owner had traded a batch of Renaissance paintings to Goering in exchange for nine Impressionist canvases, which the Field-Marshal had previously looted from France. The resulting tangle of claims and counter-claims may be imagined: that case was resolved only by a public letter of protest from Robert Murphy, the American Ambassador. Obviously, it was not to the interest of such men as the gallery owner that Siviero should keep up his probing; and the influence of Italian dealers' cartels may in part be responsible for the resistance shown the Recovery Office by the Ministry of Fine Arts. After all, as Siviero said recently in an interview with the *New York Times*, "People have kept things hidden a long time and they may think it will soon be safe to let them out. There are a lot who are just waiting for the Commission to shut down so they can sell what they have."

Despite all this, Siviero's team, working from its offices in Palazzo Venezia, has achieved some remarkable successes. The most spectacular story opened in December 1962, when a Los Angeles art restorer, Dr A. La Vinger, gave a lecture on Los Angeles television. A lot of valuable paintings, he remarked, were lying around in the homes of people who did not know what they had. One viewer, a German immigrant named Johann Meindl, who worked as a waiter in Pasadena, had two small, dirty paintings on his wall, which he had brought with him from Europe after the war. Hoping for a windfall, Meindl went to see La Vinger.

When the restorer gave the twin panels, each measuring no more than six inches by four, a crude cleaning and a quite unnecessary coat of glossy varnish, they were revealed to be the work of the fifteenth-century Florentine, Antonio Pollaiuolo: two paintings from a series of the *Labours of Hercules* painted about 1460, one depicting Hercules wrestling with the giant Antaeus, the other the killing of the Lernean Hydra. These were not merely valuable objects (their worth, at the time, was estimated at about half a million dollars): they had been among the most celebrated paintings in the collection of the Uffizi, whence they had been looted in 1943.

When the Germans gutted the collections of northern Italy, Mussolini – by then the puppet leader of a tottering party – mustered the courage to demand from the Einsatzstab Rosenberg a list of what they had taken. Page 18 was missing, because Goering wanted certain pictures, the two Pollaiuolos among them, deflected from

145

Linz into his private collection. He had earmarked them as a present for his baby daughter. Thus they did not finish in the Alt Aussee salt mine; but neither did they reach Germany – or not directly.

Johann Meindl claimed that he had been "given" the Pollaiuolos by an old (and by then dead) teacher of his in Munich after the war. Largely to smooth the recovery of the Pollaiuolos, Dr Siviero and the American art officials who descended on Los Angeles accepted his version. The West German police remained unconvinced, and began questioning other members of Meindl's old army unit – which had been in Italy during the German retreat of 1943, and had intermittently been assigned to transporting the crates of looted art northwards, from the castle of Montegna, near Florence, over the Apennines, as the battle front approached. They searched the apartment of one of these, a master baker in Munich, and discovered, hidden in a chest of drawers, five more paintings stolen from the Uffizi: a *Deposition* by Bronzino, a self-portrait by Lorenzo di Credi, *The Parable of the Vine* by Domenico Feti, a *Nativity* by a follower of Correggio, and a seventeenth-century Bolognese *Annunciation*. The baker was terrified at first, and begged that his name be kept secret; but in any case, due to the statute of limitations, he could not have been prosecuted. The paintings were returned to the Uffizi. He had no idea of their value and had never hung them in his flat. Apparently he (and, according to the German Foreign Office, his fellow-soldier Meindl) had found a crate that had tumbled from one of the art transport trucks *en route*. Three of the pictures from the crate remain unaccounted for: a *Virgin and Child* by van Dyck, a Bronzino *Crucifixion* and a still-life by the seventeenth-century Dutch artist, van Huysum. In the opinion of Dr Siviero, the first two are still in Los Angeles and the third is in a private collection in Europe.

The Pollaiuolo affair is a good example of how the discovery of one stolen item can lead to the uncovering of others, but this would not have been possible without a catalogue; and it is certain that many uncatalogued paintings, sculptures, ceramics and rare books are circulating on the open market or stored, unrecognised, in museums.[1] A great deal of unsystematic thieving was done in Europe by British and American troops, but Allied looting has not received the same attention and, because records were lost, there is no way of proving ownership now. Soon after the war, the Allied Commission

146

removed a huge haul from a group of American soldiers, who could not remember the different castles and private houses they had looted. The great recorded pieces, like the Belgian national treasure, the *Adoration of the Lamb* by Hubert and Jan van Eyck from the Cathedral of St Bavo in Ghent, presented no problem when they were found in the Alt Aussee salt mine. On the other hand, there are still a substantial number of treasures unclaimed: as late as 1965, the West German government, in an attempt to sort these out, was privately encouraging museums and collectors to compile an unofficial list of missing objects; and the Austrians recently announced that ex-Nazi loot would be distributed among state-owned galleries if owners had not turned up by the end of 1970. This particular haul, stored in the vaults of the Carthusian monastery of Mauerbach for twenty-five years, was then valued roughly at £1·5 million.

In sharp contrast to their dealings with West European countries, the German authorities have not been so eager to restore Nazi loot to the East. In the summer of 1944, a hoard of church relics, which had accumulated at the Sixteenth Army headquarters, was transferred from Estonia to Recklinghausen in the Ruhr to prevent its disposal by local Nazis. Here it was stored "privately" for twenty-seven years till 1971, when it was flushed out by Paul Neumann, a Socialist M.P., against denials of its existence by the Foreign Ministry in Bonn. Various accusations were made that the Kiesinger government had hoped to conceal the records until the thirty-year statute of limitations had invalidated any possible claim from Russia – and these accusations were not adequately countered by the Social-Democrat government of Chancellor Brandt.

Finds like the Pollaiuolos are exceptional, but so, fortunately, is the record of Italian bureaucracy. In 1945, the U.S. State Department set up an art recovery bureau, which under the direction of art historian Ardelia Hall, recovered and returned nearly 4,000 objects before being wound up in 1962. However, one thing was and still is rigorously refused, on political grounds: the return of the historic crown of St Stephen, Hungary's greatest national treasure. The U.S. State Department would not accept a proposal, made by the Communist Party in April 1951, for the exchange of the crown for the return of Robert Vogeler, an American businessman accused of spying, but replied blandly that it "did not regard the present juncture as opportune or appropriate". It continues to insist on the legal validity of the claim that, in the closing days of the war, the crown was handed over by its guardians for safe-keeping. But the crown may not even be in America: there is evidence that it has been lodged since 1947 in the Vatican, under American auspices, and that it played a part in Cardinal Mindsenty's ill-starred attempt to set up a Central European Catholic monarchy.

Some of the impediments to recovery can be illustrated by the case of two fifteenth-century portraits, of Hans and Felicitas Tucher, by Albrecht Dürer. They had been bought in 1946 by a New York lawyer, Edward Elisofon – not as Dürers, of course – and their identity was not discovered until 1966, when one of Elisofon's art-dealer friends saw them reproduced in the West German government's list of untraced works from German museums. The paintings originally belonged to the Grand Ducal Museum of Weimar, but were moved for safe-keeping to a castle at Schwartzburg in Thuringia – an area occupied by American troops in the spring of 1945. Eight paintings, including the Dürers, were filched, and offered to Elisofon in New York the following year as "acquisitions from Europe". After some haggling, Elisofon purchased the twin portraits for $500. The ensuing legal situation was excruciatingly confused. Twenty years after the theft, no trace could be found of the ex-G.I.; and although under the Hague Convention the Dürers could not be kept in the States, they could not be returned to Weimar, because, in the meantime, that city had become part of East Germany, the government of which the U.S.A. did not recognise. The East Germans promptly laid claim, announcing that the portraits were "obviously the property of the German Democratic Republic". But this did not seem as obvious to Elisofon. A complex deal was proposed, whereby the West German government would take over the Tucher portraits and give them to the East Germans in trade for paintings that it claimed to be the property of West German museums, stored in the East for safe-keeping and never returned. Elisofon "respectfully declined", and the Dürers disappeared into a New York bank vault. The tangle grew worse in October 1966, when the impoverished Grand Duchess of Sachsen-Weimar filed a claim to the portraits, in Bonn. They were, she asserted, "without doubt the property of our family. All other claims are false, including that of the German Democratic Republic." The Grand Duchess claimed, but could not prove, that they had been on loan to the Weimar Museum from her husband's collection when they were stolen in 1945. If her claim succeeded, she would sell the Dürers in America: "We are refugees from East Germany, and lost everything at the war's end." But this poignant cry from the *ancien régime* went unheeded; Hans and Felicitas Tucher still repose in their bank vault, as negotiations drag on.

The Russians plundered Germany at the end of the war almost as efficiently as the Germans had plundered Italy. A staff of experts was sent in the wake of the Red Army, collecting from Poland and the Baltic States as well as East Germany. After 1945, some 920,000 "art objects" – ranging from battered copper coins and chipped pots to Raphael's *Sistine Madonna* – were carted away from museums in Berlin and Dresden. The scale of Stalin's "appropriations" and "safe-keeping" may be judged from a single example. The department of antiquities in Berlin's Kaiser Friedrich Museum lost:

18,000 sculptures, including the large and the small frieze of the Pergamum altar;
all moveable architectural relics, except for three cornice fragments;
8,000 "miscellaneous" objects;
7,000 vases;
2,000 paste artefacts;
6,500 terracottas and Tanagra figures;
3,000 other objects of archaeological interest, together with the department's archives and reference library.

Set against such a background, Russia's own losses (as distinct from those through fire, bombing and other damage) may seem small. Indeed, though it is likely that two-thirds of the present trade in Russian icons is supplied from dispersed German war loot, they *were* relatively small. But among them are interesting cases, the oddest of which is the theft of the Amber Room from the Tsars' summer palace at Tsarskoye Selo, near Leningrad, sometimes called the eighth wonder of the world.

In 1716, Frederick of Prussia gave Peter the Great a series of panels of solid amber, the total area of which was about 180 square feet, intricately carved and embossed by craftsmen, every incision calculated to interact with the colour of the amber, which varied in shade from an almost glassy transparency to deep opaque gold. The Tsar's own craftsmen and jewellers further elaborated the panels, inlaying them with gold sheet and semi-precious stones. The Amber Room, as it became known, was not opened to the public until after the 1917 Revolution, when Tsarskoye Selo became a museum. In 1941, during the Wehrmacht's spring offensive, the palace was looted under orders from Erich Koch, Gauleiter of East Prussia. Carefully packed, the Amber Room was shipped back to Königsberg, the former capital of East Prussia; there it was set up in the Prussian Museum, supervised by the world's leading authority on amber, Dr Alfred Rhöde, a former director of the Prussian Fine Art Museum, who announced that Germany's rightful heritage had thus been restored.

With the Russian counter-offensive of 1944, the Germans could no longer hold Königsberg. Dr Rhöde made a flying visit to Saxony, possibly to look for a hiding-place for the Amber Room and other treasures from his museum. Shortly after his return, Königsberg fell to the Red Army, and Dr Rhöde was captured. But there was no sign of the amber. According to a former officer of the Königsberg fire brigade, the panels had been encased in high, narrow crates, twelve feet by six, and spirited to the mediaeval castle of Burg Lochstedt, twenty miles outside the city. Underground passages below the castle extended over a mile, to the edge of the Baltic Sea; it was rumoured that the precious crates had been shipped away. Dr Rhöde would say nothing: he had a future to remake, and stayed on in Königsberg after the war. By then the city, renamed Kaliningrad, was Russian territory, and Rhöde took a job with the Soviet administration. His Nazism became a thing of the past; gradually his professed hostility towards Communism melted, and, according to reports in *Soviestskaya Rossiya*, he seemed to be on the point of revealing the hiding place of the Amber Room. If so, he never fulfilled the Russians' expectations, for shortly afterwards he failed to report for work and both he and his wife were found poisoned in their flat. The Russians believed it to be murder, not suicide, surviving Nazis being anxious to conceal the treasure.

The first clue appeared nearly fifteen years later, in 1969, long after the Central Committee of the Kaliningrad Communist Party had set up a special commission to find the Amber Room. A West German docker named Johann Seemann disclosed that, when he had been working in the railway shops at Königsberg shortly before the city fell, his uncle – Franz Pohlenz, a Nazi official – told him "confidentially" that the Amber Room and a collection of 800 icons were to be moved; the new hiding place was in the disused vaults of the Schoenbusch brewery (of which he was director) in the suburb of Ponarth. A few days before the Russians entered Königsberg in April 1945, Pohlenz was mudered in his home by unknown Germans.

Understandably, Seemann was jittery; he refused to disclose his address, lest the Nazis who had hidden the panels so well killed him as they had apparently killed Rhöde and Pohlenz. The Communist authorities in Kaliningrad began to search for the old bunkers beneath the brewery, without success; if the Amber Room were hidden there, it had been thoroughly hidden, for several buildings nearby had been dynamited by Pohlenz and the site was lost under a mountain of rubble. But Seemann's story received interesting corroboration from Erich Koch, the former Gauleiter, who, as a war criminal, was serving a sentence of life imprisonment in a Polish jail. In the course of an interview in 1967 with a Warsaw newspaper, Koch stated that he had supervised the hiding of the Amber Room for "the day the Germans returned to Königsberg"; and that it was in "a bunker near the old church of Ponarth". On hearing this, Soviet troops redoubled their search, but still found nothing; the Kaliningrad administration concluded that the Amber Room had indeed gone, and was in the hands of the perfidious West German government. Nevertheless the search for it has gone on ever since; and the winding cellars of ancient Königsberg may some day disgorge it.

After the war, the Russians set an example of complete intransigence about restoring German works of art.[2] Indeed, the only person to have any success with them in reclaiming lost works was the indefatigable Dr Siviero, who managed to extract a few Italian paintings from the Soviet High Command in Berlin. $17 million worth had gone east from the Zwinger collection in Dresden – including not only Raphael's *Sistine Madonna*, but also seventeen Rubens, as many Rembrandts, twenty-four van Dycks, seven Poussins, and others by Tintoretto, Velasquez, Vermeer, Manet and the post-Impressionists. A group of American journalists, on a guided tour of the Russian zone in 1948, were told that though the war-damaged Zwinger was to be restored, the collection, "being in the nature of a gift", was not.

Not for ten years did the Russians follow the example of the Americans, who had sent back from store in Washington all the fruits of the Allied Military Commission's work. But in May 1955 the entire Dresden collection was taken out of hiding and displayed in the Pushkin Museum in Moscow, where long queues filed past it all summer. At a neatly stage-managed ceremony in September, the Soviet Deputy Minister of Culture completed the hand over, reminding Franz Bolz, the East German Foreign Minister, that "only the forces of the heroic Soviet army saved these valuable treasures from ruin". Bolz played his part and spoke of "wise decisions by Soviet commanders who, even in battle, never forgot treasures of art". In a way, he was right. The Russians had returned 750 paintings but nearly a thousand were still missing. The Soviet forces, apparently, were not to blame: "The vandalism of the Hitler régime," Bolz said blandly, "and the Anglo-American air raids on places of culture and art have . . . robbed the German people of invaluable treasure."

Armies are easily blamed for all the destruction that takes place in areas through which they pass; and yet no one can do more than guess at, for example, how much was stolen from their own side by Italians searching desperately for security as Mussolini's puppet régime in the north collapsed. The case of a painting that had been missing for nearly forty years was solved recently when, at the request of the Spanish police, the F.B.I. tracked down a magnificent El Greco, *The Assumption of the Virgin*, looted from a private house in Madrid during the Spanish Civil War. Since that time many honest but shrewd onlookers have picked up a few cheap masterpieces, and many more have been gulled by seemingly aristocratic refugees into buying the grossest forgeries. Pillage is an automatic consequence of war or revolution, and not all the refugees who stagger with a few possessions across friendly frontiers are heroes of the resistance. Even the Nigerian Civil War in 1969 encouraged people to despoil their own heritage. More than £1·5 million worth of antiquities vanished from the Oron museum in Calabar in south-east Nigeria,

on the fringe of the Ibo heartland. According to Ekpo Eyo, director
of the department of antiquities, most of the ornate wooden masks
were sold abroad – some for as much as £2,000 each.

Until the boom in the art market in the 1960s, this sort of skilled
looting was the preserve of a few knowledgeable amateurs, like the
two British officers who, in Seoul during the Korean War in 1950,
made straight for the city's art gallery and removed the bulk of a
magnificent collection of carved jewels and jade – which has not
been seen since in the art market. But now that art has become
totally negotiable, and widely known to be so, any future war can
be expected to produce art thieves as efficient as the pirates or
freebooters of the past. Once only governments looted systematically,
and when defeated were made to disgorge their takings; now a
national collection, like the Oron antiquities, can be dispersed
around the world, to art-hungry and uncritical dealers and museums,
simply because it is unrecorded and the legitimate authority is weak
or at war. How many collectors, having paid £2,000 for a Benin
mask in an apparently genuine sale, would afterwards compare the
purchase date with that of the theft in Calabar? How many museums
would do so, looking over their shoulders at rival departments of
ethnography and antiquities?

The days of chivalrous restitution disappeared perhaps shortly
after the war of 1812 between Britain and America. The *Marquis
de Somerueles*, under the United States flag, and carrying several
crates of Italian paintings for the newly-founded Philadelphia
Academy of Fine Arts, was captured by a British man o'war and
taken to Halifax, Nova Scotia. The directors of the little academy
appealed: "knowing that even war does not leave science and art
unprotected, and that Britons have often considered themselves at
peace with these, we are not without hope of seeing them." Sir
Alexander Croke, judge in the Admiralty court in Halifax, responded,
"Heaven forbid that such an application to the generosity of Great
Britain should ever be ineffectual. With real sensations of pleasure,
I decree the restitution of the property." Croke's decision became
a precedent for international law – and in 1942 the now-wealthy
Philadelphia Academy returned the compliment, together with three
paintings by Salvator Rosa from the *Somerueles*, to the Nova Scotia
Museum.

153

Notes

[1] As recently as September 1971, a British journalist traced a missing Rubens from the Stadt museum of Gotha to the Albright Know Gallery of Buffalo, New York.

[2] East German authorities proved slightly more vulnerable. Dr Johann Itten, director of the Kunstgewerbe museum in Zürich, waited six years while the Swiss government conducted laboured negotiations for the return of twenty-three Chinese sculptures taken by the Russians in 1945 from the museum where they had been on loan in 1939, and later given to East Germany. Itten read of the death of Titus Kammerer, who had looked after Lenin during his exile in Switzerland. Beating a Russian delegation to the dead man's home, Itten made a deal with Kammerer's son for a teacup, a strainer and two butter knives – the only remaining mementos of the great revolutionary. A short correspondence followed with the East German authorities, and in November 1951 Itten handed over his box of Soviet history to the State Art Commission in the Russian sector of Berlin. The statues were loaded onto a Swiss lorry, and two short speeches ended what an unsmiling official called "an exemplary cultural exchange".

Chapter 9   Counter-Attack

Sometime between 1961 and 1965 – the exact date is different for each country in the Western world – the authorities woke up to the threat posed by organised art theft; and began to recognise the double market for what it was. In a press interview given in Rome in February 1964, an official of the Ministry of Fine Arts' Department of Antiquities announced dramatically:

> We are in a state of alarm. In the old days very few people cared about art – now everyone wants to have something old in his house. We find every day that candelabra, chalices, paintings disappear from churches and museums ... huge sarcophagi and even entire frescoed walls have been carried off, with thousands of urns from Tuscany. Many were auctioned in Switzerland last year. ...

Until then, the Ministry had been as lax in its care for the artistic patrimony as for its recovery from the Nazis, to judge from the precipitate plans – regarded as the minimum insurance against the new crime wave – to repair the gaps left by decades of deficient security arrangements. But the note of alarm was echoed by police forces, museum authorities, government departments and insurance companies all over Europe and America. Art theft was making them a laughing stock in the popular press and undermining the confidence needed for loan exhibitions to take place. Insurance premiums rose rapidly, to the detriment of the private collector on whom the whole elaborate edifice of the art market rested. Already a few far-sighted policemen feared that the build-up of an illicit market, taken together with insurance companies' proven susceptibility to ransom, could lead to syndicated crime.

Most police forces had been worrying for a long time before the press began their clamour to know *what* they were doing. The character of files from the Interpol library changed sharply, and, from about 1963, they began to carry more elaborate descriptions of stolen objects, with better photographs and details of the circumstances of the theft and possible suspects. For the first time, the information put into circulation was likely to be of immediate help to policemen unrehearsed in technicalities, on the other side of international frontiers.

National police forces improved in three ways their chances of recovering works of art and catching criminals: by structural reorganisation; by concentration of resources and development of new techniques; and by international co-operation. In the process, they ran into a series of difficulties, some of which threatened to put them at a permanent disadvantage with the double market organisations.

The F.B.I. seems to have been the first force actually to set up and train an art theft squad. When, in 1960, the head of the F.B.I., J. Edgar Hoover, gave his annual review of American and world trends in crime, art theft was a prominent newcomer. Since, judging by the projections made by the crime record section in Washington and information from Interpol, it could be expected to develop rapidly along lines already visible in the United States, Hoover appointed a special investigator, who was to head a small bureau based in New York and be concerned solely with theft, forgery and fraud in works of art. Headed first by Joseph M. Chapman – who handled the Bright case in 1961 – the bureau is now under the charge of John Irvin. All major robberies of works of art in the United States are reported to him through the local network of F.B.I., officers in each state and city, and the squad rarely needs to ensure that the thieves have committed Federal offences before intervening.

The rewards have been considerable. While it is impossible to obtain accurate statistics, such thefts had been contained by the late 1960s and were running at a level scarcely higher than that of ten years earlier. Typical of a dozen cases in the years 1963 to 1966 was the recovery of the million-dollar W. W. Crocker collection of modern paintings, including van Gogh's famous *Ploughman*, stolen in March 1965, while Crocker's heirs were bitterly disputing the old banker's will. The style of the crime led the police within a month to a gang, one of whom had a storage receipt from a warehouse in Houston, Texas, where the paintings were discovered. One explanation for the efficiency of the organisation is that it has relatively large funds for informants and information, and, like the narcotics squads, can dispense ten or twenty thousand dollars when required. It also has the benefit of the F.B.I. crime detection bureau in Washington, and the regular contacts that Chapman built up with museums, state authorities and the Antique Dealers Association of America.

Probably the most highly organised section in Europe is in Scotland Yard. A rudimentary art squad was originally set up in 1962, by Chief Superintendent Garrard; but it consisted in effect of only one man, Detective Inspector Andrews, who for five years worked with limited authority and virtually no formal assistance. Nevertheless he created an embryo network of informers in the underworld, fringe dealers, and reputable sources such as ex-policeman John Cunningham, loss prevention officer at Sotheby's – all in all, a sensitive retina for the reception of information, which he then had to pass on to other departments in the C.I.D. for action.

The wave of specialised picture thefts in London led to an upgrading of the Art Squad in 1967. When Andrews retired, Garrard and then Chief Superintendent Ray Peeling took responsibility for assembling an organisation dedicated specifically to solving art crimes, and possessing a wide measure of autonomy. Manned now by six officers, it has two divisions: one dealing exclusively with theft of paintings and drawings; the other covering all fields of antique collecting. The present head, Detective Superintendent Raymond Connor, emphasises that he recruits

> first-class C.I.D. men, if possible with a real interest in some artistic field. If they have that interest so much the better, but they should first be good at their job. Once here, they are expected to develop an interest, and in fact they are encouraged to do so. One of our men has completed a four-year course in the History of Art. Whenever possible, they take time off to go to lectures, courses, museums. The Squad includes officers who specialise in antique firearms, paintings, glassware, porcelain, furniture, silver, coins and medals.

Unlike its American counterpart, the Art Squad has tended to work beyond the routine framework of the C.I.D. Criminal records are little use in tracing patterns in Britain, where art theft is more diverse than in any other country. Indeed, the Art Squad has scarcely any records of its own. Combined with the fact that informers are notoriously reluctant to switch loyalty when their police contact moves elsewhere, this has led to some disruption when particularly successful officers retire.

Outside London, a few regional forces have begun to develop their own specialist services. For twenty years after the war the local C.I.D. were content to treat the theft of works of art, normally from country houses, in the same way as any other form of larceny, only very rarely calling in Scotland Yard. The rivalry between them still flourishes, similarly to the case elsewhere in Europe; but recently counties that suffer a regular plague of art thefts have grown used to co-operation with the Art Squad. The speed at which a joint operation can work may be judged from a case in 1971: three eighteenth-century silver tankards were taken from the London dealers, Shrubsoles; within twelve hours two were recovered in Leicester, 150 miles away, by the Art Squad, and the other in Hampshire by the local C.I.D.

On an informal level, it is easy for the Art Squad to ring friends in the provinces and warn them to look out for a certain piece, or a shady foreign dealer. Only the Hampshire constabulary has so far established an official art section, under the charge of Detective-Sergeant John Suter. Blessed with an unusually energetic Chief Constable, the Hampshire force have even made a crime prevention film and shown it on the local television network; in 1970 they recovered, in a matter of days, £150,000 worth of paintings stolen from the Southsea Museum and trapped the thieves.

In Germany the Bundeskriminalamt encouraged the separate state police forces of the Federal Republic to set up their own *Sonder-kommissionen*, or special squads, for a period of years, but only Bavaria has maintained one on a permanent basis. In Hesse the squad can be revived at short notice to fight a new wave of crime, and in other states (Länder) a squad can be formed with elements from Federal headquarters and the state police forces – to safeguard, say, the castles of the Rhine. Each consists of half a dozen men, operating on their own, responsible to Land head-quarters, with direct access to Bundeskriminalamt records in Wiesbaden. Every six months Herr Berger of the Bundeskriminalamt has a meeting with the heads of the Landkriminalamten to co-ordinate their work. So long as the officers keep in touch, the *Sonderkommissionen* are a flexible and effective weapon, but like any specialists they grow rusty with inaction. Bavaria's squad has an impressive record; the others have scarcely had the chance to acquire experience, and the Länder see no need to burden their finances with what – in political terms – seems justifiable only when normal local police work has broken down.

The reputation of the German police stands very high among the other Interpol countries, and their output of information on stolen works of art is the best in the world. They are not, however, lavish with credit for others, save Scotland Yard, and are particularly critical of the Italians for their confusion of separate jurisdictions, inevitable clashes of temperament, and congenital over-optimism. These strictures have a good deal of justification, for despite the apparent advantage of having authority centralised in one place, Rome (unlike the case in Germany and Britain), actual direction emerges usually as the result of conflict between police, *carabinieri* and the Recovery Office. The *carabinieri* (quasi-military police, organised on a provincial basis) usually deal with small thefts in the regions and sometimes make quite notable recoveries – witness the recent case of the two who, disguised as skindivers, arrested the looters of a sunken Roman ship at the seaside resort of Albenga. But all major cases – perhaps five hundred in any year – are taken over by the department dealing with theft and forgery, run by Dr Alessandro under the general direction of Silvio Fariello of the Criminal Division, Public Security Department, within the Ministry of the Interior. Alessandro has fifteen principal agents spread over the whole of Italy, and small squads of two or three men in the regions principally at risk – currently, for example, protecting church statues in Bolzano and Ticino.

The service is not, however, so impressive as the "dignified" version suggests. Co-operation with the *carabinieri* has never been easy – and the wheels of Italian bureaucracy move with a sluggishness equal only to the degree of *bella figura* displayed by individual civil servants. Whereas in Germany, Britain and France police changes were stimulated by the concern of politicians, in Rome until very recently the clamour of public opinion was met by blank indifference. There are no votes to be won or lost with stolen pictures, and funds for protection of the thousands of church collections at risk remained low – a mere £1 million a year to cover the whole range of state property and restoration of works of art as well. Due to lack of political support, an unconscionable burden was thrown on the police.

Rodolfo Siviero's Recovery Office is quite separate from the Ministry of the Interior. In spite of cuts in his staff and finances, and the waning enthusiasm shown by officials in Rome for the recovery of wartime losses, Siviero has remained a minister with a fair degree of autonomy, able to plan special operations outside Italy as well – the source of some inter-departmental jealousy, to say nothing of overlapping of functions. Unfortunately, police and *carabinieri* reacted to the emergency of the mid-1960s by trying to outdo Siviero through setting up special groups of their own. Luigi Luglie, head of the Police College in Rome, put men from the criminal division through a one-year course in art history and recognition. The confusion between policemen dressed up as art experts and Siviero's experts with some of the powers of policemen, but lacking access to Interpol information except by courtesy of the Ministry, has not yet been resolved.

At its best the Italian system can work well, in spite of organisational inertia: during the five years after 1965, 118 receivers and 636 thieves were arrested by the central police and two hundred more by the *carabinieri* – though by no means all were convicted. Given these figures, it is hardly surprising that ordinary policemen resent the publicity given to the Recovery Office, whose spectacular recoveries from abroad have been made legendary. Nevertheless, Siviero succeeds long after the police have been forced by lack of resources to abandon the search. The case of the *Madonna* of Cossito, a thirteenth-century painting of the Roman school, stolen in 1964, has already been mentioned (see p. 89). Nothing more was heard of the large wooden panel until in 1966 a Munich art expert, identified by the Recovery Office as Heinrich Zimmerman (who claimed to have been director-general of a respectable museum in

Nazi Germany), offered it for sale for £135,000 to a New York dealer. The latter was not shown the picture, but he became suspicious at its description, informed Siviero, and agreed to try and trap the vendor. A second German dealer was persuaded to contact Zimmerman, who then telephoned his client, a wealthy Italian citizen, at his home in Uruguay. The man refused to work by telephone from South America, but was persuaded to produce the picture and to meet the New York dealer. The meeting was to take place at another of his villas, situated on Lake Lucerne, on 28th June 1967 – exactly three years after the theft. Meanwhile the dealer primed the Recovery Office, and turned up at the villa with Siviero and an assistant, while the Swiss police hid in the grounds waiting for the confrontation to take place. The *Madonna* was recovered with a number of other works of doubtful provenance, and the Italian was arrested.

In France, the police responded bitterly to what they regarded as betrayal by the politicians over the Riviera thefts of the early 1960s. At the time, they lacked legal as well as political powers, and had neither the funds nor the authority to pay informers. Consequently, information went elsewhere – principally to the insurance companies, whose bland operations the police were quite unable to stop. Some rewards were advertised actually excluding police intervention, and insurance assessors very rarely gave information of any value, in case detectives intruded before the rewards had had their effect.

These disadvantages were enhanced by the long-standing incompatibility of the Ministry of Cultural Affairs and the Ministry of the Interior. As one police chief pointed out, after a robbery of ethnographica at the Musée de l'Homme, police security instructions meant little if fifteen keys to the museum were, with permission of the director, on loan to students. Officials of the Ministry of the Interior claimed that the police could hardly be expected to mount guard on all little provincial museums and church collections without crippling their budget. Yet no art squad was set up by the Police Judiciaire, even on an experimental basis, and, equally seriously, art theft remained for nearly ten years obscured under the classification of common theft. The Brigade Centrale de Répression des Vols in Paris were left to organise themselves to meet the new threat through the existing administrative network, and to warn likely losers through a system of *mises en garde* that they had no powers whatever to enforce.

Over the years, and on their own, the Brigade succeeded in creating machinery that kept art theft in France within bounds acceptable to public and political opinion. Important cases are dealt with from Paris, while the rest are delegated to the seventeen departments. The central organisation is kept fully informed of regional developments and, in turn, sends out Interpol and central intelligence. Links have been built up with national and local museums, a score of *sociétés antiquaires*, galleries and auction houses, and with antique dealers, customs officers and private collectors. The lists of stolen objects circulate in trade papers, and are distributed to pawnbrokers, flea markets and *brocanteurs* – providing probably the most extensive coverage of any European country.

Elsewhere in Europe, structural change has been slight. Dr Köck, the member of the Austrian Interpol bureau responsible for investigating art theft, has one assistant in Vienna and nine others to cover the whole country. In Belgium, as in France, there are no special centralised arrangements. In Switzerland, where each canton has its own police, no central authority exists. The Interpol office in Zürich has an excellent set of records but, although the penal law has been generalised since 1940, there are still difficulties in pursuing a lost work of art, say between Lausanne and Geneva. Swiss law protects property and the rights of property with peculiar intensity, making recovery far more difficult than in Germany. On the other hand, the remarkably law-abiding nature of the Swiss and the degree of state surveillance, which extends, for example, to a compulsory record by serial number of the purchase of every watch ever sold in the country, makes it hard for outside criminals to dispose of their loot. Swiss dealers and sale rooms tend to be marvellously well disposed to police inquiries, and, in a society where the most serious crimes are economic fraud and the forgery of bank-notes, the police seem able to dispense with more formal organisation for art theft.

The Dutch refer blandly to the fact that "the kind of theft referred to . . . does not form a problem in the Netherlands" – this despite the theft five years ago of a well-known Rubens, from the Singer Museum in Laren. At the extremities of Europe, to complete the picture,

Scandinavia genuinely has few problems (apart from the appropriations from the Munch museum and the losses of specialised firearms from Sweden), and in Spain and Portugal the state's absolute control through the para-military Guardia Civil and the P.I.D.E. (now known as the Direcção Geral de Segurança) has prevented the worst developments of the double market. Whatever name they are given, authorities there possess greater powers of search and surveillance than in the democracies: there are fewer dealers to watch, fewer exhibitions to guard, and, outside the principal cities, fewer wealthy houses. In Madrid, the Interpol card indexes have a dusty look; the Lisbon police have never recorded the recovery of an object stolen outside Portugal and know of only one major picture that has slipped out in the last ten years.

Structural reorganisation was to some extent inspired and co-ordinated by the work of Interpol. At St Cloud, on a hill overlooking Paris, stands the grey, featureless modern block that is Interpol's headquarters, surrounded by sleek black Citroëns, pointing outwards like the lions around Nelson's Column in Trafalgar Square. Inside, however, there are few overtones of the cinema, and the overriding impression is of the clinical expertise of a computer. Interpol is, in fact, a sophisticated post-box; the "Man from Interpol" does not exist: St Cloud is international territory, like the United Nations building in New York, staffed largely by civil servants under the urbane direction of Jean Nepote, the Secretary-General. Policemen there are seconded from the various national forces of member countries. The point needs to be put this way in order to show that Interpol neither dictates nor initiates activity in the art-theft sphere. Its filing system holds complete records of art thefts, but only of those that have been reported to it; Interpol transmits messages, but only from what comes in. There are gaps in the multilateral organisation: Russia, the Communist countries of Eastern Europe, and China; and when some member countries prove less than co-operative, there is nothing whatever that Interpol can do.

The far end of the network is the Interpol bureau in each capital, staffed by nationals from within Scotland Yard, the F.B.I., Bundes-kriminalamt or whatever. Interpol in no sense overrides national law or police systems, and at the most will only issue memoranda of advice, such as the general warning on art theft, *Projet de la session*, of September 1971. The mailing list includes, for example, the General Conference of the International Council of Museums, and a member of the Belgian bureau has lectured to members of C.I.N.O.A., the international dealers' forum, and a gathering of police in south-east England. Unspectacular, but essential, Interpol's role is one of co-ordination. However much M. Nepote may deplore the practice of certain insurance companies in paying ransom, there is little he can do. In 1966 he set up an Interpol liaison committee to explore means of preventing it, but ran into such heavy opposition that he was forced to abandon the idea.

Circulation of information is, of course, vital in combating the international trade. A theft occurs, say, in Germany; if Interpol is informed quickly, with photographs and sufficient details – if these are printed quickly and circulated – if the local Interpol offices pass the information on to art squads and local police forces – then the chances of recovery improve. A typical Interpol circular, an example of which is given below, is put out in French and English.

STOLEN

Subject: Theft of a statuette from a Museum.
Date of theft: 7th January 1964.
Country: Italy.

On 7th January, 1964, between 11.30 a.m. and 12.15 p.m., a theft was committed in the "Oliveriano" museum in Pesaro (ITALY). BALENA Maurizio, UGOLINI Cesare, and SANSONI Adolfo, who are suspected of the theft, have been arrested and the stolen objects, except one, have been recovered. The missing object is a bronze statuette, covered with a green patina, of a man with the left arm lowered and stretched forward and the right hand raised holding a club. This statuette dates from the 5th century B.C. measures 12·5 cm (about 5 inches) and was in an excellent state. It was placed on a support in a central show-case on the ground floor.

Cultural value: 700,000 lire.

Fingerprints were found on the scene of the theft but they do not correspond to those of the persons arrested.

PLEASE INFORM GALLERIES, AUCTION-ROOMS, ANTIQUE-DEALERS, PAWNSHOPS, MUSEUMS, CUSTOMS.

REASON FOR THIS CIRCULATION:

Done at the request of the ITALIAN authorities for recovery or information. If found, or should anything be known of this theft, please inform: Ufficio Centrale Italiano di Polizia Criminale Internazionale, Direzione Generale di Pubblica Sicurezza, Ministero dell'Interno, ROMA 10 (EUR) (INTERPOL ROME), and also the I.C.P.O. – INTERPOL, General Secretariat, 37 bis rue Paul Valéry, PARIS (INTERPOL PARIS).

File No.: 875/OV/210/64

I.C.P.O. PARIS

May 1964

Control No.: B 709

Assuming that the national bureau can read French or English, the next step is entirely up to them. If St Cloud suggests they should watch a certain dealer, there can be no follow-up to ensure that this is done. Conversely, there is no control over Interpol: if the London Art Squad sends an urgent message for the French Police Judiciaire to intercept a man on the Channel ferry, there is no recourse if they simply receive an acknowledgement dated three weeks later. In Germany, Interpol notices are reproduced in the *Bundeskriminalamt Blatt*, if relevant, and occasionally in the very widely circulated periodical *Die Weltkunst*. Unfortunately, it is hard to judge relevance. In most countries Interpol messages are simply filed away in central police archives. The art squads in Belgium and London try to circulate what they consider items of possible interest, but only the Germans and French make a real effort to ensure that local forces know roughly what is in circulation.

The trouble is that there is so much on the illegal market that encyclopaedic records and memories could scarcely cope. The Department of Public Security in Rome gave up, having compiled the list of 683 major items for the years 1956–64; and their *Repertorio delle Opere d'Arte Trafugata in Italia* is not likely to be brought up to date. In sharp contrast, the Bundeskriminalamt in Wiesbaden has produced annually since 1968 what must rank as the most scholarly catalogue of stolen works in the world: the *Katalog über abhanden gekommene und sichergestellte Kunstgegenstände*. The photographs are of a high standard, the details are usually sufficient, and it is updated each year before circulation through Interpol. The Blue Book, as it is known, has been instrumental in solving some cases, notably that of a whole series of icons, supposedly Russian but in fact stolen from Russian Orthodox churches in Eastern Germany, which were sold at auction in London in the late 1960s; and it serves to warn owners and insurance companies to record their property, because nothing is inserted without full details and photographs. Yet its 500 items comprise only twenty per cent of the total stolen in Germany in any year; and there is something depressing about the very existence of these massive volumes. Like the *Opere d'Arte Trafugata*, they emphasise how heavily the cards are stacked against recovery.

In addition to Interpol circulars, every police force has its own internal channels of information: the *Orden General* in Spain, the *Police Gazette* in England and Italy, the *Moniteur de police belge* in Belgium. Confidential documents, these carry lists of suspects and fingerprints; *objets d'art* jostle for position with stolen cars, or jewellery. In Austria, the Ministry of Trade circulates lists of dealers and salerooms with impressive numbers of photographs. In Belgium and Spain, where all dealers have to register with the police, coverage is easier than it is with the *antiquari* of Italy. In France, the police insert notes in the *Gazette de l'Hôtel Drouot* and the *Moniteur des ventes*. In London, perhaps the most successful advertisement has been the column "Too Hot to Handle", which, for the last five years, has been inserted free of charge in each issue of *Art and Antiques Weekly*. Its author, Detective-Sergeant Whisker, calculated that, in 1969 alone, £60,000-worth of property was recovered as a result.

Publicity among antique dealers may cut the double market at an important intersection. To the certain knowledge of Scotland Yard, items listed in "Too Hot to Handle" have been sunk in the Thames, being impossible to shift through the illegitimate trade. Reaching a

166

far wider readership, the expensive European monthlies carry sponsored articles, such as "Oggetti d'arte, scomparsi delle chiese, dai musei e dalle collezione private" in *Gazetta Antiquaria*. Not to clog the memory, the Bundeskriminalamt selects its items for *Die Weltkunst* very carefully – the more so since it is published in three languages and taken by virtually all European dealers, museums and salerooms. In the last four years the police have also been able to utilise the services of radio and television – via such programmes as the B.B.C.'s "Help the police" series, and "File no. . . . unsolved", put out monthly by two German television companies.

Claims for these methods can be substantiated. In May 1970, three carved wooden figures were reported stolen from a church in Boppard in Germany. Details duly appeared in *Die Weltkunst*. When a Belgian offered one statue for sale in Brussels, the dealer recognised it from the photographs and telephoned the local police. The message reached Wiesbaden via the Hesse Landkriminalamt, and the Belgian vendor was discovered in possession of the other two, which he had bought from a German woman, wife of a dealer, whose brother worked as a restorer of churches and their treasures. Both men had been substituting figures, producing forgeries and using their receipts for work well done as advertisements for further trade. Hired men committed the actual thefts; what was stolen in Germany was sold to dealers or other clergy in Nuremberg, or vanished into Belgium. From the meticulous account books, it appeared that this traffic had existed since 1965.

Occasionally, individual catalogues put out by insurance assessors produce the same result. A finely illustrated brochure showing classical antiquities and Egyptian coins recovered by the Swiss customs from four Greeks in Zürich in 1968 led to their extradition and the restoration of over a hundred items to different museums all over Greece. But the weak links in the system of communication are obvious. Speaking quantitatively, details of no more than a quarter of stolen objects are ever put into circulation. Transatlantic information links leave a great deal to be desired: not unnaturally the F.B.I. concentrate on their internal problems, and the recovery rate of objects exported from Europe is minimal. Affairs like that of the Tillman collection indicate huge gaps in international co-ordination. While the illegal market in North America is self-contained, in

Europe it extends to supply a world demand, overloading the channels of information and dulling the most perceptive memory. It has, sadly, become impossible to do any more than pinpoint the finer, recorded things and leave the rest to haggling between the loser and his insurance company.

A policeman hardly needs to judge the authenticity of an object or a picture. For most purposes a good photograph is sufficient.[1] The essential requirement is that he should be a good detective, not a connoisseur. Information is his stock-in-trade, from liaison with dealers, salerooms, museums and, beyond the professional sphere, banks and government departments. Where a register of dealers exists, formal liaison, in the sense of circulating reports of stolen property, is easy, but the greatest value lies in unofficial contacts and informers. Every member of an art squad has his friends in the antique trade and a list of those he can trust to pass on hot tips. After the robbery from the armoury at Montacute House in 1966, a West-Country dealer rang Scotland Yard to say that a man was trying to sell him a pair of Scottish steel pistols, worth at least £500, for a quarter of their price. The man ran off, leaving the pistols behind. It took a week to track him down, and with him a fine suit of armour and eventually the greater part of the lost collection. Without a friend in the Art Squad, the dealer might never have bothered to go beyond the local C.I.D.

To register all antique dealers – a measure sometimes advocated – would be futile in Germany, the United States or Britain since there are too many. In France, where it has been tried, the returns scarcely justify the work. Belgium and Switzerland are small enough for the police to indulge in careful surveillance, and one gets the distinct impression that dealers there are careful to co-operate precisely because they fear being branded as fences and put out of business. But in countries where dozens of dealers work in a single street, the police have to befriend those whose information they can trust. Such dealers are not, in the ordinary sense, police informers, but, rather, safeguard the morality of a trade that has, in some respects, been declining since the 1930s. Unfortunately there are too few dealers of this type: even with the weight of C.I.N.O.A., the Antique Dealers' Association of America, or the British Antique Dealers' Association behind them. Salerooms, on the other hand,

168

Sir Roland Penrose at the front door of his Kensington residence. The marks show where thieves forced an entrance, to escape undetected with works of art valued at £300,000. Shown below are two of the stolen Picassos: *Gas Jet* and the celebrated *Weeping Woman*. (*Press Association*)

Hungary's national treasure, the crown of St Stephen. Its whereabouts are still a mystery. (*The Worshipful Company of Gold-Smiths*)

Thermoluminiscent testing, a sophisticated method of detecting fakes in ancient pottery. (*Topix*)

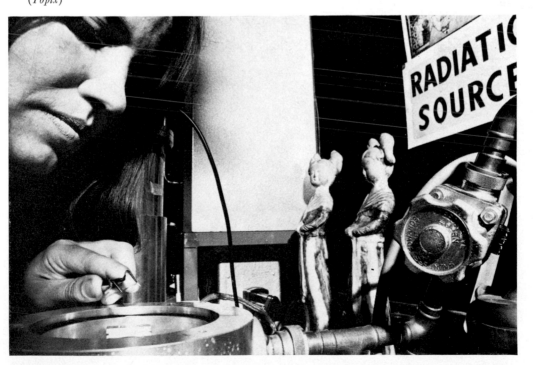

Rodolfo Siviero, head of the Italian Recovery Office, whose tireless pursuit of stolen paintings has led to many recoveries. He is shown here with Raphael's *Portrait of a Young Girl*, illegally sold to the Boston Museum of Fine Arts. (*Associated Press Ltd*)

The seal of Isabella of Hainault, bought in 1971 by the British Museum despite the fact that it was stolen from the Cathedral Treasury of Notre Dame in 1860. (*British Museum*)

The Amber Room at Tsarskoye Selo, opened to the public after the Russian Revolution, looted and dismantled by the Nazis in 1941. The Kaliningrad administration have since concluded that it is in the hands of the West German Government, but no evidence has so far corroborated this. (*Society for Cultural Relations with the USSR*)

Communication of accurate information on stolen works is vitally important. All police forces issue descriptions like this one reproduced from the *Moniteur suisse de police*. (*Zürich police*)

An extract from the Blue Book, the official West German catalogue of stolen works of art. The examples shown are statues of St Joseph and St Margaretha, and an unidentified carved figure. (*Bundeskriminalamt*)

4

5

6

Interpol's list of the 12 most wanted works of art in 1972, among them three Buddhas stolen in 1961 from the Nalanda Museum. In India and the Far East, wages paid to those guarding museum exhibits are very low. (*Interpol*)

A Still Life by Ladell with two very similar copies made by the artist. Such close resemblances illustrate the extreme difficulty of identifying stolen paintings. (*Art Squad, Scotland Yard*)

A fine example of a Greek *krater* on display at the Metropolitan Museum of Art, New York. Doubts have been raised about the legality of its export to the United States, arranged by an international dealer. (*McgrathCamera Press Ltd*)

have a vested interest in checking both theft and forgery, and, from the Dorotheum in Vienna to Parke-Bernet in New York, the police expect a high degree of co-operation and trust. Most galleries and salerooms employ ex-policemen as security officers to guard what is for sale (which in the case of Sotheby's in London may be two or three million pounds' worth at any one time); but these officers are also on the watch for that most difficult problem, the submission of things already stolen.

Other government services are available as a further defence. Customs officers in any country are a useful source of information, well placed to note a build-up in certain categories of goods, such as the flood of forged eighteenth-century paintings emanating from Spain that plagued salerooms in Western Europe in the early 1970s. Immigration authorities can watch for suspect dealers. In the United States and, much less officially, in most European countries, tele-phones can be tapped; and there have been cases in Britain and Germany where a receiver has been watched by every means available to the security forces.

Finally, there is an ingenious last resort. Many known criminals get away with receiving year after year, for lack of proof that will stand up in court. The police have to produce a case to convince a jury. But the tax men need only to suspect evasion in order to pursue a man for years. The F.B.I. sometimes pass a case on to the Federal tax authorities, who can inspect bank records. Even in Switzerland, despite the monolithic security of numbered accounts, the banks will open up. If, for example, the German Federal prosecutor makes an official complaint, pin-pointing stolen property, the Swiss public prosecutor in Berne will issue a warrant and the bank concerned will co-operate, if for no other reason than to avoid future trouble. And if a man claims rewards for a ransom case and thereby establishes himself as a professional informant, by British law he becomes liable to income tax. The mills of the Inland Revenue grind for an exceedingly long time; and they take no notice of the fact that the informant may have passed a share on to his colleagues. Protection is not a deductible expense.

Of course, every policeman needs the most modern equipment. It helps greatly if, when he finds suspect works of art in transit, they can be checked at once from a central archive. Italian records are computerised, but most other countries rely on what seem old-fashioned card indexes. Still, the police can normally hold suspected objects for identification, and the number of cases where obviously stolen property is recovered but cannot be traced is declining. But this does not solve the problem posed by the glut of stolen objects in circulation and their lack of clear identification. Say a set of Georgian silver spoons vanishes from a London flat: within a short time it will either have had any identifying motto or crest removed, for immediate resale, or it will be on its way abroad. Neither its value nor the circumstances merit circulation to Interpol. The Art Squad, overworked with major cases, cannot cope. The local C.I.D. will be courteous, helpful and, rightly, discouraging. Chances of recovery are probably 0·1 per cent.

The conclusion is simple: just as the chief of police in Marseilles could say of the Riviera thefts "it was not a case of murder", in order to explain the dilatoriness of his inquiries, so the Georgian silver is less important than a case of ransom, or the Goya *Duke of Wellington*. The net must not have too small a mesh, or it is impossible for it to move through the water. Few police officers in private conversation can claim more.

Yet to admit that in the majority of cases the likelihood of success is so small that it does not justify the trouble is precisely what the police cannot do, for fear of destroying faith in their capacity to control more serious crime. Caught in a vicious spiral, frequently over-worked and undermanned, they cannot avoid action when a crime has been committed. Temporarily reassured, the loser's frustration may be greater in the end, unless, bolstered by the security of his insurance, he does not greatly care.[2] Discredit rebounds on the police from excessive hopes as well as from the compromises that are peculiar to the search for criminals in the art market.

On the beat, a policeman is exposed to few or very simple forms of corruption. As a member of a specialised C.I.D. squad, whether dealing with art theft, horse-doping or drug-peddling, he may face bribery, blackmail, and legal haggling brought to bear with great sophistication and backed by large bank accounts. He is, above all, isolated. Although, almost by definition, his principal quarry is gangs that have specialised in art theft and not art experts taking a criminal chance, he can get relatively little help from his colleagues

170

elsewhere in the C.I.D. The important leads and arrests are not those of the thieves, but of the receivers behind them, who are not usually known as members of what old-fashioned judges used to call "the criminal classes", and who tend too often to escape with fines or light sentences on minor indictments. Evidence sufficiently strong to stand up against them in court can probably only come from close accomplices, and to get that the detective must enter a world devoid of the clear landmarks pointed out in early police training.

During the trial described in Chapter 7, police witnesses affirmed that without informants a great part of the work of the C.I.D. would run into the sands. The same is true in all countries, though circumstances vary: payments from the funds at the disposal of Scotland Yard are circumscribed strictly by results and seldom exceed three figures; conversely, in the United States single payments of $2,500 to $10,000 are not unusual. Italian law recognises the position of informants and payments are covered by police regulations, whereas the Swiss police are very reluctant to enter into relationships with the underworld at all, preferring to rely on strict surveillance of the open market.

Behind these regional distinctions, however, there is a common pattern. Official approval and the supply of money can only partially influence the outcome. There are occasionally exceptions to the rule that informants are themselves criminals and the nearer they are to the crime, the better their information. Something *may* be overheard in a café, a solid citizen *can* see stolen goods being unloaded; but a chance remark or a suspicious glimpse will probably mean much only to a person already in the know. The French police attempt to classify sources of information in three categories: first, members of the general public; second, members of professional bodies, such as dealers; and, third, members of the underworld; but they admit that ninety per cent of what is useful comes from the third category.

In this half-world, official regulation of informers is ponderous if not valueless. A policeman needs to be able to work up his own sources, to know roughly what their value is and to treat them accordingly. He may find one source in a gang member aggrieved at his small share, or resentful of a bullying boss. A girl-friend may get tired of a man who brags of other women. Most often a man will try to pull a bargain: "don't press a charge on this and I'll do you a good turn". The fear of arrest, even of the suspended sentence, brings information as often as money. A man already in prison may hope for remission; another about to be tried can win a more lenient sentence. In the United States, a criminal can win immunity from prosecution by testifying against his partners – assuming he is willing to run the risk of their revenge. But the information alone is rarely enough, consisting as it does of half-truths, hints and evasive explanations. The better a good informant is, the sooner he risks losing his cover and perhaps his life. One receiver in London has had a man blasted with a shot-gun for talking too loud in a pub, and at least two police informants on art thefts have died in New York since the 1950s. One recalls the Corsican, Guidicelli, shot by former colleagues in Nice in 1961. Most details come second-hand and lead to jigsaw work. A tip comes in; something is for sale. Gradually the search narrows down; the informer may go back, watched carefully to see that he doesn't do his own deal on the side; or perhaps a police agent goes in as a "buyer" to set the trap.

Within the limits of discretion, a detective will look after the interests of his informants, though he may sometimes be powerless. In the summer of 1968 a highly valuable altar-piece, by Matteo di Giovanni, was stolen from the church of St Agata at Asciano near Siena. The news was circulated to Interpol. In due course two German criminals came to the Bundeskriminalamt in Wiesbaden, to say that the painting was hidden in Switzerland. What would Herr Berger pay as a reward? The local bishop had already promised a reward amounting to 100,000 Deutschmarks, and this offer had been published in the Italian press, but the Germans preferred to trust their own police. From their information, the combined forces of the three countries recovered the painting and arrested both the thieves and the receiver. The bishop, however, declined to pay; since when, two furious Germans have bombarded Wiesbaden with complaints for which they can only be shown considerable sympathy. The resources of Interpol do not extend to bringing pressure to bear on the clergy of one member nation to redeem their pledges, nor those of the police of another.

Just as the files of the secret service of any country are kept secret generations after the official government papers have been opened to historical research, so the records of past agents are destroyed or locked away. It would be unwise and unfair to describe anyone now at work; and the odd lust for publicity that surrounds the best-known F.B.I. informant, who called himself Jean-Pierre Lafitte, after a Caribbean pirate, suggests that he is a conflation of several different informants and undercover agents employed by Joseph Chapman, first head of the bureau investigating art theft. His pedigree and exploits invite comparison with a number of semi-fictional characters: this "chunky man in his fifties with a wisp of hair fringing his head" has claimed more than thirty aliases and the absurd figures of fourteen desertions from the French Foreign Legion. His "background" consists of a long history of minor crime, studded with deportations from the United States. For a time he worked for the Federal Narcotics Bureau, and he has, allegedly, been on the pay-roll of the F.B.I. at $100 a week for the last fifteen years. Among his successes is the recovery of the debatable masterpieces from Bardtown Cathedral, Kentucky. His "memoirs", written for *True* magazine, groan with derivative overtones.

At the time of the Bardstown theft I was on close terms with a group of New York hoodlums. They accepted me as a hoodlum and I was circulating around on the hunt for information about an entirely different matter from the Cathedral theft. People find it difficult to believe that one can move into the underworld at will. I do not encourage amateurs to try it, but with the right background, knowledge and a certain control over your nerves it is not difficult. In 1954 I went out to Las Vegas impersonating a fictitious mobster named Louis Tabet, and within a month I was dealing with some of the sharpest crooks and fixers in the country.

The night after I got my call from the F.B.I. agent, I was drinking in a New York bar with a few mobsters. The one sitting next to me was a big man and he had had a few drinks too many. He leaned over closer to a hood across the table and said, "I hear someone in Chi has some paintings he wants to dump for a couple of hundred grand." That was all. I had a hunch that this might be the thread that would wind back to the nine empty frames in Kentucky. . . .

Almost without exception, the top echelon of informers lose their value after two or three important arrests. Very few are valuable enough to get on the police pay-roll and so to some extent preserve themselves from the need to steal as much as they restore. The rest grade sharply downwards, soon reaching the old lag, the hopeless drug-addict and the worn-out prostitute. The glamour exists only in the columns of *True* magazine, not in Lafitte's life, and certainly not lower down.

Informants have a limited life-span, and their use is also strictly circumscribed. Information is not necessarily evidence, nor in most cases can a detective expose his agent to cross-examination in court. If arrests are to be made – as distinct from the recovery of stolen paintings – then the thieves or receivers must be caught in possession, the one situation that even the most amateurish know to avoid. Hence the elaborate schemes for handover that police "buyers" have to set up.

On the night of 26th July 1966, four seventeenth- and eighteenth-century paintings and a variety of bronzes and antique clocks, worth in all £100,000, were taken from Stupingi castle, a former royal hunting-lodge near Turin. The Roman police took over the case and assigned to it one of their art agents, a policeman unknown to the Piedmontese underworld. He arrived in a large chauffeur-driven Mercedes, booked in at one of the best hotels, and began a leisurely round of the principal *antiquari*, inquiring for eighteenth-century paintings. After a little conversation he would let drop discreet hints that he was not too particular about the legal provenance of what was offered.

For a month nothing stirred. Then he was offered a bronze statuette at an absurdly low figure and bought it without question. The gang were apparently convinced. In due course came a telephone call: was he interested in paintings and antique clocks "for a big price, but cheap"? A meeting was arranged. No one turned up. The police waited. A second appointment followed (a pattern similar to that in the Rockley case in London), for a meeting on the motorway beyond the city. Here the policeman-dealer met a young Calabrian, driving a lorry containing the whole proceeds from the castle. In the open country the gang had thought themselves safe, but, as the agent left, ostensibly to collect £60,000 from his bank, he alerted his colleagues by wireless and the lorry and driver were picked up, after a chase, near the Swiss border.

Circumstances in the Penrose case (Chapter 7) prove how carefully and lightly the bait must be laid. Probably no experienced receiver would fall for a trap designed to catch him personally in the act of possession. In the balance with the pursuers he really does have weight, and sometimes thrusts back at the police, damaging reputations with innuendoes or unveiling real corruption.

Sufficient numbers of corrupt policemen exist to give a basis for such accusations. The underworld is rich, and looks after its own. While a minor criminal may deliberately be abandoned, a valuable man will be defended. Those who can afford £5,000 worth of prominent counsel can also afford a tenth of that, in single notes, handed over in the back of a squad car at night. Criminal investigation departments of all police forces are over-worked. Some detectives in Scotland Yard, the Police Judiciaire or the F.B.I. put in sixty hours a week without overtime. While Commissioners may be well paid, their subordinates rarely are, and, out of the hundreds of upright men, there are, inevitably, a few who are corrupt.

Hearsay and rumour originating from criminals multiply rapidly. There are at present three ex-policemen in all Europe serving jail sentences for receiving bribes in connection with art theft. Of past history it is harder to speak. In the early days of art squads, several bureaux found themselves plagued by leaks of information that enabled gangs to evade police traps, and one presumes that the sources were well paid for their information. After the O'Hana affair in London in 1962, a detective in Scotland Yard came under suspicion and was transferred but not suspended. Abroad, figures as high as £200 a week in protection money have been mentioned. Yet it is hard for a low-ranking detective to hide the signs of conspicuous spending.

Given a meticulous system of investigation of abuses by the police, which exists for example in England, criminals frequently make spurious complaints to smear those most dangerous to them; and this sort of frame-up is not uncommon on either side of the Atlantic. Corruption appears to be very rare in Britain, where the C.I.D. are not even allowed to accept rewards, and equally uncommon

175

among the F.B.I. Elsewhere, in countries where nepotism forms part of the social climate – in Italy, Spain and to a lesser extent in France – one cannot be so categoric.

Two other impediments work against the art squad. In spite of the facilities offered by Interpol, co-operation between individual national police forces is only as good as their mutual trust and goodwill. For example, in 1970 an informant gave in the names of two American dealers negotiating the sale of stolen property in Britain and Europe. Scotland Yard handled the case delicately and called on Germany to help trap the pair. Posing as potential buyers, detectives from both countries met the dealers in a London hotel; but the Germans immediately began to question them and gave the game away. Elsewhere the trouble may lie in stilted protocol. A British officer on holiday in Cadiz saw in the street a man he had been chasing for the theft of a picture in Holland. The Spanish police were courteous, but less than helpful. Perhaps the señor had authorisation from London, counter-stamped by Madrid? One fiasco – a detective from another country actually showing a police dossier, containing the names of suspects, to a criminal – leaves a sour taste that lasts a long time.

Finally, no ambitious policeman wants to be seconded for years to an art squad, away from the main stream of promotion, unless he is given prestige and a commensurate salary. Siviero is the only man who has lasted more than a decade in office, though Joseph M. Chapman served nearly that long. Rapid turnover in detectives is fatal for the operations of an art squad, for it is not merely a question of a policeman's own accumulated expertise: without the network of informants and confidence among friendly dealers, the art squads operate in a vacuum. A case from Switzerland illustrates the point. A thief tried to sell a stolen Pissaro to a woman dealer in Zürich; she was impressed and thought the price of 200,000 Swiss francs a great bargain. Having paid a deposit, she showed it to a well-known local expert, who authenticated it. She duly bought and exhibited it. At once questions were asked by other dealers outside Switzerland. Her lawyer persuaded her to go to the police. The same expert was called in and now gave a doubtful verdict: the picture could well have been stolen. He had actually suspected the picture from the start, but had not wished to stir up trouble, lacking confidence in the ability of detectives he did not know to handle the case with the necessary discretion.

During the later 1960s, police counter-measures hit the underworld in the art market hard. In Austria, the number of thefts, which had risen steadily each year to a peak of 215 in 1967, fell sharply to 119 in 1969, and 127 in 1970. Italian statistics of arrests since 1965 are impressive, and the recovery rate of items in the German Blue Book has run at roughly fifteen per cent, substantially higher than the European average. Although full statistics are not available, the F.B.I. claimed as early as 1963 to have recovered $5 million worth of art objects in the previous three years. Many criminals, accustomed to the easy conditions of the previous decade, were caught off balance.

1964 was something of a turning point. In Britain, the Ionides collection of Meissen and Chinese porcelain, lost after the death of the vastly wealthy Nellie Ionides, was recovered buried in a Kentish orchard. An eleventh-century ivory statue of the Madonna, stolen from Rieti in Italy, turned up, and the three thieves who looted the Olivierano Museum in Pesaro, were caught with almost the entire haul (see the Interpol circular reprinted on p. 164). In the following years, Italian police work was responsible for the recovery of substantial losses from Perugia, and the bulk of the Renaissance paintings from Prince Torlonia's collection in Rome. When the finest Cromwellian firearms vanished from the Wills collection, at Littlecote House, in 1967, the London Art Squad and the Wiltshire Regional Crime Squad got three-quarters of it back.

At the risk of overemphasising the work of one man, the story of the much-travelled *Ephebus* of Silinute should be told. The *Ephebus* is the statue of a young man, an Archaic Greek bronze, dug up in Sicily in 1886, and, like many such works, attributed by nineteenth-century art historians to Phideas. It needs no grand name added to make the thirty-three inch high figure one of the finest surviving works of art of the greatest period of Greek sculpture. For years it had stood in the town hall of Castelvetrano near Trapani in Sicily, and was conservatively valued at 500 million lire (£300,000). On 31st October 1962 it vanished, while the mayor and his officials were actually in the building. According to some reports, the robbery was done by two minor *mafiosi* from Agrigento, who took it across to the

177

mainland and offered it for sale. Others say that the thieves were working to the order of a rich Sicilian, living in New York, who had promised a fee of half a million lire. According to the same source, when the two read of its true value they decided to sell it themselves.

Every museum, gallery, dealer and likely private collector in Italy was warned, and the details circulated through Interpol. File No. 752/OV/907/62 swelled rapidly during the next six years as varied reports came in from Europe and America. Rodolfo Siviero followed all the leads. Some were mere red herrings; others indicated that the *mafiosi* had acquired colleagues, crossed into Switzerland and finally reached America. The director of a west-coast museum was offered the *Ephebus* but declined. An anonymous private collector prepared to pay out $450,000, but suffered from cold feet at the last moment. The original rich Sicilian lost interest. Unable to dispose of the *Ephebus*, the Sicilians brought it back to Europe. Once more it passed through Switzerland to Sicily, where they attempted to persuade a dealer from Palermo to act for them and ransom the statue back to the municipality of Agrigento.

Instead, the dealer telephoned the *questore* of Agrigento, and Siviero and two of the regular police from the criminal department in Rome began to haggle through the intermediary. The thieves took Siviero for a genuine buyer, representing a noted Italian art dealer. They demanded 80 million lire. Siviero offered 20 and finally agreed on 31 million (£20,000) in March 1968. The handover was to take place in neutral territory, at Foligno, about 100 miles east of Rome. On 13th March, Siviero and his colleagues waited until five men turned up in a car. Two were posted as guards. The transaction had begun when waiting police rushed in. A furious battle developed as the guards began shooting in all directions, and the police replied. A dozen shots later, all five *mafiosi* were in custody, one policeman was slightly hurt, and the undamaged *Ephebus* had been recovered. Vincenzo Ragora and Leonardo Bonafede received prison sentences of four years.

Such cases depend on detective work of a high order, dedicated, even unusual persistence over a long period, the co-operation of honest dealers and the work of Interpol. At its best, the police counter-attack was undoubtedly effective and successful in those countries, like Britain and Italy, where crime was most serious in the

178

1960s. But enough has already been said to show that the fundamental dilemma of art theft, whether police priority should lie in recovery of the object or arrest of the criminal, was by no means solved. Because of the dimension of cultural blackmail, Siviero had to walk warily; the *Ephebus* was unique, whereas Sicilian *mafiosi* spring ready-made from the stony soil. The fulsome publicity that recovery attracts should not mask the fact that, whatever their theoretical duty to prevent crime and bring criminals to trial, the police of all countries do take into account the dual nature of the job and public reaction. As the local Sicilian press claimed, the world had waited anxiously for six years for the *Ephebus* to come to light. So this chapter may end with a story which has a moral but no morality. For obvious reasons the personality and place are left obscure.

The private collection of a provincial lawyer, worth roughly £15,000 in the porcelain of a single factory, vanished in the winter of 1970. One marked piece turned up in the shop of the local antique dealer, already known to the police as the receiver of an occasional disreputable object. A member of the central Art Squad came down and discovered that the locals did not intend to do anything hastily. Fearing that the whole collection would disappear for good, the detective overrode the local man, who had twice his seniority, went to the dealer and charged him. The man was elderly and whined about spending his declining years in prison. There followed an hour of hard bargaining, at the end of which the dealer admitted the theft and agreed to hand over the whole collection; he would then plead guilty to a minor charge of dishonest handling of one piece and cheerfully pay what for him was a small fine. The locals were furious, but it was too late to prefer more serious charges. The porcelain was handed back undamaged; the receiver, out of pocket by £250, will doubtless deal again in stolen property, but he is a marked man. Is this the model of how such things should be?

Notes

1 Save perhaps in this recent case in London: a still-life of fruit and flowers, by the Victorian artist Edward Ladell, was stolen. Soon

afterwards it was spotted in an antique dealer's window. The Art Squad pounced, then retired crestfallen, having found that the main part of the picture matched the photograph supplied by the loser, but that the background did not. Further research produced two other versions of the same subject, all painted by the prolific Ladell, all with minor differences.

2 There is an eighteenth-century long rifle, bearing the arms of the Bishop of Salzburg, in the possession of a provincial police headquarters in England. In the two years since it was found, no one has claimed it. It is worth £800 and has been well advertised. One can only presume that its owner has had more than the market value and prefers to keep quiet.

Chapter 10 Remedies

Although art theft, like most other forms of crime, is cyclical in its incidence, rising and falling with demand and opportunity, the police do not pretend that it is likely to do anything but increase under present conditions. Nor is it possible to claim that they have much hope, with their existing resources, of curbing it. By itself, art theft is not subversive enough to merit massive state spending on detection. Confronted with worsening crime statistics, the majority of police forces have tended to ask for changes in the law in order to make easier the arrest and conviction of thieves and receivers, or for ways of thrusting responsibility back onto the owners, whether museums or private collectors.

The law protects private property only in so far as the climate of opinion supports it and its penalties remain a credible deterrent to thieves. For reasons discussed in Chapter 1, public opinion over the last ten years has been schooled to regard art theft as a generally trivial crime, almost a diversion compared to the problems of violence and drugs. In most European countries, the deterrent aspect has been slight. In Britain, for example, it is hard, given the basic principles of the law of theft, to prove possession (unless the accused is caught red-handed) and harder still to prove intent to steal. Usually only amateurs and the unlucky can be nailed in the process of selling, which, until 1968, was virtually the only way to prove the latter.

With the Theft Act of 1968, the definition of theft in Britain was widened so that "intent permanently to deprive the owner of possession" came within its scope. It was no longer necessary to prove that the thief had offered his loot for resale or profit. But while *de facto* possession may be contrary to the law, it is not necessarily a serious criminal offence. The sanctions are, in any case, antiquated.

Far heavier penalties should apply to the receiver than are now in fact applicable in any country surveyed in this book – except Soviet Russia. Other charges, such as conspiracy to commit a crime, are much graver, but virtually beyond proof. What thief caught by the police would implicate his master, give evidence against him and stand up to cross-examination, with the thought of revenge at the back of his mind? The police can, and do, bargain serious charges for lesser ones to get property back or gain information, but they cannot offer a criminal protection against his own side for very long. In France they cannot even offer him money. Yet, as Dr Alessandro says, wearily, "The only possibility that exists is breaking the thief–receiver link."

In the United States, a Federal offence serious enough to merit a prison sentence or a fine of $10,000 is committed if the stolen property, being worth over $5,000, is taken across a state line. Nothing like this is available in Britain. Kempton Bunton claimed that he took the Goya *Duke of Wellington* for political ends, and, under the law as it then stood, he could be convicted only of stealing the frame, which was not returned. The loss of a masterpiece was thus reduced to the same level as joy-riding in a borrowed car.

In court the policeman faces a jury that probably has no experience of the antique trade. An English jury has even been known to accept the plea, by a man accused of receiving two pictures (found by the police hidden in his wife's garden), that he had been "forced to take them" by men who threatened him with guns. He described them as "a London mob, wearing dark glasses" and claimed to have parted with £150 after being told that, if he didn't, "the bullets would fly". Once the average jury-man comprehends that there are areas of the trade that closely resemble the second-hand car market, or horse-dealing in Southern Ireland, he finds it hard to see exactly where the line between legitimate and illegitimate sales lies.

Worse, police recovery strategy may conflict with the aim of convicting thieves. Undeniably, the use of informers has unpleasant overtones, and an expert detective may find that in the eyes of the jury a subtle scheme to trap a receiver looks barely legitimate itself. This is to say nothing of the scope for defending counsel. In no activity does a policeman lay himself more open to charges of corruption, aiding and abetting, or wilful neglect of duty than in dealings with the underworld. A policeman's drink with a known thief in the course of an operation can be seen as a necessary part of an elaborate game of bluff – or it can become, insidiously, an overt sign of complicity in crime itself. Counsel must defend his client as best he can; if he chooses to do so by blackening the police, he cannot be blamed. But many cases involving art theft rest, because there is no clear evidence of possession, on the word of one side or another; and if the police are publicly discredited their reputation, both with the public and with thieves, as a deterrent to them, is diminished.

The experience of special legislation is disheartening. The declaratory aspect of the law is valuable in the sphere of public morality, but if the public reject the concept behind it no amount of legislation will help. Until recently, looted antiquities came into this category, partly because for the dealer and the buyer the offence does not appear an absolute one. What emerges from the ground, they say, is hardly theft at all.

Mussolini's decree of June 1939 is probably the best-known attempt to create a new crime and thereby to educate the public.[1] It forbids (for it is still in force) the export of anything that can be classified as part of the national patrimony, except where a licence is granted by the Ministry of Fine Arts. The penalties are fines, graded according to the offence; and the law covers both works of art and antiquities. One result has been to make the value of every-thing artistic inside Italy highly artificial, since in most cases fine paintings or *objets d'art* can be bought openly only by others resident in the country. In the underworld, it has failed to check the trade in stolen art and antiquities, which has flourished in the last five years. As a fiscal measure, the law has come under attack because it demands an export tax of thirty per cent. The International Court of Justice at the Hague has therefore defined it as a customs duty, and the Common Market Commission objects to it as a breach of Market rules. Hardly a deterrent, it strikes hardest at the honest, those who apply for licences or fall within its ambit through no fault of their own. Such was the American woman who bought two French paintings in a sale in Florence, for a trivial sum. They were both signed by Chardin. Disbelieving, she took them to the experts at the Uffizi, who verified them as genuine. Now, the law allows the state

183

to buy in pictures intended for export at cost price. The officials apologised: but these were required for the Uffizi's rather meagre French collection; and they duly reimbursed the unlucky buyer with her money – £200.

After many years of haphazard attempts to enforce the law, the Ministry of Fine Arts has recently fired off a salvo of accusations, the most notable being against Baron Heinrich Thyssen-Bornemitza, who had bought in Switzerland in 1965 two fine early Italian paintings for his private museum. They had been on view there for four years before the Italian authorities, pursuing a warrant from the State Attorney in Florence, accused him of complicity in smuggling. It is fairly certain that the pictures were smuggled into Switzerland; the question lies in the bona-fides of the sale. Thyssen showed a bland disregard for the attempts to put pressure on him, even though the case was set down for trial in Florence, for this law can achieve little in a Swiss or any other court if the paintings were actually sold legitimately by the original owner.

Police and other authorities outside Italy are usually unsympathetic. For instance, in October 1970 the British Foreign Office was asked to check that Scotland Yard had actually attempted to recover works of art supposedly stolen in Milan. But were they stolen? The British police believed that they had simply evaded the 1939 law – that the owner had smuggled them out and that, under British law, the new owner had a perfect title.

The Foreign Office gave a polite but firm refusal. To have acceded might have required British legislation and would certainly have upset the London art market. The Italians then claimed that, since the pictures in question had been resold in Europe, British law on export had been evaded. Not so, came the answer: a painting brought into Britain and re-exported within fifty years does not need any licence.

A somewhat different response was made in the celebrated case of the Raphael acquired by the Boston Museum of Fine Arts. On 15th December 1969 the museum director announced with glee, at a press conference, that the museum had "discovered" a previously unknown Raphael of great beauty, which it was about to display. The small, delicate portrait of a young girl, Eleonora Gonzaga, or possibly Maria della Rovere, in a rich dress, wearing jewels and a curious gold head-dress, had been painted by Raphael about the year 1505. Although it was reported as coming from "an old European collection", the director later told the *New York Times* that it had come from "an elderly private collector in Switzerland, who, as he is nearing eighty, had expressed a wish that his favourite painting should go to some great institution where the public could appreciate the beauty of Raphael".

Fine sentiments indeed, not shared by Rodolfo Siviero, who read the reports in Rome, where the existence of the painting, though not well known, was recorded by several scholars. Commissioned from Raphael by Pope Julius II, it had passed into the Fieschi collection and had last been seen in 1947, when sold to a Genoese dealer. Records of this transaction had been lost but, working on the theory that the frame, which Boston claimed to be the original, was a later copy (nineteenth-century records showed that the two had been separated), Siviero tracked down first the frame-carver, and then the dealer, Ferruccio Bossi – then aged eighty-five. When first confronted, Bossi suggested that he had bought the frame and used it for the portrait of a young girl, but years before, and not for a portrait of great merit. Then the police found that Bossi had a criminal record, with a conviction for smuggling under the 1939 law, for which he had been banned from dealing in Italy. Finally, he admitted that he had known the portrait was a Raphael: he had offered it to many museums, asking £1 million. All but one refused, assuming that the Ministry of Fine Arts would never give it a licence. He had sold it to Boston, he said, in July 1969.

Bossi died in May 1970, while the inquiries were still proceeding. The question of how the picture and its frame were taken out of Italy remains obscure. Siviero found out that Boston had insisted on an independent assessment, and that an expert had visited Genoa in 1969 and had authenticated the picture. The final price was alleged to be $1·5 million. The offence was flagrant and the Italian government were more or less bound to act. They asked for the Raphael to be sequestrated and the U.S. Customs complied – a decision that must be seen in the light of Turkish protests about the gold treasure put on view by the Boston Museum, the UNESCO draft convention that was then in preparation, and also the political circumstances of the first state visit to Washington of the new Italian

Premier. Finally, in September 1971, the U.S. Treasury ordered the return of the Raphael, to the bitter astonishment, and substantial loss, of the museum.

What is most important here is the fact that the U.S. Customs did act, although they had no more than a technical excuse: the museum's failure to declare the import of the Raphael. A change of public attitudes may be on the way, evident at the UNESCO Conference in Paris in January 1971, when the United States and a dozen other countries voted in favour of the convention outlawing illicit export of antiquities. Under the terms of the convention it would become possible for any member country to secure the extradition of a work of art that had been illegally exported. None of the legislatures of the countries concerned has yet ratified the convention, but if and when they do (remembering that it took from 1960 to 1971 to get the draft prepared) it will have the force of international law. The part that the affair of the Boston Museum and many other cases played in awakening the public conscience is reflected in the convention document itself: "Museums as cultural institutions should ensure that their collections are built up in accordance with universally recognised moral principles." If the vultures' diet really does change, the voices of Mexico, Spain, Italy, Peru, Zaire and Turkey will at last have been heard as well. But all this illustrates the limits of legislation: it will do very little to check theft, except of ancient art; and it does nothing to convict the thieves that the police arrest.

Those who look to the courts tend therefore to demand exemplary sentences and applaud judges who, as in the case of the Sir John Soane Museum robbery in April 1969, make their position clear: "This sort of offence must be discouraged . . . whether the people who take part in it are rich unscrupulous art dealers or people who form the necessary link in the chain of disposing of property of this enormous value." But even then, where the famous Watteau *Les Noces* was involved, the two caught in possession by the police trap were given only three years' imprisonment. The Theft Act, 1968, provides for a maximum sentence of ten years for theft, and fourteen for robbery with violence. In the U.S.A., the maximum is ten years. Art theft scarcely ever seems to merit half these terms, and in Italy and France receiving is normally punished by fines –

which are scarcely more than a turnover tax on established criminals.

Modern criminologists tend to disparage the supposed deterrent effect of long prison sentences where areas of very high cash reward are concerned. From this study of the art-theft field, it would appear that the only effective reform would be to alter, generally, the law relating to the title of whoever buys the stolen object. While it could hardly affect the final private client (unless he were offered an obviously suspicious bargain), it might create unease among those dealers who buy now at one or two removes from the receiver.

At present, the law of title is different in almost every country considered in this book. The Austrian police were justifiably proud when, in October 1968, they at last arrested a gang who had been milking castles and churches all over the country since the previous July. There had been no pattern to their thefts: eighty antique weapons from the Forchtenstein castle, home of the Esterhazy family, altar-pieces from churches, carpets and clocks from less exalted houses. The leader turned out to be a coal merchant, employing half a dozen professional thieves, who operated in fast cars, equipped with two-way radio. Caught red-handed loading the contents of Schloss Sebenstein, they admitted guilt and told the police that everything had been taken across the frontier to a German dealer living in Switzerland. At this point the real difficulties began. The receiver had sold nearly everything to private Swiss collectors, either directly or through an equally crooked colleague, who had a side-line in renting squalid flats at high rents to immigrant Italian workers – themselves a profitable source of stolen property from Italy. By Swiss law a bona-fide purchase from a registered dealer gives absolute title to property, even if the dealer himself knows the property to be stolen. Consequently the Austrian owners had no claim in Switzerland beyond the small amount recovered from the receivers. Many of the private buyers offered to return the works, but, reasonably enough, only if they were reimbursed. Unfortunately, the Austrian state and church property had not been fully insured, and the Ministry of the Interior and the Archbishop of Vienna would not, or could not, find the money. Even what the receivers held was sequestrated by the Swiss authorities, pending the trial; and the rest – including some exceptionally fine late-Gothic church statuary and seventeenth-century tapestries – will remain legitimately in Switzerland. On the other hand, the coal merchant got eight years in jail: police triumph, individual loss.

Another instance of a case involving title can be found in the postscript of one of the Riviera robberies in 1961. Armand Drouant's pictures were recovered after the sort of legal imbroglio typical of the disposal of stolen works of art. The thieves tried to sell to a Milanese businessman who asked an expert what value they were. The expert was Drouant himself. The police set a trap but failed, and the pictures were sold instead to a dealer in second-hand cars, in settlement of a debt. The police interrogated him but he disappeared, having already resold the pictures, through a go-between, to a Genoese dealer, who exhibited them in Milan. The Italian Ministry of Fine Art intervened and prohibited re-export, since the Genoese could prove that he had bought them in good faith. Drouant sued, but litigation dragged on for over a year. The dealer then sold the pictures to another dealer in Nice for $11,200. He tried several ways to deliver them, finally by boat; but they were seized in Nice harbour on 9th December 1964 by court officials acting on behalf of Drouant. The Genoese suffered, because he had not been paid and, having offended against Italian law, could hardly claim his money in those courts.

Under German law, however, the buyer never acquires title, and nor do his decendants, unless he bought the object at public auction. If it were traced to his possession, he would have to restore it and take civil action to recover his loss from the dealer or individual from whom he bought it. These are the poles; in between lies great variety. In Belgium, under Section 2280 of the Penal Code, purchase from a legitimate (i.e. a registered) dealer or at any public sale[2] gives title.

In Britain, title is secure to the buyer, but the vendor is open to prosecution unless the thing is sold, under ancient French law, in the "open markets", the Bermondsey and the Caledonian markets in London. In Italy, however, the onus is on the buyer to prove his innocence: he must produce evidence of bona-fide purchase if he wants to retain the right to compensation.

The importance of these distinctions lies not in their historical significance, nor in the division between Roman and English common law, but in the likely location of the eventual buyer. The cases that can be documented right through indicate that the most frequent resting places for stolen goods are those countries whose laws most strongly defend the institution of private property: Switzerland, Britain, Belgium, Holland and the United States. If a rich European or an American decides whether to buy a suspiciously cheap masterpiece, it will not escape his sophisticated calculations to take into account whether the laws of his home state or country will or will not support his acquisition. Otherwise there may be a very embarrassing scene when he presents the painting to his local museum or sells it to pay for his own retirement.

If, however, he is in any doubt, it pays him to buy the painting in another country, for in this field international law is at a disadvantage. Say, for example, a statue, stolen from Germany, where the laws are strict, turns up in France. The German authorities will have to ask the French to seize it as evidence; and they must then settle down to discover whether the case is subject to German or French law. That may take a long time. The case of Fidel Castro's "secret treasure", for example, is still *sub judice*. According to a rich exile from Cuba, Señor Loba Olavarria, a shipload of religious and artistic objects (mainly altar plate and private collections, sequestrated after the Cuban revolution) was sent for sale in Europe in June 1965. Olavarria and members of the self-styled Recovery Committee blocked the sale by injunctions and the parties have settled down to what promises to be a generation of litigation.

The difficulties encountered in attempting to restore stolen things to their owners when they *are* found are legion. It may not even be possible to decide who is the original owner. A van Dyck belonging to a man prominent in Viennese society was reported stolen in August 1969. The German police later recovered the painting, and, before returning it, asked for proof of ownership. Naturally, the Austrian police asked a few questions. The van Dyck had been in the family for generations – but the man's wife denied this. Eventually it turned out to have been a present from a friend who did not know its value. Later the two had agreed to sell it through a third party, the "thief", and split the profit and, presumably, the insurance; but even the final story left the police in considerable doubt about whom to prosecute, if anyone, or to whom to restore the painting.

Even when ownership is clear, returning objects across national frontiers can raise tricky legal and political problems. The two East German Dürers (see Chapter 8) have remained in New York since

1946, because no one can compel their restitution nor can the U.S. State Department arrange it on behalf of the East German government. The most protracted case is that of the three paintings stolen from the Grand Ducal Museum of Weimar in April 1922: a Rembrandt self-portrait, painted in 1663 and fully authenticated by Dr Jacob Rosenberg, a portrait by Ter Borch, and another. Nothing was heard until 1934, when a German-born resident of Dayton, Ohio, met some German seamen in New York. They offered him the pictures and, after a night on the town, the man found himself without his wallet but in possession of the canvases. He hid them at home. Later he married, and his wife, suspecting the pictures were valuable, did some research. In 1946 she took them to the Dayton Museum, where they were eventually recognised. But whose property were they now? Dayton kept them in the vaults until, in February 1947, the United States Bureau of Alien Property vested them (under the Trading with the Enemy Act) in the possession of the U.S. government – despite the fact that they had been stolen nearly twenty years before America declared war, and discovered after it was over.

This Act was annulled in 1952, and the Bureau began to dispose of its acquisitions by sale. What was not in question for the private property of German citizens, however, was quite different for the property of a museum. The State Department worried; yet under the law it could do nothing. Eventually, in 1966, two bills were introduced, one in the Senate and one in Congress, to amend the Act: not, sadly, to permit the paintings to go back to Weimar, now in East Germany, but to the Federal Republic, "for eventual transfer to the Weimar Museum, state of Thuringia, Germany, etc., etc.", after a hypothetical German reunification. Reasons of state lay behind such persistence with special legislation: perhaps the State Department really has a conscience and would like to restore the Rembrandt to its home if it could, just as officials are rumoured to be seeking ways of handing back the crown of St Stephen to the Hungarian government.

No one wants to resort to the ponderous and expensive machinery of the law of whatever country unless there is no other resort. It can be most embarrassing to have paintings withdrawn from a sale-room by court order, or seized, like a Winslow Homer water-colour, from a display in a Long Island gallery by two deputy sheriffs armed *cap à pie*. But even if it were, by international law, accepted that no title can ever be established to a stolen work of art, time sets its own statute of limitations: the British Museum showed no qualms in buying, in 1971, a small silver seal of Isabella of Hainault, Queen of France from 1180 to 1190, which had been stolen from the Cathedral Treasury of Notre Dame, Paris, in August 1860.[3] Perhaps the only answer to those who object to new legislation, or the UNESCO convention, would be for the new statutes to run only from the present. Even so, it is doubtful whether the double market could be crippled in less than twenty years.

The alternatives that have been suggested are expensive, time-wasting and, if they involve increasing the powers of the police, or the routine work of surveillance, unappetising. It is true that in a small country like Belgium, or one where antique dealing is not highly developed, a register of dealers and their transactions may help in checking theft. France, which possesses 15,000 dealers, 2,000 of whom operate in Paris and 1,000 in the Flea Market alone, has also made the experiment; a new scheme was introduced by a decree of August 1968 under which all fine-art dealers (as opposed to *brocanteurs*, who include even scrap merchants) must register every single purchase they make where the value is over 500 francs.

The form to be filled in reads as follows:

DATE de L'ACHAT ou du DEPOT	NOM, Prénoms, Surnoms PROFESSION et DOMICILE du VENDEUR ou du DEPOSANT	NATURE et NUMERO de la PIECE D'IDENTITE présentée Indication de l'autorité qui l'a délivrée
	NATURE et DESCRIPTION DES MARCHANDISES (marque, style, qualité, éventuellement dimensions, teinte etc. . . .) (pour les véhicules automobiles: marque, type, numéro d'ordre dans la série du type, couleur)	PRIX D'ACHAT en toutes lettres

These registers are automatically open to police inspection. As yet it is too early to know whether the practice has succeeded in checking the operations of receiver-dealers. The fines for *not* registering a piece are not very high, and one must presume that, if caught with a stolen object, the receiver would plead forgetfulness, or ignorance of the law. A total of 2,000 shops or stalls in Paris alone presents a field almost beyond the powers of any police force to inspect. How much harder would it be in Britain, where the number of dealers is half as many again, or in Italy, where the police say, "Everyone is a 'fence' today, even accountants and dentists."

Siviero demands greater power, heavier fines and swingeing prison sentences, as well as the registration by dealers of all objects in their possession. "To close the gaps we need adequate legislation", he said in a recent interview. "Drug peddling was cut back by anti-drug squads. We cannot hope to succeed in the fight against art thieves unless we have all this, and special police teams".

But who will recruit them, and who will pay? Say that each of the 2,000 dealers in Paris has, on average, 100 objects worth over 500 francs in his possession at any one time. Multiply this by all the cities and provincial towns in Europe; what computer would take such records? Would these descriptions, even accompanied by all the paraphernalia of photographs and measurements, assist in identifying a single piece? How can a police force, however well trained, hope by random searches to do more than put receiver-dealers slightly more on the defensive? The open market itself would hardly take kindly to such surveillance. The Swiss, being peculiarly law-abiding and respectful towards authority, do not seem to resent the recording and filing of their transactions, but one can imagine the reactions elsewhere, not only of tax-conscious investors, but of private collectors offended by state interference.

Certainly, there are strong arguments for giving police forces more control over the often wayward and anti-social behaviour of some insurance companies. In London, ransom deals appear to have been checked since the affairs described in Chapter 7; but neither Scotland Yard nor the F.B.I. have any actual power to prevent the offer of rewards. In Italy the police try to handle all recovery payments between the authorities and the informers, but no one would claim they succeed any better than the French Police Judiciaire did with the missing Cézannes in 1961. Only in Germany does there appear to be a reciprocal understanding: most insurance companies require owners to prove that they have reported losses to the police, as well as to them – a fairly obvious precaution against fraud, but one frequently neglected. In many cases they will not pay out on the claim, let alone on the reward, without police agreement; and claims may equally be held back by the Prosecutor's Office. At an informal level, the Bundeskriminalamt has occasional conferences with the heads of German insurance companies, and they have begun to work out a system of graded payments for different classes of information: (1) payments for general or background information, relevant to art thefts but not to any particular cases; (2) payment for definite information on a particular case; (3) funds required for infiltrating agents into gangs; and (4) funds for the purchase of stolen property (usually from legitimate buyers) as evidence for criminal proceedings.

The basis of this tentative agreement is that the insurance companies collectively will be responsible for finding the money, but that the police alone will dispense it. Rewards would be carefully graded, the higher ones being paid only when recovery is followed by an arrest and conviction. It is by no means certain that the system will be put into practice permanently, for such an arrangement virtually destroys the main function of the insurance assessor; but if it does succeed then the ransom technique, as described earlier, will surely die. The model is certainly worth examining in other countries, not least in Great Britain; but it is open to two objections: it places greater power in the hands of the central police, which is not necessarily desirable, especially when the "intangible value" of a work of art is at stake; and, by formalising what is essentially an immoral practice (since most informants are themselves criminals), it does by rational compromise give a certain licence to the underworld.

Scotland Yard has recently suggested a total ban on the payment of rewards except where criminals are arrested *and* convicted. Most loss adjusters, only too well aware of the moral dilemma, would like to be let off this hook.[4] Until then, however, insurance companies' first reaction to a wave of art thefts is to raise premiums, chiefly on their private clients, since their other clients, museums and state collections, cannot be tapped excessively without suffering diminishing returns. Few, if any, museums insure all their contents to their full value against theft, since the premiums would be astronomical. A spokesman for the Louvre said in 1969, with splendid bravado, "*Bien entendu*, you can't put a monetary value on any painting in the Louvre. As far as insurance goes, any figure you might see in the press is pure fantasy. There is a clause in every insurance contract enjoining secrecy." It is just as well; the figure quoted is usually as high as the reality is low:[5] witness the provincial collections at Dulwich and St Tropez, both covered only against fire and damage. The Italian dealer Bruno Grossetti stated, after his gallery in Milan had been robbed in September 1970, that the paintings were not covered "because the cost of premiums is absolutely insupportable. The most important galleries could spend tens of millions [of lire] a year. Much better install electric alarms, or, as I think, have a guard or security officer twenty-four hours a day – that would cost only 300,000 lire a month."

Lack of insurance cover may be a sort of deterrent against ransom but not against the double market, and, unless the cost of cover is overwhelming, the private collector is ill-advised to ignore it. Insurance companies can do a great deal to help their clients, quite apart from giving them "peace of mind"; and in the process they can reduce their own losses and the scope of thieves.

The first step *should* – because by no means all companies insist on it – be to request an adequate description of any object with a value of over £500: measurements, identifying marks, and, above all, photographs. These records are the basis of any recovery operation and the practice of keeping them ought to be made mandatory, as it is already in Austria,[6] where they must be supplied before the company can legally accept the risk. If, for tax reasons[7] or avoidance of death duties, the client objects, then they ought to ignore him: they are not in business to compound evasion. Insistence on proper records is no more than enlightened self-interest, serving to cut down the free flow of stolen works and to prevent more flagrant forms of insurance fraud.

Safeguarding a museum presents no insuperable problems. In practice, however, it is far easier to secure the great endowed state collections of European capitals than the monastic treasure of a poor convent in Southern Italy. The price of full security in an age of technological innovation is high. Some museums, housed in antiquated buildings with badly fitting windows and easily scaled walls, are like great fat carcasses tied up waiting for the tiger. Yet even these have advantages over the more exposed private collector: opening hours restrict legitimate access, paid guards patrol the corridors, and, in the last resort, governments will probably bail them out. After the loss of the Goya *Duke of Wellington*, for example, an almost panicky examination of internal security at museums and galleries was ordered by the British government, and the fallout of improvements reached most provincial collections.

The Rijksmuseum in Amsterdam suffered an irreparable loss when Rembrandt's vast and macabre canvas, *The Anatomy Lesson*, was burnt by an insane student. Only the centre part, fire blackened, remained. Guards now stand around like secret police, blank-faced but effective, and visitors are stripped of cameras, briefcases and even overcoats. Similar precautions followed the loss of the *Studies of a Negro Head* in Brussels; and Interpol took the occasion of a conference of museum directors in 1962 to urge the audience to check all systems, record everything, weed out aged, sedentary guards, take special care during repair works, and to give no details to the press.

In the last ten years, museum security has grown highly specialised; guards watch automatically for particular risks, at opening and closing times, or during repairs. Scaffolding against an outside wall is almost an invitation to a thief and small objects and pictures, being most at risk, need to be specially secured. Science steps in with closed circuit television, ultra-violet and infra-red beams, photo-electric cells, magnetic fields and what one American museum describes as "a seismo-electronic beam of unprecedented sensitivity". Ultrasonic waves are disturbed by any movement in a room, once the pulsator has been switched on. Trap boxes fitted to the back of the picture can produce any variety of alarm, from a high pitched buzz to a bang like a shot-gun's. Chemical sprays scatter stain onto a thief's clothes or blind him with smoke. An "art mat" – two layers of foil separated by a thin piece of foam rubber, which makes contact and sets off the alarm when an object is lifted or if the wires are cut – can be fitted to almost any piece on display, and can now be run off 12-volt current so that it remains effective even if the mains fail. By night the system can be wired to the nearest police station, and by day the alarm can automatically seal all the exits.

The best of these devices are theoretically fool-proof, and any museum with adequate resources should, by second nature, fit them. Yet, *Rififi* and *Topkapi* are not just idle exercises in ingenuity. Beams, even scanners, can be avoided, and criminals know, too, that some museums would rather claim precautions than spend the money to buy them. Cost-conscious until too late, the staff may take the cheapest quotation from a security firm in preference to the expensive best. Even the most sophisticated device may not work properly, or activate in a thunderstorm or in a sudden change of humidity. One French museum installed a machine that was so sensitive that it rang because a cloud had passed over the moon. There are other security risks: underpaid or discontented members of staff may talk too freely, or simply sell information. Co-operation with the police may be a source of conflict: the police want the alarm to go off not in the museum, but at headquarters, so that the thieves can be caught in the act; museum directors, fearful for their treasures, want the alarm to scare them away. The usual compromise, a few-minute gap between the external signal and the alarm, has the worst of both worlds, for the police tend to arrive just as the thief vanishes.

All security decisions are compromises. The National Museum of Panama, for example, had no lack of good advice. Wealthy Panamanians sat on the board of trustees, together with Americans from the Canal Zone. To guard their pre-Colombian gold treasure, they studied a variety of methods and finally settled on a steel case, six feet by six by two and a half, fronted with a door of safety glass one inch thick. No one could carry it away. Unfortunately the committee failed to ensure the safety of the outside windows, so that when the thieves came they had a whole night to chip at the glass with pick-axes and diamond cutters until they had smashed a hole wide enough to pick out everything with a long, flexible pair of tongs.

Over ninety per cent of absolute security should be the minimum aim of any museum. But outside Western Europe and North America the standard is far lower. In 1967, the authorities in Cairo staged an exhibition of paintings on Gezireh Island and promptly lost a Rubens. It was found near the Pyramids, after the director had received a letter pointing out, in the most outraged terms, just how lax his security was. Yet even in London as recently as February 1970, and despite all the recriminations after the theft of the Goya, lack of security lost the National Gallery a thirteenth-century Italian primitive, *Virgin and Child with Two Angels*. It had lain in a shallow box to protect the surface and was replaced with a notice saying "Temporarily Removed". Only then did the gallery admit that, after the earlier security review, they had decided that during the daytime they would protect only a few selected masterpieces, rather than spend a large part of their pitifully low annual grant on total precautions.

Such a decision is difficult to make, especially when the gallery is under much greater political and public pressure to lay out funds for new acquisitions or "to save for the nation" a major work in danger of export. £450,000 (the National Gallery's annual grant) goes hardly anywhere in competition with American institutions and collectors, and, against the argument that the opportunity to save a particular masterpiece will never recur, it is hard to argue for the priority of things that can equally easily be done next year. All expenditure on defence, from locks to guided missiles, is inherently unpopular. Hence the introduction of schemes for renting the newest forms of protection. For a flat payment of £300 a room, or a rental of £36 a year, one firm in Britain offers protection twenty-four hours a day.

If museum authorities really are indolent, sanctions can be used against them. In 1966 the Italian government ordered all smaller state and private museums to overhaul their security. The Ministry of Education made it the responsibility of local officials in charge of the national patrimony to report what had been done. If government experts were not then satisfied, exhibits in private museums would be declared state property, and those already in the care of the state would be withdrawn and exhibited elsewhere.

It is too early yet to know whether there was any intention actually to enforce this Draconian edict. Failing government intervention, the withdrawal of private patronage may serve. Avery Brundage, the elderly Chicago industrialist, once controversial president of the Olympic Games Committee, was uneasy at the lack of precautions taken by the San Francisco Art Museum to safeguard a collection that he had loaned them, and he threatened to remove it and donate it elsewhere unless his own security recommendations were carried out, at a cost of half a million dollars. This covered the appointment of more guards, humidity control equipment, an endowment fund, with a final target of $5 million, for the care of the collection, and the appointment of an independent committee to "advise" the directors. At the expense of the city, the money was duly voted and the collection made secure; and no one seems to have questioned the social priorities of those who voted in favour.

Whether or not museums are as secure as they appear, they present few calls on police resources, except during the transport of loan exhibitions like the treasures of Tutankhamun's tomb. Much more debatable is the extent to which the responsibility of safeguarding works of art can be thrown back on the private owner. To ask a theoretical question: how far is it his duty to provide adequate precautions, and what claim has he on the authorities to enforce the law of property if he has not taken them himself?

To a very large extent, "normal" theft of antiques could be cut down by owners themselves, and it does not require an especially radical turn of mind to envisage the use of scarce police time, in defence of property that has been lost partly through negligence, becoming a charge on either owners or the insurance company that failed to insist on proper security. An art-theft squad properly organised, equipped and, if need be, financed is the only effective way to check the operations of the double market; yet since virtually no police force outside the totalitarian countries runs at its theoretical full strength, it is a luxury to second able detectives – and the less able are of no use – to a specialist branch. Commissioners and Chiefs of Police tend to allow it only when the crimes and public outcry make an overriding case for doing so. Hence the existence of only one permanent *Sonderkommission* in Germany; of a small over-worked office in Scotland Yard; of a single officer with responsibility for art theft for the whole of Vienna.

In the past, the initiative for cajoling and warning private owners has usually come from the police, but however much they, or interested government departments, may, through broadcasts, television or door-to-door visits, urge collectors to fit mortice and window locks and take elementary care,[8] they cannot *compel* people to look after themselves. But if the owner knows that he cannot get insurance cover unless he does take precautions, and that if he doesn't and is robbed his claim will be met only in part, or not at all if he has not locked his locks,[9] then the onus lies on him. *Caveat possessor.* For once, social justice is served by such an attitude, for it is usually the well-to-do who are thus called on to help themselves.

Commissioner La Vallette of Marseilles was not joking when he said, of the St Tropez affair, "After all, it was not a case of murder." While there is no police force that could not improve its methods, given more money and more men, there are a dozen higher priorities than recovering stolen art. Prevention must start with the potential loser rather than with illusions that the double market can be broken *after* the loss occurs. Security firms, ranging from Pinkerton's to Securicor, offer patrols, permanent trained watchmen, guard dogs (which thieves hate) and useful advice, most of which is surprisingly cheap: a twenty-four hour trained guard, with a contact system to his headquarters, rarely costs more than £1 per hour. A firm such as Chubbs, oldest and most experienced of locksmiths, will provide the mechanics to suit the house or the owner's purse. One of the finest devices available is the standing safe, which has bolts on all four edges of the doors. It is too large to carry out of the house and greatly frustrates the thief, who, with great trouble, saws through the hinges, only to find the door as secure as before he began.

Significantly, most of the police who retire from art squads give their experience to private clients. Joseph M. Chapman, formerly of the F.B.I., is now a security consultant for several dealers, museums and insurance companies; Chief Superintendent Garrard is loss-prevention officer at Lloyds, and Sotheby's employ Frank Cunningham, formerly of Scotland Yard. The services of such men and firms, if properly used, give as great a protection as is possible, remembering that anything short of turning one's house into a bank vault must be a compromise between enjoyment of possession and total security.

Private collectors are not the only ones to have to face their responsibilities. In May 1970, the Vatican ordered a world-wide census to be taken of the treasures of all Catholic churches and religious houses, and warned that any person selling without authorisation would lose his office and risk excommunication. Cardinal John Wright, head of the Sacred Congregation, declared at the time, "The faithful are pained to see today, more than in the past, so many illegal sales, thefts, so much usurpation and destruction of the churches' historic and artistic heritage." Bishops were instructed to ensure that all parishes drew up full inventories of their possessions, and the services of experts were to be used in cataloguing, describing and valuing. The survey is expected to take several years.[10]

One should not complain too much that the order might have been given ten years earlier. Even a body so closely interested as C.I.N.O.A. (Confédthat the order Internationale des Négociants en Oeuvres d'Art) waited until its fourth congress in Florence, in September 1969, before touching on the subject. "Worried by multiplication of art thefts" they concentrated on two remedies: better description and recording of works of art, and tighter control of national frontiers. Since their own members felt increasingly under attack, C.I.N.O.A., to the pleasure of their guest speaker, Rodolfo Siviero, recommended them all to liaise more closely with their own national police forces and insurance companies.

By then it was eleven years since UNESCO had first debated ways of protecting museums and passing on to their staffs relevant technical information. In 1965, one volume of *The Museum*, quarterly publication of the International Council of Museums, was given over to details of the most modern ultrasonic devices, automatic flash cameras to record a thief's appearance, trap boxes and chemical sprays. Wearily, however, the report concluded:

> The present study reveals no information that would endanger the security of museums against theft, but is simply designed as a compilation of first principles and basic information. The information has long been thoroughly familiar to the thief who keeps abreast with all developments in this field.

No one, save a millionaire recluse, like Paul Getty at Sutton Place, can prevent the *expert* thief, all the time. Good advice, sensible care and liaison with the police can greatly cut down the risk. If a collector or a museum loses to a casual thief, in a simple breaking and entering job, then the fault should be the owner's. Without precautions, the owners of property have no great claim on the services of the state. When they have, they should expect the full use of the law to smash the practice of ransom and the double market at all points.

Notes

1 In Spain, Articles 7 and 9 of the law of September 1953 prohibit the unauthorised export of works of art. This was promulgated by General Franco, after a period in which the government had become alarmed at the number of private sales by noble families impoverished as a result of the Civil War. The code provides for licensing of exports by the Fine Arts Department of the Ministry of Education. It has been operated sporadically. One notable case concerned an American dealer who took out a painting by Goya and was fined $100,000 after a trial *in absentia*, which took three years to prepare. Ponderous and easy to evade, the law cannot be said to have done more than slow the illegitimate export traffic. Theft hardly comes into the picture.

2 For this reason, the Belgian police vet public sales carefully. Commissioner Lues once inspected a big house sale in 1966; but the vendor produced a sheaf of sales receipts showing that he had bought nearly all the 246 lots within the previous year in London. It was a put-up job, familiar enough in Britain but rare on the continent, where the glamour of a "country-house" sale is used to enhance prices.

3 Shortly after this event, Lancing College put in for sale at Sotheby's a twelfth-century manuscript. Written on it in a fourteenth-century Latin hand was the message "This belongs to Salisbury Cathedral". The cathedral authorities objected to the sale, though they were somewhat vague as to the date of loss: somewhere between 1622 and 1670 seemed probable. Leaving them to argue it out, Sotheby's said, sardonically, "We are satisfied that this is the property of Lancing College. It is not the only manuscript from Salisbury Cathedral library to be elsewhere; a number are in the Bodleian at Oxford. If everyone claimed ownership of books and manuscripts that were in their possession centuries ago, half the libraries in the world would have to return many of their books."

4 At the time this suggestion was made, in July 1970, a spokesman

for the London loss adjusters said, "Any proposal that would eliminate payment before conviction would be welcomed by many adjusters."

5 Figures are hard to come by, but, in 1963, sources in the American insurance world estimated that in the previous year, 1962, $4,108,000 were spent on insurance of works of art by individuals in the United States, but only $2,119,000 by museums and dealers together. The total figure had been rising steadily during the previous ten years, but, in a country with astonishingly rich museums and some of the biggest dealers in the world, the latter figure was remarkably low.

6 The central archive of the Österreiches Bundesdenkmalamt houses a collection of photographs and descriptions of major works of art in most public and private collections, and the task of completing the survey of churches has now nearly finished. With the development of computers, similar projects for larger and wealthier nations are brought within the bounds of possibility – though at the C.I.N.O.A. Conference in Florence in 1969, the UNESCO scheme for registering all items within the national patrimony was dismissed as "utopian".

7 One of the complications of taxation law concerns capital gains tax, principally in Britain, where the rate is thirty per cent on the profit, taken from a base line of 1965, or from the most recent transfer of ownership, on all objects worth over £1,000. If the object is stolen, capital gains tax is payable on the insurance payment as if the object had been sold. Thus, if a Canaletto, worth £25,000, vanishes, the owner may not be able to replace it with something of equivalent merit, even though he had no intention of selling the original. The catch is that, under the existing law, he cannot insure for the excess, because that would be either to over-insure the picture, or to compound tax evasion – both of which are illegal!

8 Every European and American police force has an advisory bureau for museum security, which also offers advice to private collectors. Most of them, unfortunately, rely on the public to request help, thereby reaching only the already enlightened. Usually it takes a wave of particular crimes – châteaux in France, castle armouries in Germany, country-house silver in Britain – before they take the initiative.

9 As, for example, insurance companies already do with motor cars that infringe the laws on tyres and maintenance standards.

10 In Greece, the military régime ordered, in 1969, a similar survey of the treasures and manuscripts of the monasteries of Mount Athos, but with less success. The monks reacted furiously, fearing that their peculiar isolation was threatened and that the central government might remove the best things to state museums. Above all, they feared intrusion of foreigners as being a moral danger to an already declining community. (Not for nothing has the Greek hierarchy incorporated a prayer into the liturgy to ward off the plague of tourists, who threaten to undermine the traditional values and relationships of their society.)

Chapter 11 Archaeological Theft

When receivers transfer their attention to new categories of artistic objects, it may be because old long-term sources have become too heavily protected or because of a shift in customers' demands. The wave pattern, discernible since the late 1950s, suggests a restless, protean aspect in the double market. Within the last seven years, there has developed a rash of losses of manuscripts and rare books from libraries and institutions – once a field in which only occasional scholars and bibliophiles turned to genteel, almost imperceptible crime.

When cat burglars broke open the glass case containing the finest of 50,000 manuscripts in the Apostolic Library of the Vatican, in November 1965, they publicised a new field for thieves. They took two manuscripts: the *Cansoniere* of Petrarch (1304–72), seventy-two parchment pages of sonnets and love lyrics, mostly in his own handwriting; and a book of poems by Torquato Tasso (1544–96), some in his own hand and others corrected by him. "It is impossible to put a value on them," library officials said. "They are worth whatever an unscrupulous collector may be willing to pay for them." The details cried out the commissioned crime: expert technique, knowledge of the corridor between the Sistine Chapel and the Borgia apartments, and the fact that equally rare manuscripts by Aquinas, Michelangelo and Galileo were ignored.

These thieves may well have worked to the orders of a bibliophile or dealer. Already in 1964, a series of manuscripts that had been stolen over a twenty-year period from a church in Saragossa in Spain was discovered by a Spanish scholar in the library of Yale

University. The thief had passed them to a dealer, who sold to another unsuspecting colleague in the trade, who sold to Yale. Many European collections housed in libraries were highly vulnerable, often being only partly catalogued, and the access given to scholars proved a grievous temptation when set against the widespread publicity given in the 1960s to high prices paid across the Atlantic. The sums that were laid out for manuscripts of living artists by, for example, the University of Texas, seem to have inspired the raid, in March 1969, on the London publisher John Murray, from where £25,000-worth of Byron manuscripts, including his last diary, as well as contemporary letters by Queen Victoria, Darwin, Dickens and Browning, were taken. Six months later, after a tip from the rare-book trade, all this was recovered in a North London cemetery, at the moment of handover to a prospective buyer.

Losses have multiplied since. The Vatican was robbed again, of a unique illustrated volume describing the setting-up of the obelisk of Pope Sixtus V in 1590; the Bodleian library at Oxford lost two pages (worth at least £1,000 each) illuminated by the del Foà brothers of Florence for the edition of Pliny's *Natural History* in 1476. One of the worst cases occurred in Buenos Aires, where an Argentine collector's flat in the Avenida Callao was ransacked. A marvellous collection of books from the presses of Venice and south Germany in the 1470s and 1480s was taken, these having formerly belonged to the famous library of Dr Jorge Auerestein. Few of them were worth less than £1,000 on the open market. Ransom theft has reached out even to this sphere: in 1971 an American university was nearly robbed of a copy of the immensely rare Gutenberg Bible, on which the thief intended to claim the insurance.

But the area of most recent growth has proved to be disposal of treasures looted from archaeological sites, and, since the traffic goes through and augments the double market, it is worth mention. Wherever ancient civilisations that laid out their dead with presents for the nether world flourished, tomb robbers have been at work for centuries. This has taken place in Greece, Turkey, Italy and Egypt, and in Latin America since the Spanish and Portuguese explorers of the sixteenth century. But the present, organised business of looting has despoiled more in the last twenty years than in all previous history. To take a single case: when the Peruvian police uncovered a smuggling ring in April 1971, they calculated that the gang had been responsible for the illegal export of more than 2,000 pieces of pre-Colombian art, mainly gold ornaments and pottery worth at least £1 million on the foreign market. They arrested an official of the Archaeological Monuments Section in Lima, together with a Swiss receiver and half a dozen Peruvian agents. The organisation they found had been trading almost openly, circulating coloured slides of particularly fine pieces to agents and customers in Europe and America. Some of the objects were the result of illegal digging, but a large part came from museum robberies similar to that of the National Museum of Panama.

Fashion in the West has steadily built up the artistic repute of Maya, Inca, Olmec, Toltec and all other cultures that flourished in South and Central America before Columbus, of the Khmer civilisation of Thailand, and the great ages of Indian art. However, venerating these objects for their artistic merit divorces them from their primarily religious context. Just as the saints from the Bavarian *feldkapellen* became menu holders, the Khmer Buddha's head is cut from its body and launched into the limbo of the commercial market of the United States. The loss is partly religious – as a Thai scholar complained, "We do not use Christian statues as ornaments nor crucifixes as hat stands in Bangkok" – and partly cultural. The artistic wealth of an under-developed country, unable to bid high enough to redeem its own heritage on the Western market, can never be replaced. Such is also the case in Nigeria, as regards the vanished Benin bronzes and the sculptures looted during the Biafran war.

Some collectors would argue that this is inevitable; that if Lord Elgin had not "stolen" the marble frieze from the Parthenon, it would long ago have disintegrated. Safe-keeping was the argument put forward by André Malraux, who fictionalised his experiences of hunting for ancient sculptures in Indo-China in 1923 in his novel *The Royal Way*. Depicting himself as the hero, Claude, he expressed, ironically enough, the illusion of Western identification with Eastern art:

> Thanks to the fallen statues, he was suddenly in harmony with the forest and the temple. He pictured the three stones as they had been, one above the other; the two dancing girls were some of the finest work he had ever seen. Well, the next thing was to load them onto the truck.

207

At the age of twenty-two, Malraux, deeply in debt, had obtained permission from the French colonial administration to explore an area containing the almost unknown temple of Banteay Srei, on the way to Angkor Wat in Cambodia. He discovered that though his saws soon blunted, he could topple uncemented *devates*, or guardians of the temple, with ropes. He and his wife smuggled them back to Phnom-Penh by river. Later, Malraux was arrested, convicted and sentenced to three years in jail; but on appeal, the sentence was commuted and finally suspended. The episode disgusted him with French colonialism and turned him towards a decade of revolutionary activities; yet it may also have served to preserve some of the best Khmer sculptures from later, less high-minded, thieves, for it jolted the French administration into taking rudimentary precautions. Malraux's statues were all returned to Banteay Srei in 1925, when the temples were cleared of vegetation and restored. As Clara Malraux recalled years afterwards, "Of course it was illegal, but no more so than for all those others who had Khmer heads in their houses."

From a few thousand dollars' worth of statuary a year in the period before 1939, the shipments to America and Europe had, by 1961, reached an estimated value of $600,000, only half of which went through official channels. Forgery, though skilfully done with the use of acid or by burying carvings for months in damp earth to give them the right colour, failed to fill the gap. Temples throughout South-East Asia have been ransacked with increasing ferocity. Altar-pieces have been pulled down, temple doors torn off and sawn up into decorative panels, rows of carved Buddhas have been decapitated, all for the stock of antique shops in Bangkok and the smugglers' route to the West.

After the magnificent carved and gilded sixteenth-century doors from Wat Pra Ngarm had been unhinged in 1961, the Thai authorities attempted to retaliate. Bangkok police swept through the storerooms of the local dealers and impounded 3,500 heads and statues of Buddha. Of all those, only a handful were recognised by the priests and restored; after holding the rest for three months, the police had to hand them back. Raids interrupted the traffic only for a moment. Given the attitude of the hordes of foreign officials, the United States military missions, embassies, representatives of international aid (each with a diplomatic privilege), and the fact that corruption is endemic, the law requiring export licences proved unenforceable. As Clifford Evans, of the Smithsonian Institute in Washington, told a symposium on "Looting the Past" in December 1971, in Cambodia, Turkey, India, Ecuador and Peru, "American diplomats and aid missions view cultural sites as places where they could go to picnic and loot while they were there." The Metropolitan Museum in New York has itself bought a rare bronze Thai Buddha for which no licence had been applied.

Eventually the Thai government brought in legislation designating all temples as national monuments, imposing regulations on every piece sold, and funding a proper national museum in order to take the better pieces off the market. But thousands of ancient sites lie in remote areas of jungle, and since Buddhists, whose objections to the traffic were primarily religious, believe that the statues lose all significance once they have been broken or moved from their niches, the incentive to protest is lacking. In 1965, some of the charges of embezzlement against the late premier, Field Marshal Thanarat, related to stolen Buddhas. The Bangkok expert, Thamay Myan, put the value of losses during 1968 at nearly half a million dollars, which figure takes no account of the loss of 518 statues in one raid on the unfortunate new National Museum. No sooner had the government begun to check the traffic in the jungle than it opened up more fiercely in the capital. What has happened since war engulfed Cambodia in 1970 cannot even be guessed at.

India suffers equally. According to Amdananda Gosh, Director-General of the national Archaeological Survey, looting of ancient sites is "a very serious business". Western demand, particularly for sculpture of the Gupta period, is reflected in high prices in the sale-rooms and expensive vandalism at home. In 1967, the complex of temples, dating from the tenth century, at Khajuraho in north-central India, was despoiled by thieves who took particular care to strip façades of erotic sculptures such as might have illustrated the *Kama Sutra* – republished in unexpurgated editions in Europe in the previous year.

In an interview reported in the *Washington Post* in November 1967, soon after the Nalanda Museum in Bihar had been robbed of seventh-century bronze figurines, Gosh said flatly, "We have about one thousand chokhidars [watchmen] to look after three thousand monuments. They are paid one hundred rupees [£5] a month. They are, let us say, careless." In other words, for a few rupees more, they avert their eyes. The big exporters in the cities have agents who recruit village labour to carry out the thefts. Some are carefully planned. It takes many men with saws, ropes and ladders to dismantle a figure twenty feet high. The authorities could double the guards, pay the customs men a better wage. But the government has other priorities – irrigation, advancement of new crop techniques and the avoidance of famines. It is not for the West, where the demand originates, to criticise India or South-East Asia, or countries like Zaire and the Ivory Coast, where the looters fly in by helicopter.

How far gangs of thieves are prepared to go to despoil the relics of ancient civilisation may be gauged from the experience of Mexican police since the introduction, in 1971, of legislation banning the export of pre-Columbian antiquities. The gangs, who are normally Americans, fly across the border in light aircraft to reconnoitre among the thousands of uncharted Maya temples in the jungles of Yucatan and Quitana Roo, then instruct local Indians, who are hired to dig up remains. These are given a small downpayment and a much larger reward when the relics are handed over to the gangs, who use old Second World War airstrips to pick them up. For large statues and carved stones, they bring in portable power-operated drills and digging equipment, run off lightweight generators.

The Mexican judicial police, acting under authority from the Attorney General and the National Institute of Anthropology and History, have succeeded in bringing more than a hundred prosecutions under the new law, and have broken up four gangs and recovered over £5 million worth of items. They are fortunate in serving a government prepared to back them with a dozen light aircraft and helicopters; but they are up against an enormously wealthy and persistent organisation, which can stack away even famous things, like the Mayan *Señor de las Limes*, which was buried for three years in the grounds of a receiver's ranch at Oaxaca, until smuggled over the American border by car.

There is no doubt that the U.S. market is the most voracious and greedy of all for antiquities from all over the world. A single example will serve: in May 1973 it was revealed that the collection of Mr

Norton Simon contained a magnificent five-foot high bronze statue, dating from the tenth century and depicting the Indian god Shiva, dancing in a circle of flames. It had been stolen from a temple at Sivapura in southern India, replaced by a fake, and offered for sale in New York for $1 million (£400,000). Mr Simon, of course, bought the statue legitimately, from a dealer, Mr Ben Heller, who had acquired it from an Indian collector in Bombay, on the understanding that the Indian government knew that it had left the temple. This was hotly denied by the authorities, who claimed back what they called "possibly the greatest work of Indian art now outside India". Mr Simon, with the frankness of possession, told the *New York Times*, "Hell, yes, it was smuggled – I spent between $15 and $16 million over the last year on Asian art and most of it was smuggled. . . . I believe that the authorities in Indian temples have the right to sell works. It's not like Italy where the work belongs to the state."

The West has its own troubles, bred of similar tastes; but since archaeology is a science that Mediterranean countries value highly and can afford more easily than the Third World, archaeologists form a powerful lobby. For them the contents of Etruscan tombs and lost Turkish cities are landmarks in charting ancient history. Without precise identification of the site and analysis of the layers deposited around it over the centuries, an antiquity is almost value-less to scholars. To the avid buyer, whether tourist or collector, these considerations are less relevant. For them beauty is enough, beauty conceived of in modern terms, as Picasso's *Demoiselles d'Avignon* drew on and popularised the art of primitive Africa.

Of course, the approach to ancient art through the collector's own mental *outillage* is nothing new. The eighteenth-century tomb robbers selected what their clients wanted; *conquistadores* destroyed vast numbers of Inca treasures, and the crusaders who sacked Constantinople in 1204 melted down the seven-branched candela-brum of King Solomon, which had survived the sack of Jerusalem a thousand years before. Very few gold hoards have had the luck of the great Petrossa treasure from Romania and remained undisturbed, retaining an impeccable pedigree. Yet so much survived until recent times untouched in the earth that it is a tragedy that the application of modern methods of investigation and the development of scholarly techniques should have coincided with looting on a scale wider than the depredations of Attila and all the Goths.

After the end of the war, in 1946, the Italian government set up watch-towers with searchlights in the marshes of the Po delta, in an attempt to restrain illegal excavation on the site of the lost city of Spina; and former eel fishermen, deprived of their living by land reclamation, fought a ten-year battle with the police to recover the remains. Night patrols through the Tuscan hills failed to dislodge grave robbers from Etruscan tombs, and by the late 1950s antiquities worth, at an informed guess, $8 million a year were vanishing across the frontier or, via antique shops in Rome, into the hands of tourists. According to the Rome police, the network then comprised upwards of a dozen receivers, employing twenty-five middlemen and probably 200 thieves. In August 1957, following up information from a customs post on the Austrian frontier, Rome police, using agents disguised as American tourists, complete with cigars and cameras, penetrated the façade put up by a fashionable antique shop near the Piazza di Spagna. In the raid they collected 15,000 items without permits, a quarter of which they ranked as "important objects" in the national patrimony. The authorities claimed it as "the greatest hoard of looted archaeological treasures ever found in Italy", but the elderly dealer denied that he was a receiver and told reporters, "Nonsense, nonsense; it's a small collection of little things. So I let my friends come and look at my collections. So I let them buy a few things. So I export something to America once in a while. What is all the talk of Etruscan antiquities? No one can prove the Etruscans even existed."

Few perhaps now read for pleasure Livy, who described the glory of Etruscan civilisation as filling both earth and sea; but many collectors worship the bronzes and the gold jewellery of their mysterious tombs. By the mid-1960s the Department of Public Security was, at last, seriously alarmed. At the same time as the official list of stolen works of art was published, the Italian government appealed to UNESCO and the Council of Europe in an effort to control the illegal traffic by international agreement. As well hold back the sea by act of parliament. From Germany, America, Switzerland, and so on, came buyers not only of Etruscan pieces but all classical remains, some of them literally chipped off palaces and gardens in Rome. The worst outrage happened in 1963. Equipped with electric saws, a gang broke into some of the most famous of all Etruscan monuments, the painted tombs of Tarquinia, and one by one cut out large sections of the frescoed walls. They cut deep channels in the walls, then inserted steel wires behind and sliced the panels out like slices of cheese. Night after night they worked, loading the fragments into a specially adapted car, which was then driven across the Swiss border; and were only found out when inspectors discovered one tomb open with the walls ready-cut for dismantling. The *carabinieri* informed Interpol. Three young locals were arrested and confessed that they had done the work for $8,000 on behalf of a Swiss-Italian dealer. But the latter escaped and, although some fragments were recovered in Switzerland and others in a farm house on the Italian side, the bulk has vanished, including the celebrated painting of a dancer, one of the best known of all Etruscan works.

A special squad of *carabinieri* was formed under a tough police veteran, Guiseppe Scordino, to put an end to looting, but it is noticeable that although the law of 1939, which claims all finds as state property, provides penalties of from six months' to five years' imprisonment, no one has ever actually been jailed under it. Fines range up to a trivial maximum. Far too many Italian peasants augment their meagre living by digging for profit and fun. It appears that over seventy-five per cent of everything dug up in Italy surfaces illegally; and the police do not recover more than five per cent. The small fry are pulled in and fined at intermittent intervals, but it is very rare for the authorities to throw the book at a big dealer. Once, however, an American from Baltimore, Robert E. Hecht, was accused, in the words of the indictment, of being "a danger to the artistical patrimony of Italy". It was alleged that he had organised clandestine shipments to Switzerland, Britain and the United States amounting to hundreds of thousands of dollars' worth – a charge confirmed, but secretly applauded by many Italians who had dug for him on their own land. Later the charges were withdrawn.

The Italian government does pay up to twenty-five per cent of the value of declared antiquities, but its own experts fix the value and the money may take months or even years to arrive. In contrast receiver-dealers pay ten to fifteen per cent of market value on delivery, and, as recent thermoluminescent testing at Oxford has proved, augment this sizeable profit by slipping brilliant forgeries into the same channels of distribution. The true proportion of genuine to faked Etruscan objects may be less than half of what was regarded as a reasonable estimate ten years ago.

In Italy, as in the Far East and Africa, the problem of looting has resolved itself into a question of priorities. The state will not, or cannot, afford to spend more. State museums are full, their cellars bulging, but they are not allowed to sell the surplus. There are not nearly enough guards to protect them, let alone the hundreds of ancient sites in what is archaeologically the richest earth in the world. Arguably, the illegal channels make a useful contribution to Italy's balance of payments. On the other hand, the Greek and Turkish authorities, with securer frontiers and fewer tourists than Italy, still believe that they can check smugglers.

The introduction of deep ploughing in Greece and the extent of new building in the 1960s brought to the surface hundreds of ancient artefacts, and, despite the stringency of laws against illegal export and the work of a special commission made up of police and archaeologists, substantial numbers of Attic figures, pots and coins began to disappear. Four years later a Supreme Archaeological Council was set up, with wide-ranging powers, and the number of custodians was increased. Under the régime of the Colonels, the profession of the receiver was no longer as safe as formerly. The pleas of archaeologists for what one recently called "Draconian legislation to put the thieves on the same level as drug peddlars" have been heard. But prison sentences can apparently still be exchanged at will for a fine of 500 drachmae against each month of sentence.

The export channels are similar to those of India: in many villages there are local tradesmen who will buy things for a few drachmae or a crate of wine and then pass them on to agent's touts who tour the villages. In due course the antiquities will swell some dealer's stock, awaiting a foreign buyer and a discreet shipment, which may travel on the main lines from the Piraeus, by caique or yacht at night across the Adriatic, or by way of Jannina and Yugoslavia into Switzerland.

One difficulty in tracking down these losses is that the empire of ancient Greece covered a large part of the Mediterranean, including

Sicily and southern Italy; and the red-figure vases, for example, found in transit beyond Greece, could have come from a dozen different sites. This could not be said of the loot from buried Turkish cities. The Turks have seen the finest hoards of pure gold objects from the area between ancient Troy and Dorak vanish overseas. Schliemann took the celebrated treasure from Troy itself to the Berlin Museum in 1873. Within the last decade, three more have been discovered – one, dating from the third millenium B.C., now in the University of Pennsylvania; another, since disappeared, shown at Dorak by a village girl to the British archaeologist James Mellaart; and a third, which may be called simply the Boston hoard.

In January 1971, Landen T. Clay, one of the trustees of the Boston Museum of Fine Arts, donated to the museum 137 pieces of gold jewellery, including a unique Egyptian cylinder seal said to have belonged to an official at the court of two Pharoahs who ruled between 2497 and 2450 B.C. Clay was alleged to have paid more than $1 million for the hoard, which had already been offered privately to the Berlin Museum and rejected because of lack of authentic provenance. The same, or a similar collection, had also been refused in England. The purchase was apparently made in Switzerland.

This acquisition was not the first contested item, nor is Boston the only American museum to put on display things that have manifestly evaded the laws of the country of origin. In this case, poker-faced museum officials admitted only that the hoard had come from "somewhere in the Eastern Mediterranean". Unfortunately, without documentation, the hoard is academically worthless and may even be artistically suspect, for the famous gold seal has since been the subject for searching criticism by many archaeologists. Gold does not date in any measurable way and, in the absence of archaeological evidence, authentication must rely purely on stylistic grounds. It is, for example, of great importance to establish whether a collection is homogeneous, or whether it is the result of haphazard acquisition by dealers, as some experts consider the Dorak treasure to have been. A few of the great collections from South America have been proved in recent years not to be homogeneous, and a generation from now scholars may well mock the Boston hoard as they now do Piltdown Man. The Turkish authorities, however, furious at such open provocation, demanded from the United States State Department

215

the return of the Boston hoard, and threatened to ban all future digging inside Turkey – to the horror of reputable archaeologists at work on the neolithic site of Catal Huyuk.

One scholar said angrily, "International crime is taking over the antiquities business, like narcotics smuggling." Turkey had prepared a list of more than a thousand smuggled items lost within the previous fifteen years and suspected to be in collections in the West. Together with Mexico and Guatemala, the government appealed to UNESCO, but ran into opposition from Britain, centre of the world market, and America, home of the purchasers of most antiquities, neither of which countries is likely in the present climate of opinion to ratify a convention designed to stamp out the illegal trade. The pursuit is probably hopeless once the treasures are installed. The Boston *Globe*, seeking to mitigate some of the charges against the museum, accused the Metropolitan of having a similar hoard, "the treasure of King Croesus", concealed in its cellars; and a spokesman for the Turkish Department of Antiquities complained bitterly that even the vanished Dorak hoard "is nothing compared to the treasures that we know have been smuggled out". Since then, the Metropolitan Museum has been embroiled with Italian authorities because of an outstanding Greek *krater*, or decorated vase, supplied by the ubiquitous Mr Hecht.

Preventing illegal export at the frontier or other checks to the smugglers' trade routes are the only means of halting their trade. None of the countries mentioned can afford to redeem their losses at world market prices, even if they regarded such ransom as a legitimate use of scarce foreign exchange. It cost the Greek government $15,000 to buy back an archaic bronze *kouros* or statue of a young man, stolen from the Jannina Museum in 1935 and later bought by the Metropolitan. Nor is there any reason why a poverty-stricken country like India should reverse its priorities and allow a Western ideological approach to art to be imposed on it. If Italy cannot stem the flood, and if Greece can check it only under a despotic military autocracy, how can the Middle East and Far East do more?

Unfortunately, the process is circular. By attacking the legitimate trade in antiquities, the countries of origin help to raise the price on the world market, thus ensuring even greater penetration by the illegal diggers. If it is virtually impossible for new museums to buy antiquities in any other way, they will negotiate on the double market or accept tax-deductible donations collected in the same way by individuals. Prestige is at stake. Attendance in the antiquities section at Boston went up ten times after the display of the gold hoard.

Why not, one may ask, legitimise the trade and make a proper export out of it? In Italy, Carlo Lerici, a Milan industrialist, has devoted his retirement and a great deal of money to the application of ultrasonic detection to finding Etruscan tombs. These are then photographed in minute detail by drilling a hole in from the top and lowering a special camera. In the first ten years he has done as much for archaeology (despite a good deal of official harassment) as the whole staff of the Ministry of Fine Arts. Why not turn over a proportion of the findings to such experts? At Selinute in Sicily (where the *Ephebus* was found a century ago) the local authority has tried a daring experiment: former tomb robbers are paid a regular wage to dig, with a bonus for discoveries. The practice could well be extended and paid for by selling the lesser objects. Control would have to be strictly preserved to retain the best things, but it might be more effective than at present; it is a question worth returning to.

Chapter 12 An Endless Case?

In studying the growth and flowering of the double market and its offshoots, art theft has been treated here as a product of a particular time and condition of society. It would be wrong to suggest that any new insights into criminology can be obtained when the great majority of thieves and receivers are in this market in preference to others only because of distinct opportunities and acquired skills. Deviancy theory has little to learn except that a higher degree of protection and rate of profit exists among receivers of stolen art than almost any other type of fence.

On the other hand, an understanding of the reasons for the market's growth and immunity is essential for crime prevention. No other inquiry has so far given the complete picture; and the conclusions are extremely depressing. There seems to be no reason why art theft should not remain a feature of criminal activity until the last major painting is absorbed into the vaults of the latest new museum. Already, criminals live off legitimate art dealers, as they have done off private collectors: during the summer of 1970, a gang not un-connected with the Great Train Robbery amassed a haul of nearly £35,000-worth of modern paintings, all from galleries in the West End of London. Consequently insurance premiums add yet another inflated cost to the overheads of a profession that is at its worst parasitical and underhand, but at its best dedicated and scholarly; and oriented not to investment scales of profit, but to the uncertain future of the private collector.

It is not enough to induce skilled, indefatigable detectives to take up service in an art squad, nor to place some of the onus of prevention on the owner. Detectives are likely to be policemen first, art historians and politicians second. For some, a stolen Rubens is only a stolen piece of canvas. This is how to catch thieves; but, because the painting loses priority, the owner, the politicians and, by implication, the public tend to cry that this is too important a job to be left to the police. Implicitly or not, all detectives in search of stolen art are aware, at the back of their minds, of the risk that if their quarry is destroyed[1] they will be exposed to the same sort of press attacks as follow the death of a victim in ransom negotiations.

The double market can really be damaged only by attacking the demand which creates it. Autonomous decline is unlikely. Fashion may conceivably spin back to the 1930s, shattering the price structure of the art market as it goes. Some investors in antique silver feared this during the slump of 1969–70; but since then the market has, within two years, more than made good the losses caused by bursting of the speculative bubble, and has progressed beyond fashion itself. So much money (in professional, rather than amateur hands) is involved that fashion is too dangerous to be allowed free range. Demand outruns supply – as it must for the advantage of those who manipulate the market. On their backs climb the illegal entrepreneurs, performing, in purely economic terms, a service that perhaps prevents an even more violent inflation.

Since demand has social origins and is based, broadly speaking, on the wealth of the modern industrial middle class, persuasion or legislation are unlikely to alter the pattern. But could the appetite be slaked by other means? Could the trend whereby museum acquisition diminishes the total available supply be reversed, to the advantage both of the private collector and the maintenance of the law? The obvious way would appear to lie in the hands of the great museums themselves, who could off-load some of the contents of their bulging cellars, either by loan to less fortunate institutions, who would then withdraw from bidding, or by actual sale. Yet the objections are serious. First and simplest, there is the fact that every antique, being hand-made, is unique. Every Greek vase, Philadelphia high-boy or Benin carving has its own special characteristics and cannot in the true sense be a duplicate. Even if one says that museums should confine their collections to representative works, there is merit in the argument put by Bruno Molajoli, Italy's surpeintendent of museums:

There are in the first place not thousands of identical vases in our museums, but thousands of unique ones, each one a little different from the others. We must remember that museums are like libraries: they contain items which perhaps nobody wants to see for ten years, and when a scholar comes to find that one item, it must be there. Besides, think of the difficulties of organisation, if the museums were allowed to sell. You need experts with knowledge, judgement, awareness of what is most important.

Secondly, it is hard, both in equity and law, to override the principle of donation. Museums rely heavily on pious gifts, whether tax-deductible or not. To hint to a prospective donor that in a few years, when the novelty has worn off or the gift become unfashionable, it might be sold, possibly at a profit, is scarcely good politics. On the other hand, rules might be made to allow surplus collections to be loaned, a century later, to poorer museums, or to new ones in areas of cultural deprivation. If the donor wants his bequest to be seen, surely it is better that it enliven the town hall of a slum borough in Glasgow or Detroit, than repose unremarked in an air-conditioned cellar?

Some churches have a more realistic, pragmatic approach. The Vatican circular of May 1971, which ordered a census to be taken of all church treasures, strictly enjoined that changes imposed by the new liturgy should never be used as an excuse for disposing of artistic masterpieces. But permission can be granted for more urgent needs, just as in the Anglican church silver that is not actually altar plate can be, and has been, sold to raise money to keep the church roof from falling in.

On the same principle that the institution is worth preserving more than the individual items belonging to it, there is a case for saying that if a museum wants a new, striking acquisition, it should be allowed to sell off something it needs less. The safeguards that surround the disposal of church property, or the sales that do take place, such as the auction of surplus weapons from the armoury of the Tower of London, could be extended and enforced. In Italy, Carlo Lerici has often suggested that the impoverished superintendents of antiquities could solve most of their problems by turning archaeological exploration over to private experts, giving them half the value of their finds as an inducement to hand in what the museums require. Others among the younger museum officials have dared to suggest selling off the excess of discoveries – a taking over, in effect, of the illicit trade, giving the profit to the Italian state, rather than to Swiss dealers.

An economic argument against museum sales is put by antique and fine-art dealers, and supported by many museum staffs who depend on the trade for new acquisitions. Sales on the scale likely, if they were legitimised, would break the ring of the market, just as if de Beers suddenly flooded the world with their stockpile of diamonds, instead of doling out a percentage at a constant price each year. It is much more likely in fact that the pendulum will swing the other way. In Britain, for example, pressure has been building up for ten years to introduce something similar to the American system of tax allowances for donations; and the recent controversy over the sales of the Velasquez *Juan de Pareja* and Titian's *Diana and Actaeon* may undermine the opposition of the Treasury to a new category of tax discrimination. At the fourth C.I.N.O.A. conference in Florence, Signor Predieri, professor of art history at the University of Florence, emphasised the duty of the state to stimulate and facilitate private gifts by taxation policy. A bill to validate the practice is at present under consideration by the Italian Parliament. Other European countries are expected to follow suit. Optimistic advocates of the change claim that the abuses of the United States scheme (substantially lessened since the reforms of 1966 and 1969) can be avoided altogether. Perhaps they can;[2] but the effect on prices will be the same as in the United States and will ramify through the entire fine-art market. It is not beyond the limits of possibility that in Europe, as in America, the scramble to endow museums will develop so fast that the market for the private collector will be irredeemably wasted. Amateurs in the twenty-first century may yet praise the life-enhancing side-effects of the illegal market, the end product of which is usually reserved for the private, rather than the public, sphere.

If demand itself cannot be dried up, there is no recourse but to accept art theft as a fact of modern life, an endemic parasite. Wearily the police will deal with each new outraged loser. Commissioner

Matthieu, in charge of the theft department of the Police Judiciaire in Paris, recorded that in June and July 1972 a theft occurred in Paris once every four days, and in none of these cases was the total value of works lost less than 100,000 francs. It is discouraging for him to know that only five per cent of these works will be recovered. If the new French methods work, the proportion may rise to eight per cent, or, to break all records, ten. But the summit will not be reached, the corner will not be turned, because the double market is beyond the control of police, Interpol, C.I.N.O.A. or anyone. A single aspect, like ransom, may be strangled, but the pattern will only change.

Too many half-truths veil the nature of the art market today. Seventy years ago, Soames Forsyte was at least honest about his attitude to modern painting as a form of investment.

> He stood before his Gauguin – sorest point of his collection. He had bought the ugly great thing with two early Matisses before the War, because there was such a fuss about those Post-Impressionist chaps.

On the other hand, he knew very well that

> aesthetics and good taste were necessary. The appreciation of enough persons of good taste was what gave a work of art its permanent market value, or in other words made it "a work of art".

Rooted in our consciousness of that term, "work of art", is the antithesis between "art as beauty" and "art as investment". As the prosecuting attorney said, during the *Jung Waldteufel* trial, "a painting is not a loaf of bread or a can of beans or a Cadillac convertible . . .". If it were, the parameters of the double market would resemble those of the stolen car trade. In some respects, of course, they do: the techniques of theft, the skilled conversion and disguise and the "legitimate" resale bear comparison. But the response of authority and owners differs. The loss of a painting or a Greek vase creates not merely a sense of outrage, but also a fear of diminishing the world's stock of a precious heritage. Tough laws and police work are sometimes both vitiated by the associated dilemma that stolen works of art trail with them. Because society has in a sense

223

made works of art independent of private ownership – "a Rembrandt belongs to the world" – they possess, beyond personal and cash value, a quality that gives as much unease to the pursuer as it does advantage to the thief. All art theft is therefore a form of moral blackmail, to which twentieth-century Western society is peculiarly vulnerable.

Thence arises the threat of theft for political ends. After the *Duke of Wellington* was stolen from the National Gallery in London in August 1961, the first ransom note demanded, for an unspecified charity, £140,000, the price the gallery had just paid for it. When Kempton Bunton, an unemployed North-Country lorry-driver, was finally accused, after the painting's return four years later, he denied the charge of theft and his counsel sought to establish that he had never intended to deprive the gallery, only to use the £140,000 to buy television licences for old-age pensioners. (Bunton had earlier campaigned against what he regarded as the injustice of the licence fee and had served two short prison sentences for refusal to pay his own licence.)

Hardly a revolutionary cause; yet Bunton, unknown at the time of the theft, can claim to have been one of the first to have seen the possibilities offered by hi-jacking the world's greatest paintings. So too can the Irish students who stole Berthe Morisot's *Jour d'été* from the Tate Gallery to protest against the British government's refusal to return the Lane Bequest pictures to Dublin. Since then, political aims have intruded on the criminal sphere. A group of ultramontane Catholics removed the Romanesque statue of the Virgin of Nuria, famous in Catalonia, to protest against the domination of the church by the Franco régime. And, in January 1963, a band of terrorists, armed with automatic pistols and shouting slogans, invaded the Museum of Fine Arts in Caracas, herded the crowds of onlookers into a hall, together with the armed guards, and cut down five major nineteenth-century French paintings on loan from the Louvre and the Museum of Modern Art in Paris. A young man who stood in the way was shot and badly wounded.

The raid was the culmination of a series of guerilla attacks (including the petrol bombing of Shell and U.S. Rubber installations) and bank raids, which had plagued the government of President Romulo Betancourt. The Venezuelan National Guard fanned out across the city in their search for the terrorists, and wounded three students as they forced entry onto the University campus, where the N.A.L.F. (Armed Forces for National Liberation) were known to have many sympathisers. The N.A.L.F. were at once blamed for the incident by the Minister of the Interior, who had a good deal of justification for doing so: Venezuela had been a prime target for Cuban revolutionary propaganda, and the tactics of Che Guevara were already in evidence.

The Communist party leader, Gustavo Machado, announced to the press that the raid "was a political propaganda operation that had repercussions, not only nationally but internationally". The pictures would be returned, but "only after they had served their purpose". There were rumours of negotiations for the release of political prisoners (foretaste of the Tupamaros' demands in Uruguay), but, judging from a captured letter, the aims appear rather to have been to expose the government's campaign against the guerillas in western Venezuela and to publicise the N.A.L.F. campaign against United States oil interests. In the document N.A.L.F. charged that American military advisers and F.B.I. agents were "leading the police forces of repression".

The National Guard retorted by arresting José Monterrey, a Communist and union official, whom they charged with complicity. Monterrey talked. The police discovered that the guerillas were planning to transfer the pictures and intercepted their car in a Caracas suburb. In the resulting gun battle two students were shot and captured. The five pictures were found safe in boxes labelled "Fragile. Handle with Care".

The N.A.L.F. design was intended to cause such disruption that Betancourt, the first democratically elected President for many years, would not be able to finish his five-year term of office; and the main target seems to have been to deprive the government of the fifty per cent of its budget that it derives from oil revenue. Sacking the art gallery, however, hit the world headlines far more effectively than sniper shots and petrol bombs, just as Henrique Galvao's seizure of the vessel *Santa Marta* in the same year brought to public notice the opposition to Salazar inside Portugal.

Unless the Viet-Cong occupation of the famous temples of Angkor Wat in Cambodia is included as a form of military-artistic blackmail,[3] these examples have not, until recently, been followed assiduously. The fashion for hi-jacking aircraft supervened. But artistic blackmail, less horrifying than the blowing-up of aircraft, or capturing of ambassadors, may yet be a danger. It is no longer a question of asking whether Al Fatah will take over the ruins of Palmyra, or Basque Nationalists hold the Spanish government to ransom with Velasquez's *Surrender of Breda* from the Prado in Madrid. The loss of the great Vermeer from Kenwood House in March 1974, and of Sir Alfred Beit's collection of paintings from Russborough House in Ireland – both crimes a form of blackmail by I.R.A. sympathisers demanding the release of prisoners held in England – are only too recent.

The thought of blackmail using the world's greatest treasures hits a most vulnerable point: assumptions about value – cultural or cash – are exposed. Should a government, in such a case, take a high moral line? The precedents are ambiguous. The Swiss suffered a severe crisis of conscience in 1970, when faced with Arab guerilla demands to release three Arabs already sentenced to prison. Eventually, since lives were involved, the Federal government advised the canton of Zürich to concede. More recently, the Austrian authorities have submitted to similar blackmail. But for works of art, no matter how famous? Recovery of the lost pictures from Dulwich College saved the British government from the dilemma in 1964, but France had already given way three years earlier to redeem Cézanne's *Card Players* for the Louvre.

Rhetorical questions will be answered only in specific circumstances and there is little point in debating whether the safety of the *Mona Lisa* is worth the risk of a single human life. But it is relevant to the subject of art theft to ask whether the heaping up of treasures in museums demonstrably enhances the standard of life of a community or merely its sense of prestige. Again, do those who file past have their critical ability blunted by stereotypes, like the thief who knows that if he takes a Picasso the master's signature is as good a bond as American Express travellers' cheques? More pertinently, does concentration on the virtues of retaining "national treasures" (the majority of which, in Britain, are the proceeds of European shopping tours by wealthy eighteenth-century aristocrats) indicate anything more than crude nationalism, a feeling that the stock of status symbols is running low? One can make a valid distinction between eighteenth-century spoils and works of art in a genuine national tradition; but, if so, why did the British Committee on the Export of Works of Art allow the export of the Oscott lectern, the finest example of English mediaeval metalwork? Why did we have to rely on the generosity of an American citizen in order to retain the *Ovid* of Caxton, our most famous printer?

One may question whether our feelings about loss are as profound as those of the defeated Greeks who suffered religious sacrilege and symbolic castration as they watched the Roman wagons loaded with marble statues. Hence our difficulty in taking the moral line. It is easy enough to cast in emotional terms an argument about the nature of value, to contrast the hypothetical Texan millionaire's tax-deductible operations with the actual loss in U.S. Federal revenue. That may not necessarily force a cut-back in the slum-improvement scheme for a Negro ghetto. But the clamour for protection of the cultural heritage appears to come only too often from an art establishment, or from fine-art dealers with a vested interest in supporting price levels. The issues not only of state patronage of the arts, but also of the rights and duties attached to private property are raised.

Given the standards of modern society, these questions will not be answered. Art theft will continue. The man out in the front-line is, of course, the private collector. The world of the enthusiast, the amateur (in the proper sense of the word) and the dealer – himself at best a collector – who supplies him, has, mercifully, not yet been swamped by the practitioners of investment. Their wealth and demand, however, creates and sustains the whole chain of art thefts. The double market cannot be eradicated; immoral but inevitable, it is, in truth, as much a phenomenon of our times as share-watering and company fraud were of earlier, brasher stages of industrial society.

Notes

[1] Very little publicity has been given, for this reason, to cases where stolen works have been destroyed. The author has come across a few cases, among them the fact that some of the Cromwellian

firearms stolen from Littlecote House were dumped in the Thames, and that two paintings supposedly by Tintoretto were burned in Brighton in 1969, when they became too well known to be disposed of more profitably. Naturally most of the stories are largely rumour, and one can only suggest that, since thieves are not normally connoisseurs, they have no more compunction about dumping Sèvres vases than they have about ditching a stolen Mercedes over a cliff, if it becomes too hot to handle.

² Will one see in Britain advertisements to compare with the splendid example quoted by Gerald Reitlinger? Issued by the Department of Fine Arts of the Immaculate Heart College of Los Angeles, it read: "We wonder if you, dear reader, would like to add to our collection. Your gifts are tax reducible, not only here, BUT ESPECIALLY IN HEAVEN." (*The Economics of Taste*, vol. II, page 1.)

³ The Viet-Cong, it is worth noting, gave assistance to Cambodia's only resident archaeologist, Chea Thay Seng, in burying or safe-guarding several hundred of the finer sculptures during their occupation of parts of Cambodia. Both belligerents co-operated in his efforts to bring thousands of Khmer bronzes and statues from Phnom-Penh during the fighting in 1970–71, but, of course, thieves and smugglers took the chance vastly to increase their trade to New York and London.

Index

134, 205; London 56; Mafia 80; penalties 182; risks 172; stockpiles 63; Swiss 207

Recovery 54, 64, 90, 128, 130, 141–80 *passim*

Recovery Office, *see Italy*

Rembrandt 16, 27, 45, 51, 73, 114, 118; *Girl at a Window* 119; *Saskia at her Toilet* 27; *The Anatomy Lesson* 195

Renaissance 6, 15, 28, 36; paintings 85, 144, 145, 177

Reni, Guido 41

Renoir 33, 44, 45, 108, 116; *Andrée assise* 116

Restorers 81, 145

Rewards 23, 24, 26

Riemenschneider, Tillman 36, 38, 114–15

Rijksmuseum, Amsterdam 68, 195

Riviera 80, 109, 115, 161

Rodin: *Le Baiser* 91; *Psyche* 91

Romania 211; Brackenthorn Museum 71

Rome 2, 3, 4, 8, 10, 26, 40, 51, 65, 141, 155; *carabinieri* 64; Fine Arts Ministry, Recovery Office 160, 161

Rothenstein, Sir John 119

Rothschild 52; Baron Ferdinand de 23; jewel collection 6

Rouault 101, 129

Royal Academy 118, 119

Royal Armoury, Vienna 56

Royal Museum, Brussels 97

Royal Ontario Museum 45

Rubens 43, 59, 72, 85, 118, 154; *Flaying of St Bartholomew* 43, 44; *Studies of a Negro Head* 97, 195, 197

Russia 70–1, 147, 151; looting 149; press 71; recovery 148; refugees 33; Stalin 149

St John the Baptist (figure) 42

St Joseph's Cathedral, Kentucky 43

St Paul de Vence 100, 102

St Stephen, crown of 147–8, 190

St Tropez 101–8 *passim*

Sales 50

San Francisco 411; Art Museum 197

San Isidro (Mattias Stumer) 49

Satyricon (Petronius) 8

Schiller 5, 7

Schliemann 215

Schott Museum, Brussels 68

Schuman Plan 35; *see also* Common Market

Scotland Yard *passim*; Art Squad 64, 80, 128–32 *passim*, 157, 189; criminal intelligence 128

Sculpture 5, 76; Chinese 154; Hellenistic 142, 146; Henry Moore 129; Indo-China 207; Khmer 207, 208; *Virgin & Child* 114

Security 194–9 *passim*

Segonzac, Dunoyer de 103, 104, 107

Sicily 109, 113, 177, 214–15, 217

Silk, Det. Supt Len 129–32 *passim*, 136

Silver 27, 32, 41, 114; boom in 50; candlesticks 11; chandeliers 55; Georgian 60, 61; statues 44; wine-coolers 61

Silver-gilt plate: Cellini 142; Portuguese 93

Singer Museum, Laaren 59, 128

Siviero, Rodolfo 49, 63, 88, 143–5, 178–9

Soane Museum 186

Sonderauftrag Linz 6, 7

Sotheby's 26, 61, 67, 93, 94, 157, 159, 201n

Southsea Museum 158

Spain 39, 59, 67, 69, 186; civil war 34, 152; export legislation (1953) 201; palaces 33

Spina, lost city 212

Stamps, postage 59

Statistics (thefts) 76

Statues 39, 42, 45, 54, 69, 92, 208, 211; Khmer 228; *kouros* 216; Shiva 211

Statutes of limitations 64, 88, 146

Stern magazine 115

Stolen goods: "legitimised" 11; on sale 77

Surrealists, International Exhibition 133

Sweden 56, 69–70

Appendix

Values

File #
485234

Gertrude Diamond
516 - 295 - 0970